ELEANOR MARX (1855–1898)

ELEANOR MARX (1855–1898)

Life · Work · Contacts

Edited by
John Stokes

Ashgate

Aldershot • Burlington USA • Singapore • Sydney

Published by

Ashgate Publishing Ltd
Gower House, Croft Road
Aldershot, Hampshire, GU11 3HR
England

Ashgate Publishing Company
131 Main Street
Burlington, Vermont 05401
USA

Ashgate website: http://www.ashgate.com

ISBN 0 7546 0113 7

British Library Cataloguing-in-Publication Data
Eleanor Marx (1855–1898) : life, work, contacts. – (The nineteenth century series)
    1. Marx, Eleanor, 1855–1898 – Political and social views 2. Marx, Eleanor, 1855–1898 – Friends and associates 3. Women socialists – Great Britain – Biography 4. Socialists – Great Britain – Biography 5. Feminists – Great Britain – Biography I. Stokes, John, 1943– 335'.0092

US Library of Congress Cataloging-in-Publication Data
Eleanor Marx (1855–1898) : life, work, contacts / edited by John Stokes
        p. cm.   Includes bibliographical references
    1. Aveling, Eleanor Marx, 1855–1898. 2. Socialists–Great Britain–Biography. I. Stokes, John, 1943–
HX244.7.A83 E44 2000
335.4'092–dc21
    [B]   00–040614

This volume is printed on acid-free paper.

Typeset on a RISC OS workstation using EasiWriter Professional (Icon Technology). Set in the Electronic Font Foundry's (www.eff.co.uk) 'LondonA' typeface.

Printed and bound by Athenaeum Press, Ltd.,
Gateshead, Tyne & Wear.

Contents

The Nineteenth Century General Editors' Preface

The aim of this series is to reflect, develop and extend the great burgeoning of interest in the nineteenth century that has been an inevitable feature of recent decades, as that former epoch has come more sharply into focus as a locus for our understanding not only of the past, but also of the contours of our modernity. Though it is dedicated principally to the publication of original monographs and symposia in literature, history, cultural analysis, and associated fields, there will be a salient role for reprints of significant texts from, or about, the period. This, we believe, distinguishes our project from comparable ones, and means, for example, that in relevant areas of scholarship we both recognize and cut innovatively across such parameters as those suggested by the designations 'Romantic' and 'Victorian'. We welcome new ideas, while valuing tradition. It is hoped that the world which predates yet so forcibly predicts and engages our own will emerge in parts, as a whole, and in the lively currents of debate and change that are so manifest an aspect of its intellectual, artistic and social landscape.

Vincent Newey
Joanne Shattock
University of Leicester

Preface

The essays contained here are all based on papers delivered at the Eleanor Marx Centenary Conference which was held at the Centre for English Studies, University of London on 27 March 1998. Thanks are due to the Director of what is now the Institute for English Studies, Professor Warwick Gould, and to his staff for their enthusiastic support and efficient organization of that event.

In the preparation of this book I have benefited from the professional advice of Andrew Davies and Louis Marks and the editorial skill of Faith Evans. I owe a special debt to Stewart Brookes whose computer magic and sharp eye brought it to life.

John Stokes

List of Abbreviations

Daughters: *The Daughters of Karl Marx. Family Correspondence 1866–1898*, Commentary and Notes by Olga Meier, translated and adapted by Faith Evans, introduction by Sheila Rowbotham (London: André Deutsch Ltd., 1982)

Kapp, I: Yvonne Kapp, *Eleanor Marx, Volume I, Family Life (1855–1883)*, (London: Lawrence & Wishart, 1972)

Kapp, II: Yvonne Kapp, *Eleanor Marx, Volume II, The Crowded Years (1884–1898)*, (London: Lawrence & Wishart, 1976)

Tsuzuki: Chushichi Tsuzuki, *The Life of Eleanor Marx 1855–1898. A Socialist Tragedy* (Oxford: Clarendon Press, 1967)

Woman
Question: Edward and Eleanor Marx Aveling, *The Woman Question* (London: Swan Sonnenschein, Le Bas & Lowrey, 1886)

Notes on the Contributors

Simon Avery is a Lecturer in Literature at the University of Hertfordshire. He teaches nineteenth- and twentieth-century literature and gender studies and has published work on the Brontës, Christina Rossetti and Mary Coleridge, as well as on teaching and learning in higher education. He is currently co-authoring a monograph on Elizabeth Barrett Browning.

Bridget Bennett is a Lecturer in the School of English, University of Leeds. Her publications include two edited books, *Ripples of Dissent* (1996) and *Grub Street to the Ivory Tower* (1999), and a monograph *The Damnation of Harold Frederic* (1997). She is currently preparing jointly edited works on transatlanticism, and on the representation of Egypt in nineteenth-century American and British literature, as well as a book on nineteenth-century American spiritualism, gender and radicalism.

Laurel Brake is Senior Lecturer in Literature at the Faculty of Continuing Education, Birkbeck College, University of London. Her recent publications include *Walter Pater* (1994) and *Subjugated Knowledges: Journalism, Gender and Literature in the 19th Century* (1994).

Faith Evans is an editor, translator and literary agent. Her editions include *The Daughters of Karl Marx. Family Correspondence 1866–1898* (1982) and Rebecca West's *Family Memories* (1985); she translates the work of the Belgian writer Madeleine Bourdouxhe.

Emma Francis is a Lecturer in the Centre for the study of Women and Gender, University of Warwick. She is the co-editor of *In a Queer Place: Sexuality and Belonging* (Ashgate Publishing, forthcoming) and is currently at work on a monograph study *Women's Poetry and Women's Mission: British Women's Poetry and the Sexual Division of Culture, 1824–1894*.

William Greenslade is Principal Lecturer in English at the University of the West of England. He is the author of *Degeneration, Culture and the Novel 1880–1940* (1994) and a number of articles on late nineteenth-century British literature and culture. He has edited George Gissing's *The Whirlpool* (1997) and is currently editing Thomas Hardy's *'Facts' Notebook* for Ashgate Publishing.

Lynne Hapgood is Principal Lecturer at the Nottingham Trent University where she specializes in late Victorian and early twentieth-century fiction. She has published in a variety of edited collections and journals, and is currently completing a book on the literature of the suburbs. She is co-editor with Nancy Paxton of *Outside Modernism: In Pursuit of the English Novel, 1900–1930* (2000).

Sally Ledger is Senior Lecturer in English at Birkbeck College, University of London. Her publications include *The New Woman: Fiction and Feminism and the Fin de Siècle* (1997) and *Henrik Ibsen* (1999).

Gail Marshall is a Lecturer in the School of English, University of Leeds. Her publications include *Actresses on the Victorian Stage: Feminine Performance and the Galatea Myth* (1998) and she is currently working on a study of nineteenth-century women and Shakespeare.

Lyn Pykett is Professor of English at the University of Wales, Aberystwyth. Her books include *The Improper Feminine: The Women's Sensation Novel and the New Woman Writing* (1992) and *Engendering Fictions: The English Novel in the Early Twentieth Century* (1995). Recent work includes two edited collections, *Reading Fin de Siècle Fictions* (1996) and *Critical Essays on Wilkie Collins* (1998); an edition of Mary Elizabeth Braddon's *The Doctor's Wife* (1998); and essays on the New Woman fiction and the fiction journalism of May Sinclair and Rebecca West.

Ruth Robbins is a Lecturer in English at University College Northampton. She has published a number of articles on late nineteenth-century literature, is the author of *Literary Feminisms* (2000) and co-editor (with Julian Wolfreys) of *Victorian Gothic* (forthcoming).

Carolyn Steedman is Professor in the Department of History at the University of Warwick. She is author of *Landscape for a Good Woman* (1986), *Margaret Macmillan* (1990) and *Strange Dislocations. Childhood and the Idea of Human Inferiority* (1995), and numerous other books and articles. She is currently working on eighteenth-century servants, and the role of service and servitude in the making of modern identity.

John Stokes is Professor in the Department of English, King's College London. His books include *In The Nineties* (1990) and *Oscar Wilde: Myths, Miracles and Imitations* (1996 and 1998). He reviews regularly for the *TLS* and other journals.

Introduction

John Stokes

I

In 1905 Bernard Shaw described the suicide of Eleanor Marx as a 'romantic tragedy', and went on to imply that her personal narrative paralleled the failure of orthodox Marxists to appreciate the progressive Fabianism which he now endorsed.[1] Shaw had known Marx well, had described her in a letter as 'a clever woman',[2] nevertheless, given the opportunity, even he could not resist falling into the casual cliché, the facile attempt to link her misguided devotion to her lover, Edward Aveling, with her fidelity to the revolutionary ideas of her father.

The truth is that experiences never mesh as neatly as one might sometimes wish – which, paradoxically, is always the lesson of a well-told life. Eleanor Marx has been excellently served by her biographers. In 1967 Chushichi Tsuzuki published the most rounded account of her to date, a solid and useful résumé of events, but it was Yvonne Kapp's extraordinary two volumes of 1972 and 1976 that established Marx's unique position within the political environment of her time as well as providing a remarkably thorough account of her personal activities, her dealings with her family, her friends and her lover. We are short not of details so much as the perspectives through which to view them.

With Kapp's achievement respectfully in mind the contributors to this collection have set out to explore, more deeply than Shaw chose to do, the ways in which the political and the personal might – or might not – relate to one other. Boundaries are retraced and, sometimes, redrawn. As Lynne Hapgood puts it in an essay on her friendship with the novelist Margaret Harkness, Marx excelled in two seemingly opposed fields.

There always has been a difficulty in linking the political, an arena characterized by conflict, with the personal, a space where traditionally the highest goal is love. One response to this conceptual dilemma is to register the private passion fuelling political activity, another tactfully to politicize love by putting it in context, by making comparisons and connections with the emotional

---

[1] Letter to Archibald Henderson, 15 July 1905 in Bernard Shaw, *Collected Letters 1898–1910*, ed. by Dan H. Laurence (London: Max Reinhardt, 1972), p. 538.
[2] Letter to Ellen Terry, 5 January 1898 in *Collected Letters 1898–1910*, p. 8.

experience of others. With her citations of those who knew her, Lyn Pykett, in one of several essays on Marx's social and intellectual contacts, shows that her career must not be cut off from those of her female contemporaries, nor would she have wanted it to be. After all, she shared their enthusiasms, and their problems – even when, as Laurel Brake demonstrates in her parallel account of the life of the academic classicist, Clara Pater, the immediate milieus were very different. Marx's intellectual relationships – with Amy Levy (analysed here by Emma Francis), with Olive Schreiner, with Dollie Radford and (as Simon Avery investigates) possibly with Mathilde Blind – were made and tested in the turbulence of ideological debate. At the same time she showed tough but genuine understanding of men, from Bernard Shaw to Tom Mann, from Havelock Ellis to Will Thorne, and, who can doubt it, to Edward Aveling himself.

Some of these essays go so far as to contrast Marx's life with that of the man she loved precisely because what he so conspicuously lacked she so famously possessed. According to Gail Marshall it was Aveling's lack of 'sympathy' that prevented him from becoming an instructive literary critic, while William Greenslade connects Aveling's personal coldness with his predilection for the ugly discourse of degenerationism. Aesthetic interests certainly played a strong part in Marx's political outlook. Through a comparison with Oscar Wilde's 'Soul of Man under Socialism' Ruth Robbins shows how she made an essential connection between the appreciation of art and radical attitudes, radical action. If Wilde creates his public persona by apparently doing nothing on a grand scale, Marx realizes herself in work, group activity, political organization. Consequently, as Carolyn Steedman powerfully if disturbingly insists, she must be firmly distinguished from those ardent female observers of poverty such as the novelist Isabella Ford who, for all their wry self-consciousness, sometimes used the claims of 'personal growth' to justify their theft of other people's lives. That famous 1960s slogan – 'the personal is the political' – can be misleading. If Steedman is right to be suspicious of the claims made for individual development then it is because if they are properly to be understood, the undoubted fascinations of human difference must always be placed within an historical spectrum.

The love affair (for that is what it was) between Marx and Aveling belongs with those other modern relationships where the partners are of rival but not necessarily similar or equal talents. It is as hard to write dispassionately about the pair as it is about Eliot and Lewes, West and Wells, Wilde and Douglas, Rhys and Ford, Tom and Vivien Eliot, Hughes and Plath. Most accounts have been blatantly partisan; even so, there is a feeling of intrusion, of prurience. Women, it has been said, are the sex associated with, often defined by 'privacy' – yet 'privacy' is precisely what they are never allowed to possess.[3] To enquire too closely into

---

[3] See Catherine MacKinnon, 'Feminism, Marxism, Method, and the State: Toward Feminist Jurisprudence', *Signs*, 8 (1983), 635–58 (p. 656).

Marx's unhappiness can seem like a violation of her dignity, especially when it is compounded with curiosity about her death, a particularly cruel take on her sexual identity.

As with her friend and contemporary Amy Levy (and later female suicides including Virginia Woolf, Anne Sexton and Sylvia Plath) there is a temptation to let the final moments summarize everything that went before, to decide the whole narrative. These lives are test cases, they tell us something (but what?) about madness, sexuality, creativity; they also prove that the balance of power, of agency, between individuals, as between classes, is continually shifting, always pre-determined yet always provisional in outcome. No wonder that, in more recent times, the phrase 'sexual politics' has established itself so rapidly, and that it has left so many questions unanswered.

The politics of the home and of the bedroom supposedly differ from those of the platform and meeting hall: private loyalties in the one case, public responsibilities in the other; fidelity to an individual against obligations to a group. Yet, though the boundaries between them are ideologically conceived, both spheres expect authenticity. We can take up Greenslade's distinction here, between the various 'lives' and roles played out by Aveling – 'dandy and man of the theatre, earnest evolutionist, romantic visionary, fearless freethinker – which were bound in with the improvised nature of his position in the cultural and political life of the period', and Marx's own very different interest in questions of identity. Aveling claimed that the playing of parts was a form of bad faith forced upon him by unfortunate circumstances not of his own making; Marx planned at one point to go on the stage because she felt she had a vocation. As Lyn Pykett suggests, by January 1882 her 'acting ambitions had become much more clearly a way out of a life crisis – a response to that sense of life slipping away which was experienced by so many self-sacrificing unmarried dutiful (if resentful) daughters in fact and fiction in the 1890s'. For women of the *fin de siècle*, the 'New Women', the embodiment of roles, on or off the stage, constituted an extension of reality.

A fully 'qualified' actor, insisted Bernard Shaw, only half-jokingly, in an article of 1885, 'is a man [sic] who knows the visible symptoms of every human condition, and has such perfect command of his motor powers that he can reproduce with his own person all the movements which constitute such symptoms'.[4] In the first respect Marx was well qualified for the stage. The complex relationships she had with her political allies, or near allies, her exposure to the facts of working-class existence, meant that her experience of life was anything but closed. There were, in addition, the endlessly varied types she came into contact with thanks to literature – through her work as translator, her enthusiasm for drama and, from earliest childhood, through books of many kinds, including the forbidden.

---

4 'Qualifications of the Complete Actor', *Dramatic Review*, 19 September 1885, 64–5.

'Madame Bovary, c'est moi', claimed Gustave Flaubert in a famous act of self-identification to which, given the gender divide, even he, as her creator, was not fully entitled. In her cautionary essay on Marx's 1886 translation of the great French novel, Faith Evans suggests that the relationship between author, translator and character is never fixed. Marx, a radical woman with a sense of history's sexual imbalance, approached all available roles, in life and in literature, as options, seeing them as the products of actual – that is to say political – situations. But there was nothing hesitant about her recognition of Ibsen as a great exemplar and she was at the heart of the small, at first rather select group of men and women who at once saw the playwright as the herald of change, a radical pioneer whose plays, as Sally Ledger writes, seemed to 'resonate with the conflicts and contradictions in Marx's own *modus vivendi*'. At the same time, along with many of her female contemporaries, Marx looked to the plays of Shakespeare for moral and political inspiration as well as for lyric beauty and, as Gail Marshall shows, she found in his heroines – from Juliet to Lady Macbeth – evidence of a capacity for passionate commitment she was anxious to emulate. In 1882 this made her impatient with Ellen Terry's controversial interpretation of Juliet (described by Henry James as 'too voluminous, too deliberate, too prosaic, too English, too unversed in the utterance of poetry')[5] on the grounds that 'she gets weaker and weaker as the tragic element appears till in the poison scene she collapses altogether'.[6] It was Henry Irving – brooding, powerful, masculine – who not just Eleanor but the whole Marx family admired.

Like the great actress she once aspired to become, Marx had a notably strong presence; how much was inherited, how much acquired, is hard to say. The perfect command of 'motor powers' that Shaw also thought a basic qualification of the actor may have been more difficult for her to achieve. Yet though she was not as successful at acting as she would have liked, she did excel at oratory, a skill that nineteenth-century women who intended to make their mark in the public sphere knew they had to possess and, if they were tenacious, could learn to perfect. Indeed, Bridget Bennett's essay makes explicit comparison between Marx and the American agitator and spiritualist Victoria Woodhull in just this respect: both women set up unacceptable domestic ménages that were, at best, passed by in silence; both participated in social controversy by speaking out.

II

In his 1885 article on acting, Shaw makes the point that it is extremely hard for bit-part actors to develop their talents: 'Repeating that minor part every night for six months will not advance him as a skilled actor as much as half-a-dozen public

---

[5]   Henry James, *The Scenic Art* (London: Hart-Davis, 1949), p. 164.
[6]   Kapp, I, 234.

meetings on different subjects will advance a candidate for a redistributed seat at the East End'. Moreover, the public speaker must 'learn their business on the platform at the expense of audiences who interrupt, cough, and groan in a manner unknown in the theatre'.

Triumphing over such an audience means, at the very least, convincing them of one's own sincerity, but although Marx's oratory was invariably praised for the way in which she appeared to identify totally with what she was saying, it was probably not until the late 1880s that she discovered how to incorporate an appreciative audience response within her own delivery. This was a political lesson.

Renewed proof of the real dangers involved in political protest had come with the brutalities of 'Bloody Sunday', on 13 November 1887. Although it seems that Marx was not scheduled to speak she was certainly present, and in the aftermath sent an article to the *Pall Mall Gazette* complaining about the way the police targeted the most vulnerable members of the crowd:

> In the fight for free speech now being waged in London a great number of women are doing their fair share of the work, and are fully prepared to bear their fair share of the blows and the ill-usage. No woman who enters such a movement as this has the right to ask – and so far as I know not one does ask – for different treatment from that dealt out to the men by whose side she is fighting, simply because she is a woman. But my experience on Sunday was that women were singled out by the police, and received a good deal more than their fair share of blows.[7]

Personal observation testifies to collective experience. On platform or on page, the power of activism was exemplified by Marx's role as a witness, on behalf of others, to the world about her.

It is perhaps for that very reason that, in the panicked reports of the great assemblies of the mid-1880s provided by the main national newspapers, Marx's presence and her articulate speech-making are often noted but rarely described in much detail. An exception is the vignette from the *Daily Telegraph*'s report of the meeting held in April 1887 to protest against the 'Irish Coercion Bill'. One speech was said to have been

> delivered with excellent fluency and clear intonation by Mrs. Marx Aveling, who wore beneath her brown cape, a dress of green plush with a broad hat trimmed to match. The lady has a winning and rather pretty way of putting forth revolutionary and Socialistic ideas as though they were quite the gentlest thoughts on earth.[8]

This is particularly intriguing because, of all Marx's physical qualities, her voice is the most obviously irrecoverable. Like other women of her generation she took the

---

7 'How the women fared on Sunday', *Pall Mall Gazette*, 15 November 1887.
8 *Daily Telegraph*, 12 April 1887.

art of speech seriously and, when she was still hoping to become an actress, paid for elocution lessons from Mrs Vezin, a highly reputable coach and wife of a well-known actor. These started well but the tutorial relationship ended unhappily in 1887 when a critic, commenting on Marx's poor performance in one of Aveling's adaptations from the French, noted that she was 'said to be a pupil of Mr. Herman Vezin'. Vezin wrote in to the paper repudiating the claim that he had taught her, but failing to point out that, in fact, his wife had done so.[9]

There appear to be no records of Mrs Vezin's methods but it is reasonable to assume that husband and wife would have been in accord about first principles. Herman Vezin wrote on more than one occasion about the nature of elocution, paying tribute to two great pioneers of voice training. One was John Hullah, who taught 'Public Reading' in the Theology Department at King's College, London, and whose published works counsel the importance of standing still, of starting gently and building up, and of dealing with noisy audiences not by raising one's voice but rather by decreasing its pitch and intensity so that that the audience's hubbub is exposed to itself.[10] Vezin's other hero was Emil Behnke, who took a more physiological approach, stressing the importance of diet and breathing and, for women in particular, of loose clothing.[11] Behnke was to become a crucial figure in transmission of new ways of thinking about the voice, largely through the influence of the educational pioneer Margaret McMillan who, introduced to voice production by Behnke himself, was later determined that children in elementary schools be taught elocution according to his methods.[12]

Like Hullah and Behnke, the Vezins believed that the technical secret of effective speech lay in developing the human voice as a resourceful instrument under the absolute control of its owner. The ideal result, as far as the modern increasingly realistic theatre was concerned, was a more low-key, allusive style of delivery: 'Let the pupil remember that the essential quality of good elocution is that the speaker succeeds in conveying the full meaning of the author to his hearer's brains, without giving the latter any trouble to catch that meaning'.[13] In other words speakers should neither shout nor whisper. Vezin admired a certain actor's performance as Hamlet because 'all *his* tears were in his voice … his art was eminently suggestive, not demonstrative'.[14] If on stage Marx never quite attained the Vezins' high ideal, nevertheless it seems that in her speech-making she

---

[9] Kapp, I, 234.

[10] See John Hullah, *The Speaking Voice* (Oxford: Clarendon, 1870).

[11] See *The Mechanism of the Human Voice* (London: Macmillan, 1881), and Lennox Browne and Emil Behnke, *Voice, Song, and Speech. A Practical Guide for Singers and Speakers from the Combined View of the Vocal Surgeon and Voice Trainer* (London: Sampson Low, Marston, Searle & Rivington, 1883).

[12] See Carolyn Steedman, *Childhood, Culture and Class in Britain: Margaret McMillan 1860–1931* (London: Virago, 1990), p. 216 and p. 232.

[13] 'My Masters No. 9', *Dramatic Review*, 25 July 1885, pp. 410–11 (p. 411).

[14] 'My Masters No. 4', *Dramatic Review*, 18 April 1885, pp. 184–5 (p. 185).

managed to adapt theatrical methods to her own particular ends, to be suggestive in circumstances where the demonstrative was far more common, to persuade her listeners by telling the truth as she felt it. Clarity of vision conveyed by purity of delivery: a style appropriate for a woman who brought her unique qualities of moral imagination to bear on an all too real world.

But public speaking is as much a matter of knowing one's audience as it is of being in control of oneself. What may have been effective in Hyde Park – the 'excellent and clear intonation' that impressed the male reporter of the *Daily Telegraph* in 1887 – might not be so powerful in the East End. It was perhaps only through her involvement with the Silvertown strike in 1889 that Eleanor Marx discovered her full vocal resources, and she did so by identifying her own special constituency of women and, in her speech-making as in her other activities, by collaborating with working-class groups. Interestingly, the latter seems to have been a talent that Aveling also demonstrated on occasion.

The strike had begun in the third week of September, with workers protesting against appallingly poor pay, filthy conditions and a working week that could reach eighty hours. Marx, now representing the National Union of Gasworkers, first addressed the strikers early in October, as the *Stratford Express* reports:

> She had come down, she said, because she had heard they wanted help, and would come again as often as she could. (Applause.) Having spoken about the conditions under which most of those present worked, and the wages they received, Mrs. Aveling referred to the enormous profit made by Messrs Silver last year. That those profits amounted to £160,000 had never been denied. That sum was wrung from the labour of her hearers. (Applause.) Literally it had been created by their work. (Renewed applause.) That being the case the demand they were making was a just one – nay, it was less than fair – and they must be determined to obtain it. (Cheers.) The speaker then appealed strongly to the women. They must form unions and work in harmony with the men's trades unions. As the dock strike had taught them the great lesson that skilled and unskilled labour should work together, so the present strike should teach them the further great lesson, that they could only win by men and women working in combination. The capitalist was using women to underwork men and that would be the case until women refused to undersell their brothers and husbands. (Loud applause.)[15]

Some of these accounts of Marx's political speech-making have an antiphonal quality of call and response as if speaker and audience, leader and led, were tightly bonded together in mutually reinforcing declarations of faith – as, in this case at least, must surely have been true. Three days after their first visit to Silvertown the Avelings accompanied the strikers on a march of some twenty miles into the City of London and back, followed by an open-air meeting in front of the works, where 'notwithstanding the soaked condition of the ground and the steady downpour of

---

15 *Borough of West Ham and Stratford Express,* 9 October.

rain, the crowd was as large and listened as patiently as ever'.[16] On the 18th Marx and Aveling both spoke:

> Dr. Aveling first addressed the meeting. It gave him pleasure, he said, to see those present, and to see them still so resolute. He wished any words of his could give his hearers half the pleasure which seeing then gave him. They were going, he said, to have another meeting at 12 o'clock – the women were going to meet the girls coming out of the jam factory. There would be no difficulty there, because the girls in the jam factory wanted to help them. At one o'clock there would be another meeting which would not be so pleasant – one with the women still working in Messrs. Silver's.
> The girls were going to talk to them. He knew what that meant. (Laughter.) He did not think many of them would go in on Monday. (Applause.) Then in the evening they were going to hold a meeting of the newly formed women's union.[17]

Within a few days Marx was busy setting up meetings between this newly formed women's union and the girls working at a nearby jam factory – solidarity in action. Although we now know that the Silvertown strike, threatened and betrayed from outside, would collapse in December, the inspirational energy of Eleanor Marx – and, it has to be said, of Edward Aveling – can still be felt.

III

When the aural evidence is out of earshot historians are confined to the written records – which leaves others free to suggest what these may leave out. There have been a remarkable number of attempts to recapture the overall presence, including the sound, of Eleanor Marx through fictional invention. In Judith Chernaik's extremely well-informed novel *The Daughter* (1979), the narrator remarks: 'It was a great asset to know something about voice projection, especially when hecklers got out of hand. Tussy might never make a Juliet, but she could reduce a crowd of hard-fisted miners to tears with her recitation of "The Cry of the Children."'[18] Chernaik devises an electioneering routine in which Marx recites the poetry of Elizabeth Barrett Browning or Nora's speech from *A Doll's House* before the local candidate speaks, and Edward finishes the whole thing off with Shelley's 'Ode to the West Wind'.

This is a thoroughly satisfying scenario for which there is only partial evidence, as has so often been the case. The custom of re-imagining Marx and Aveling probably begins with Dollie Radford's story of infatuation, betrayal and

---

[16] *Borough of West Ham and Stratford Express,* 12 October.
[17] *Borough of West Ham and Stratford Express,* 19 October.
[18] New York: Harper & Row, pp. 56–7.

possible suicide, *One Way of Love*,[19] and Shaw's *The Doctor's Dilemma* (1906) in which Louis Dubedat bears a certain resemblance to Aveling in that, although a brave and successful artist, he is careless with money.

Half a century later the Marx–Aveling story had become raw material for fictional explorations of 'the political and the personal'. In Piers Paul Read's *Game in Heaven with Tussy Marx* (1966) Marx looks down on the louche England of the 1960s alongside the anonymous narrator and a dead Duchess. All three watch closely as a would-be revolutionary hero named Hereward, goaded by a decadent Marxist, betrays his destiny by taking up with Miranda, a 'little rich girl' who, in the fashion of the day, is anxious to study sociology at university. While the narrator resembles Karl Marx in his fondness for improvising romantic tales, the function of the Eleanor Marx character is not only to critique Hereward's manoeuvres from a position of ideological orthodoxy, but once again to embody the tussle between politics and love.

'Yes, you see it was for love that I betrayed my father and the revolution', says Marx.[20] 'Aveling, I think now, now I see, was an enemy because he was bad. He meant to be with us in his head, but he was bad and a bad man cannot help a good cause', she comments.[21] And, 'You know, I believed in the emancipation of women but with Aveling I was no more than a thing, a litmus paper that changes colour in touching dampness; a piece of ferrous metal that bends at heat. I should have learnt from my father how to use my will and work'.[22]

But Read's novel declares its intellectual moment when it has Tussy maintain that 'Communism and Christianity are on different sides of the coin – as different and intertwined as body and soul, heaven and earth', asking 'What true Christian can fail to be a communist?' and 'Who but revolutionaries have ever shown a true charity towards the poor?'[23] This is Eleanor Marx for hippies, for the love generation.

Chernaik's more considerable book achieves its air of reality by offering a multiplicity of viewpoints, by imagining the memories of her friends, by inventing a 'Dollie Radford file' full of letters from others who knew her, including a fictive Shaw who writes self-betrayingly of Marx's 'awful integrity'. The novel tells Marx's story in parallel fashion, alongside those of her sisters and their husbands, of Olive Schreiner and Havelock Ellis, May Morris (another troubled daughter of a formidable father) and Dollie herself, but a major concern of the book is Marx's physical relationship with Aveling who is seen as increasingly pathetic, a sick man and wasted talent whose forms of sexual degradation only deepen Marx's sense of her own inadequacy. This theme of emotional desperation is strengthened by the

---

19 London: T. Fisher Unwin, 1898.
20 *Game in Heaven with Tussy Marx* (London and Sydney: Pan Books, 1979), p. 56.
21 *Game in Heaven with Tussy Marx*, p. 24.
22 *Game in Heaven with Tussy Marx*, p. 250.
23 *Game in Heaven with Tussy Marx*, p. 149.

use of a repeated line from *Madame Bovary* as a framing device: '*Alors sa situation, telle qu'un abîme, se représenta*'.[24] Erotic feeling, Chernaik seems to be suggesting, may take more perverse directions than economic determinism alone can account for. What remains is the strength of Marx's intellectual conviction, despite the turmoil within and around her.

The 1970s mark the moment when a rapidly developing feminism, and a consequent interest in the heroines of history, is accompanied by a widespread desire to understand the origins not only of Marxist factionalism but of British radical sects in general. Nor was it by chance that this flurry of activity came at the very moment when the most celebrated 'strong woman' of modern times, Margaret Thatcher, was in the political ascendant, busily denying the existence of 'society' and the need to teach history in schools. Within weeks of the showing, in January 1977, of the three fifty-minute episodes of Andrew Davies's play *Eleanor Marx* on BBC2,[25] the same channel broadcast a dramatization of letters between the Ibsenite actress Janet Achurch and Bernard Shaw, along with a series of six specially commissioned studies of influential women of the past (Edith Cavell, Marie Stopes, Mary Baker Eddy, Elizabeth Fry, Annie Besant and Lilian Baylis).

Davies's version of Marx's life (which is based on Chushichi Tsuzuki's compact biography rather than Kapp's two-volume opus, which was only just appearing) is much concerned with supposed female psychology. This, above all, is a father's daughter. The first episode begins and ends at Marx's funeral in Highgate cemetery, and to underline the power of the relationship makes heavy use of the family tradition of domestic Shakespeare performance, giving us not just young Eleanor's girlish rendering of 'To be or not to be', innocent of any suicidal inflection, but an excerpt from *Othello* performed in the presence of Lissagaray, briefly her fiancé, in which as Desdemona she gives a nudging rendering of 'My noble father, / I do perceive here a divided loyalty ... / I am hitherto your daughter; but here's my husband'. The emphatic pun on the 'Moor' who is Shakespeare's military hero and 'Mohr', Karl Marx's nickname, is not simply coincidence; it turns, in roughly Freudian fashion, patriarchy into romance.

It was said at the time, and not without justice, that throughout the three episodes Eleanor Marx, though vigorously and youthfully played by Jennie Stoller, was continually subordinated to male figures. Nevertheless, Alan Dobie's Aveling, for all his heavily-lidded, deep-sunk, brown eyes, does not always look the predator and the studied brilliance of his performance almost makes up for the gender imbalance of the script by showing just how and why – moral intensity, apparent political commitment, the promise of camaraderie – Marx might have been drawn, in all her strength, to the man who determined her ultimate decision.

Following suggestions in Tsuzuki (Yvonne Kapp was to be more circumspect when it came to details of Marx's death), Davies increases suspicions of Aveling's

---

24   *The Daughter*, pp. 68, 212.
25   10, 17, 24 January, directed by Jane Howell, produced by Louis Marks.

malevolence by having him issue directly to their maid an order for poison apparently required in order to dispose of his dog. Davies then has him quieten the girl when she points out that he does not actually own one. In fact there seems to be no record of this conversation. Along with such absences of fact, psychological gaps are also filled: Marx speaks of suicide as 'an old friend', and at the moment she loses consciousness the screen fills with images of her father. What follows is a long, painful and very physical agony, as realistic as television can make it.

If the intensity of the sexual interest can be said to anticipate nude Jane Austen and the other ratings-related shenanigans of the 1990s then from our present vantage point in the year 2000, Davies's interpretation of the life of Eleanor Marx looks like the close of one phase in the output of British television drama and the beginning of another. Intelligent, literate, strenuously 'researched', it tells a respectfully historical story but, in the end, prefers to concentrate upon emotional temptations rather than ideological demands.

In the more politicized works written after the fall of the Berlin Wall in 1989 representations of Eleanor Marx came, inevitably perhaps, to resemble attempts to recoup after loss. Now she stands for an original Marxist humanism, and it is the family life – picnics on Hampstead Heath and the rest – that counts above all else. Howard Zinn's one-man play, *Marx in Soho* (1999), has her father recall the little girl, wise beyond her years, who would 'dress her dolls … while sipping from a glass of wine', whose room was 'a Shakespeare museum,[26] who insisted on being read *Romeo and Juliet*, who understood the pull of religion even as she disapproved of it, who maintained pride in her Jewishness, and felt intense love for Lissagaray. There is, perhaps logically, no place whatsoever for Aveling in this idealized account. On both macro and micro levels the Marxist vision survives, almost unsullied.

By contrast, Barry Maitland's *The Marx Sisters* (1994),[27] a complex thriller which explores the archaeological layers of London in the manner of a novel by Peter Ackroyd, imagines the survival of some Marx letters, and even late manuscripts relating to the fourth volume of *Capital*, in the corrupt and tawdry environment of post-Thatcher London. These relics of the Marxian *Nachlass* are held by Marx's great-nieces, granddaughters of Freddy Demuth, Marx's illegitimate son. Inspired by their distant relative the sisters keep the true faith and, when their home is threatened with demolition by wicked developers, respond with violent action. It takes two other women, an American academic and a police officer, to comprehend the power that the legend of Eleanor Marx still possesses over her descendants, to realize that these murdering old ladies believe themselves to be working in a strangely courageous tradition. Marx's image retains its talismanic

---

26 Cambridge, Mass.: South End Press, p. 15.
27 Barry Maitland, *The Marx Sisters* (London: Hamish Hamilton, 1994).

power. Her framed photograph hangs in a corner of their home: 'She was wearing a dark velvet dress with a white lace collar, and a pair of spectacles was hanging from a cord round her neck. She was smiling gently at someone off to the left of the frame'.

Still we look at her, still try to imagine the object of her smile. In a rather different novel of recent years, Sarah Waters's lesbian picaresque, *Tipping the Velvet*, published in 1998, set in the 1880s, Marx (as Bridget Bennett has spotted) plays yet another off-stage role. Now she is a fabled angel of promise, inspiring the socialist women of the East End but, in this case, never actually appearing among them. Again her photograph works like an icon: 'a heavy-browed woman with untidy hair dark hair: she seemed to be sitting very squarely, and her gaze was grave'.[28] The conclusion of Waters's novel, though, is anything but grave, since this is a story of sexual and political survival, of happiness even, in a world that Eleanor Marx helps to make possible but which she never completely inhabits, never witnesses. That awkward but undeniable disjunction between a slow collective achievement and a truncated single life not only returns us to the dilemma of the political and the personal, it may also help explain why Marx remains unforgotten and yet, for all the efforts of historians, of playwrights and of novelists, is still not fully understood. Her historical meaning resides in the present.

When told of the contributions made to the Eleanor Marx conference Yvonne Kapp, then in her ninety-sixth year, replied by letter: 'It would be splendid if you could produce a book of essays based on the conference ... It would shed much light on the distance travelled, not only between the late nineteenth century in the spheres of both socialism and feminism, but in the past two decades since my book was written.'

There could have been no more welcome endorsement of our quest.

---

[28] London: Virago, 1999, p. 363.

Chapter 1

'A Daughter of Today':
The Socialist-Feminist Intellectual as
Woman of Letters

Lyn Pykett

The would-be student of Eleanor Marx is likely to have an experience that is the reverse of the one described by Virginia Woolf in *A Room of One's Own* when she went to the British Museum to research the topic of 'Woman'. On consulting the Museum catalogue, Woolf experienced 'five separate minutes of stupefaction, wonder and bewilderment' on discovering that woman is 'the most discussed animal in the universe'.[1] The present-day researcher on Eleanor Marx, whether electronically scanning the British Library catalogues, searching other databases, or poring over the indexes of dusty tomes, is more likely to be filled with stupefaction, wonder and bewilderment on discovering how little discussed their subject is. To be sure there is Yvonne Kapp's monumental two-volume study, and Chushichi Tsuzuki's terser biography. However, when one turns to the dictionaries of women writers, of feminists, or of socialists, or when one searches the indexes of histories of socialism or feminism in Britain, one is likely to be disappointed.

On looking up 'Marx, E.' one is usually directed to 'see Aveling', but seeing Aveling often results in disappointment – as Eleanor Marx repeatedly discovered to her cost. Indeed, the experience of trying to look up 'Marx, E.' brings to mind Jean McCrindle's review of the 1977 BBC television series about Eleanor Marx's life, written by Andrew Davies, in which she laments that 'The *Radio Times* publicity and the credit sequence where the men in her life loom up and disappear beyond her left ear, place her firmly in a male context, dominated by her "father's overpowering personality"'.[2] My essay, like others in this collection, seeks to examine the numerous things that loom up behind Eleanor Marx's left ear other than the men in her life. It will look at Marx not as the daughter of the father of socialism, but as 'a daughter of today', to quote the title of a novel published in 1895 by the British-based, Canadian novelist Sara Jeanette Duncan (Mrs Everard Cotes). For, although Marx was an exceptional woman, born into an exceptional

---

[1]   Virginia Woolf, *A Room of One's Own* (London: Hogarth Press, 1929), p. 36.
[2]   *Spare Rib*, March 1977, pp. 37–8.

family, her story is, in many ways, a stereotypical story of the modern woman, at least as this creature is represented in the press and in fiction at the *fin de siècle*.

Marx died in 1898, only four years after the *annus mirabilis* of the New Woman. 1894, in many ways *the* year of the New Woman, saw the publication of several important novels and collections of stories: Emma Frances Brooke's *A Superfluous Woman*, Mona Caird's *The Daughters of Danaus*, Ella Hepworth Dixon's *The Story of a Modern Woman*, George Egerton's *Discords*, Annie Holdsworth's *Joanna Traill, Spinster*, Iota's *A Yellow Aster*, Elizabeth Robins's *George Mandeville's Husband*, George Paston's [Emily Morse Symonds] *A Modern Amazon*; there were articles in the *North American Review* by 'Ouida' and Sarah Grand discussing the phenomenon, and W.T. Stead's *Review of Reviews* essay on 'The Novel of the Modern Woman', as well as numerous *Punch* cartoons and lampoons.[3] However, although Marx barely outlived the zenith of the New Woman, her life in the early 1880s prefigured those numerous narratives which poured from the presses in the latter years of that decade and the early years of the 1890s, and which became a torrent in 1894 and 1895. In the last fifteen years or so of her short life, Marx recapitulated – or anticipated – various stages or aspects of the New Woman identity – from 'Revolting Daughter'[4] to suicide, acting out various versions of the New Woman struggle on the way.

The picture that emerges from her letters, from contemporary accounts, and from modern biographies, reveals Marx as a relative creature, shaped and limited by her daughterly and later 'wifely' roles, and as a 'revolting daughter' who resisted the roles in which her parent sought to cast her. Yet at the same time she was also a dutiful daughter who sacrificed her own health and well-being to look after her ailing parents and sisters, and her sisters' children. Her own sense of this role and of some of its costs and injustices are powerfully revealed in a letter to Olive Schreiner in 1881:

> My mother and I loved each other passionately, but she did not understand me as father did. One of the bitterest of many bitter sorrows in my life is that my mother died, thinking, despite all our love, that I had been hard and cruel, and never guessing that to save her and father sorrow I had sacrificed the best, freshest years of my life.[5]

---

3   See Sarah Grand, 'A New Aspect of the Woman Question', *North American Review*, 158 (1894), 270–76; 'Ouida', 'The New Woman', *North American Review*, 158 (1894), 610–19; [W.T. Stead] 'The Book of the Month: The Novel of the Modern Woman', *Review of Reviews*, 10 (1894), 177–90.

4   'Revolting Daughter' was the soubriquet given to those female rebels against parental (and particularly maternal) control, whose doings filled the pages of middle-class periodicals in the early 1890s. See, S.M. Amos, 'The Evolution of the Daughters', *Contemporary Review*, 65 (1894), 515–20; Blanche Crackanthorpe, 'The Revolt of the Daughters', *Nineteenth Century*, 34 (1894), 23–31; S.M. Jeune, 'The Revolt of the Daughters', *Fortnightly Review*, 61 (1894), 267–76; and Alys Pearsall Smith, 'A Reply from the Daughters, II', *Nineteenth Century*, 35 (1894), 443–50.

5   Quoted in Havelock Ellis, 'Eleanor Marx', *Adelphi*, 10 (1935), 342–52 (p. 349).

Like many New Woman daughters of the day, Marx was, simultaneously or by turns: a British Museum hack, a teacher, an aspiring artist, and a journalist and reviewer; she set herself up in the business of typewriting; she visited the East End with Margaret Harkness; she was a public speaker who could sway her audience with her eloquence or simply by her stage presence; she was a freethinker, a proponent of free unions (and a troubled participant in one), a wild woman as politician and social insurgent (to borrow the terms of Eliza Lynn Linton's articles in the *Nineteenth Century* in 1891); she was a proponent of literary innovation (in her introduction to her 1886 translation of Flaubert's *Madame Bovary*), and a proponent and promulgator of 'Ibscenity' through her involvement, with Edward Aveling, George Bernard Shaw and others, in readings and performances of Ibsen's plays, as a translator of *An Enemy of the People* (as *An Enemy of Society*) and *The Lady from the Sea*, and in her satire on the English response to Ibsen (written with Israel Zangwill) '*A Doll's House* Repaired' (1891).

Marx also acted out, or was perceived in terms of, that most typical of New Woman roles: the hysteric or neurotic, the degenerate or erotomaniac. It is striking to note precisely how closely some of Freud and Breuer's descriptions of the dispositions and circumstances of their hysterical patients in *Studies on Hysteria* resemble her situation. Take, for example, Freud's description of Fraulein Elizabeth Von R:

> The youngest of three daughters, she was tenderly attached to her parents ... Her mother's health was frequently troubled ... Thus ... she found herself drawn into especially intimate contact with her father, ... who used to say that this daughter ... took the place of a son and a friend with whom he could exchange thoughts. Although the girl's mind found intellectual stimulation from this relationship with her father, he did not fail to observe that her mental constitution was on that account departing from the ideal which people like to see realised in a girl. He jokingly called her 'cheeky' and 'cocksure', and warned her against being too positive in her judgements and against her habit of regardlessly telling people the truth ... She was in fact greatly discontented with being a girl. She was full of ambitious plans. She wanted to study or to have a musical training, and she was indignant at the idea of having to sacrifice her inclinations and her freedom of judgement by marriage. As it was she nourished herself on her pride in her father and in the prestige ... of her family, and she jealously guarded everything that was bound up with these advantages. The unselfishness, however, with which she put her mother and elder sisters first, when an occasion arose, reconciled her parent completely to the harsher side of her character.[6]

Like Frau Elizabeth, Marx had a sick mother and a intimate emotional attachment to her sisters and father. She also enjoyed a particularly close intellectual companionship with her father. Moreover, the intellectuality, and what was

---

6   Sigmund Freud and Josef Breuer, *Studies on Hysteria* [1895], trans. by James and Alix Strachey, The Penguin Freud Library (Harmondsworth: Penguin, 1991), III, 207–8.

perceived as the 'cheekiness', and 'cockiness' of both young women, together with their shared aspiration for an independent life and an artistic career, marked them – as it did many New Woman of the *fin de siècle*, in fiction and in fact – as untypical of their gender. Indeed, some of her contemporaries simply decoded her in terms of current representations of the New Woman as hysteric and/or degenerate. This is clearly what Beatrice Potter (later Webb) did in this diary entry for 24 May 1883:

> In afternoon went to British Museum and met Miss Marx in refreshment room ... Gains her livelihood by teaching 'literature' etc., and corresponding for socialist newspapers ... In person she is comely, dressed in a slovenly picturesque way with curly black hair, flying about in all directions. Fine eyes, full of life and sympathy, otherwise ugly features and expression and complexion showing signs of unhealthy excited life kept up with stimulants and tempered by narcotics. Lives alone ... evidently peculiar views on love etc., and should think she has somewhat 'natural' relations with men! Should fear the chances against her remaining long within the pale of respectable society.[7]

Speculations about sex and drugs apart, this description shows a remarkable overlap with Marion Skinner's (later Comyn's) description of Marx as the New Girl she knew in the early 1880s – a girl whose wilfulness was indulged by her father:

> Wilful indeed she was, but she was also an unusually brilliant creature, with a clear logical brain, a shrewd knowledge of men and a wonderful memory ... She either passionately admired or desperately scorned, she loved fervently or she hated with vehemence. Middle courses never commended themselves to her. She had amazing vitality, extraordinary receptivity, and she was the gayest creature in the world – when she was not the most miserable.[8]

One of my aims in insisting on the typicality of some of the particularities of Marx's history is precisely to historicize that history. It is instructive to stand back from the heroinism of accounts such as Yvonne Kapp's, and to see Marx as the protagonist of a different kind of story. I tell this 'different' story, not in order to privilege it, but rather to think about its politics.

Kapp claims that Marx 'went her own way without fuss, feminism or false constraint ... objectively alive to the social injustices that shackled women's freedom, subjectively free'.[9] Certainly Marx had little time for the causes taken up by those whom she regarded as the parasite women of the middle and upper

---

[7]   Quoted in Kapp, I, 283–4.
[8]   Marion Comyn, 'My Recollections of Karl Marx', *The Nineteenth Century and After*, 91 (1922), 161–9 (pp. 166–7).
[9]   Kapp, II, 89.

classes, but on many occasions she revealed herself as an instinctive feminist: for example, when she wrote to her sister Laura in 1890 about the injustice with which the party seemed to be treating Louise Kautsky:

> I am sorry for Louise. Bebel and all the others have told her it is her duty to the Party to stop [with Engels]. It hardly seems fair to her. She was getting on so well at Vienna & to sacrifice her whole career is no trivial matter. – No one would ask a man to do that. She is still so young – only just 30. It seems not right to shut her up, & keep her from every chance of a fuller and happier life.[10]

Far from going her own way 'subjectively free' and 'without fuss, feminism or false constraint' Marx, like so many of her contemporaries – in fiction and in life – struggled to find her way and to define a direction for herself. She made a great deal of fuss and suffered extraordinary turmoil; and she repeatedly came into conflict with both the material and the subjective constraints (false or otherwise) of the circumstances of the life of the middle-class woman of the late nineteenth century.

As the daughter of a world-historical individual, whose home was a frequent meeting place for European intellectuals and political activists, Marx's upbringing was in many respects exceptional. However, in other respects it was not, since her parents sought to give their daughters the upbringing and social acquirements that were proper for middle-class girls who were destined to be wives. Like many girls of her class, Marx first sought independence in a teaching job, beginning work at a girl's boarding school in Brighton in 1873. This was a move for which her parents had little enthusiasm, despite their precarious financial position. Her mother tried (without success) to get her to leave the Miss Halls' school in order to accompany Helen Demuth on a visit to her ailing sister in Germany. This subterfuge was attempted despite the fact that Mrs Marx claimed, in a letter, to understand the importance of work to her daughter: 'I alone understand how dearly you long for work and independence, the only two things that can help one over the sorrows and cares of present day society'.[11] 'Work' and 'independence' were words that were to become a kind of litany in Marx's letters of the 1880s. However, this early attempt at resisting parental pressure ended in failure: she soon retired hurt from her foray into teaching, suffering from one of the nervous collapses which were to punctuate her life, as they did the histories of many fictional New Women in the 1890s.

For much of the 1880s Marx followed the path taken by many of her female contemporaries and foregrounded in much New Woman fiction, becoming a sort of woman of letters by undertaking hack work or devilling at the British Museum. A great deal of her work came through F.J. Furnivall, whom she probably met

---

10 *Daughters*, p. 224.
11 Quoted in Kapp, I, 147.

through his associations with the Christian Socialists. Furnivall was a great founder of societies. Among many others, he created the New Shakspere Society, the Early English Text Society, the Browning Society, the Shelley Society and the Philological Society. Marx took an active part in various of Furnivall's societies and undertook research and other intellectual work for them. For example, she translated from German Professor Delius's lecture on 'The Epic Element in Shakespeare' for the New Shakspere Society, and she undertook work for Dr Murray for the *New English Dictionary*, an offshoot of the work of the Philological Society. Like many of her contemporaries she would turn her hand to almost anything in the devilling research line. In June 1881 she reported to her sister Jenny that she had been invited to become a précis writer at £2 per week, for a scientific journal with which one of her acquaintances was connected,[12] and in June 1888 she reported wryly to Laura that she was doing jobbing work, 'sweating' for a Miss Zimmerman, writing essays and reviews for 5s and 7s 6d, which Miss Zimmerman would, in turn, sell on for 30s and 35s.[13]

Like many of her fictional counterparts (for example, Gissing's Marion Yule in *New Grub Street*, 1891, and Ella Hepworth Dixon's Mary Erle in *The Story of a Modern Woman*, 1894), Marx had a love-hate relationship with hack work. It brought her much needed funds (and was assiduously sought for this reason), but perhaps even more important was the simple fact that it was work, and thus gave her life a direction and a purpose. As she wrote to her Jenny in January 1882, 'After all work is the chief thing. To me at least it is a necessity. That is why I love even my dull Museum drudgery. You see I am not clever enough to live a purely intellectual life, nor am I dull enough to be content to sit down and do nothing'.[14] At the same time as she was doing her dull museum drudgery, Marx was also giving lectures on Shakespeare and taking part in readings and performances of poems and plays: Browning's *Pied Piper* and *Count Gismond* were part of her repertoire. She recited the latter at the summer entertainment of the Browning Society at University College London in 1882, which she described as a nerve-racking experience, since 'all sorts of literary and other "swells" were there'. Nevertheless, she also felt that she 'got on capitally' and was invited to a 'crush' at Lady Wilde's, 'the mother of that very limp and nasty young man, Oscar Wilde who has been making such a d—d fool of himself in America'.[15]

Marx's letters to her sister Jenny in the early 1880s suggest that her life of surface busyness concealed an inner frustration and struggle; an experience which was shared by many of her female contemporaries, and which was articulated so powerfully in a number of New Woman novels. Thus on 18 June 1881 she wrote: 'I've a goodly number of irons in the fire, but I feel I've wasted enough of my life,

---

12 *Daughters*, p. 135.
13 Quoted in Kapp, I, 284.
14 *Daughters*, p. 148.
15 Quoted in Tsuzuki, p. 68.

and that it is high time I did something'.[16] The letters to Jenny in the years of the final illnesses of their parents are full of references to last chances, and to time running out, as Marx professed herself impatient to 'do something before it's too late'.[17] In the early 1880s this crisis about what was to be done with her life became focused on her struggle with her father over her desire to express herself by training as an actress. As in so many novels by women in the 1890s, Marx represents her artistic ambitions as, on the one hand, a pragmatic route to a profession and economic independence, and, on the other, as the true pathway to self-expression and self-definition: she represents herself as looking for a vocation as well as for work.

Her first mention of her intention to take acting lessons with Mrs Vezin was couched in pragmatic terms in a letter to Jenny on 18 June 1881:

> Even if, as I fancy will be the case, Mrs Vezin finds she has much overrated my powers, the lessons will still be useful to me, and I can always make the recitation venture ... I feel sorry to cost papa so much, but after all very small sums were expended on my education, compared at least to what is *now* demanded of girls – and I think if I do succeed it will have been a good investment.[18]

By the following January, however, Marx's acting ambitions had become much more clearly a way out of a life crisis – a response to that sense of life slipping away which was experienced by so many self-sacrificing unmarried dutiful (if resentful) daughters in fact and fiction in the 1890s (and before and after, for that matter). As she broke down under the strain of caring for her recently dead mother and her ailing father, she asserted that the rest recommended by her doctors and her father was the last thing that she needed. 'I should be more likely to "get strong"', she wrote, 'if I have some definite plan and work than to go on waiting and waiting ... It drives me half mad to sit here when perhaps my last chance of doing something is going'. She went on to lament the lack of money that prevented her from going in for the more intensive work with Mrs Vezin which might bring success:

> Really, Jenny, I think I *could* do something ... in this I think I could get on. I have seen it too often – and with such different people – that I can move an audience – and that is the chief thing.[19]

Just a week later she wrote to Jenny that 'much and hard as I have tried I could not crush out my desire to *try something*. The chance too of independence is very sweet'.[20]

---

[16] *Daughters*, p. 135.
[17] *Daughters*, p. 146.
[18] *Daughters*, p. 133.
[19] *Daughters*, p. 146.
[20] *Daughters*, p. 148.

It would appear that both she and Jenny – again like many of their contemporaries – conceived of the intellectual, and more especially the artistic life as a means of transcending traditional gender roles[21] and the constraints of the life of the middle-class woman (even the middle-class woman who was the daughter or wife of a political revolutionary). For example, in April 1881 Marx encouraged her sister not to despair of her writing: 'It would certainly be a great pity if you had to give up writing but by and by when you've settled down and have a good servant you'll find more time. Just now naturally every moment is occupied with the house or the children, but that will only be for a time'.[22] In her turn, Jenny rejoiced at Marx's prospect of 'living the only free life a woman can live – the artistic one'.[23]

In the years leading up to and immediately following the death of her father, this was precisely what Eleanor Marx tried to do. At the same time as she was moving into politics on her own terms – through her involvement (successively) in the Democratic Federation, the SDF and the Socialist League, and her unpaid work as a political journalist for the publications of these groupings (*To-Day, The Monthly Magazine of Scientific Socialism,* and *Commonweal*) – she was also involved in organizing readings and performances of Ibsen's plays as well as translating and commenting on them, as part of her self-appointed mission to explain Ibsen to the British public. As she wrote to Havelock Ellis in December 1885: 'I feel I must do something to make people understand our Ibsen little more than they do.'[24]

A similar mission to explain was announced in her introduction to her translation of Flaubert's *Madame Bovary*, published by Vizetelly in 1886, in which she claimed that Flaubert 'is still so little known in England, his work so completely misunderstood'. In fact, Marx's main mission in undertaking the Flaubert translation – obtained through her contacts with George Moore – was to earn money. She found the work of translation onerous, but she also found much with which to identify and sympathize in Flaubert's work and in his project. Marx's introduction to *Madame Bovary* idealized – even idolized – Flaubert as a revolutionary and as an artist who sacrificed himself for his art: 'He fell dead at the foot of his writing table, that altar on which he had offered up his whole life in the pursuance of his one aim and ideal.'[25] Among several overwrought passages in this

---

[21] Elfrida Bell, the heroine of Sara Jeanette Duncan's *A Daughter of Today* (London: Chatto & Windus, 1894), clearly conceives of the artistic role as a means of transcending gender. In the 'charmingly apologetic' letter which she leaves for her parents when she commits suicide, Elfrida 'commanded' that these 'three little French words' should be inscribed on her tombstone: 'Pas femme – artiste' (II, 243).

[22] *Daughters*, p. 129.

[23] Undated letter, quoted in Tsuzuki, p. 67.

[24] Quoted in Kapp, II, 103.

[25] Introduction to Gustave Flaubert, *Madame Bovary*, trans. by Eleanor Marx-Aveling (London: Vizetelly, 1886), pp. vii–xxii.

introduction, there is one expressing a hyperbolic admiration for Flaubert's dedication to Art. 'That Art was to Flaubert "a jealous god", who must be worshipped unreservedly; that Flaubert was "ready for martyrdom" in the service of his divinity', she asserts, was not appreciated by M. Du Camp (whose words she is quoting in this extract, and who was responsible for cutting the text of Flaubert's novel for publication in the *Revue de Paris*).

Marx espoused the de Goncourts' view of Flaubert:

> Yes, he was striving after the heaven of the artist – ideal perfection; that ideal ever eluding the grasp, but that the great ones of the earth must still strain after, yearn for – 'or what's a heaven for?' ... It is only we who come after them who know how much that striving has achieved.

If there is, perhaps, a suggestion of personal investment – even over-investment – in Marx's reading of Flaubert's dedication to Art and aesthetic goals, there is also a sense of personal investment or identification in her reading of Emma Bovary. For Marx, Emma (in an interesting distinction) 'is the embodiment of the artistic temperament as opposed to the temperament of the artist'. She 'has not the power to work off her emotions in music, or painting, or poems. She has no means of expression, and her passions consuming her, they must result only in disappointment, disillusion and disgust'.

Marx's reading of Emma offers a significant perspective on both the Woman Question, and the acculturation of women. It also provokes questions about her own acculturation:

> Marriage has been shown to her [Emma] as the be-all and end-all of a woman's life; even prostitution, so it be to a king, she has found does not entail much of a disgrace ... there is nothing actually depending on her. Her life is idle, useless and this strong woman feels there *must* be some place for her in the world; there must be something to do – and she dreams. Life is so unreal to her that she marries Bovary thinking she loves him. She does her best to love 'this poor wretch'. In all literature there is perhaps nothing more pathetic than her hopeless effort to 'make herself in love'. And even after she has been false, how she yearns to go back to him, to something real, to a healthier, better love than she has known.
>
> She is foolish, even vile; but there is a certain nobleness about her too. She is never mercenary ... Emma Bovary is in search of an ideal. She has intellectuality not mere sensuality. It is part of the irony of her fate that she is punished for her virtues as much as for her vices.

Marx's possibly overgenerous reading of Emma Bovary as unmercenary and intellectual rather than merely sensual is, perhaps, the consequence of her reading Flaubert's heroine as a version of herself. Certainly, when she finally closed the door of her 'doll's house' in Jew's Walk, Sydenham, it was Emma Bovary's death scene that she apparently re-enacted.

From the time of its discovery, Marx's suicide has given rise to a great deal of speculation. As with most suicides, the causes of and motives for this act of self-slaughter must remain speculative. However, many of the questions raised by Marx's death are precisely the questions raised by and in the New Woman fiction, particularly in its repeated plotting of the life of its aspiring and/or 'revolting' heroines as ending in death, physical or mental breakdown, frustration, betrayal, disappointment or disillusionment. The dying fall of their endings is one of the ways in which the New Woman novelists pose the woman question at the end of the nineteenth century. It is a way of figuring the conflicts and confusions of women's sexual, familial and social roles and of the aspirations of some women to redefine those roles. It is a way, too, of figuring the tensions (which many of these writers experienced) between the aesthetic and the social or political. In her death as in her life, Eleanor Marx was very much 'a daughter of today'.

Chapter 2

Fictions of Engagement: Eleanor Marx, Biographical Space

Carolyn Steedman

Anyone who has worked on English socialism in the late nineteenth century, who has considered its involvement of women in the workers' movement, in trade-union organization and in laying the intellectual foundations of the British parties of the left, will have encountered Eleanor Marx at the edges of the story they make familiar by their writing of it.[1] She is to be found living the same kind of story and the same kind of politics as the Independent Labour Party (ILP) and Social Democratic Federation (SDF) women who are now, at the start of the twenty-first century, irremovably written into the historiography of the socialist movement in Britain.[2] Yvonne Kapp's two-volume account of Marx was a component of the same kind of restorative endeavour of the 1970s and 1980s. After reading this extraordinary work no one was able to think of her as she had been known in the eighty years after her death, as just Karl Marx's daughter, as just a minor worker for the workers' cause, who lived with a most unsavoury man, and who killed herself, in a most painful manner, when he made his final betrayal of her.[3]

And yet, even with Kapp's account in place, Eleanor Marx has not been made familiar to us, in the way that other British socialist women have been. All historiographical meetings with her are something like Beatrice Webb's (then Miss Potter) actual one, in May 1883, when over tea in the British Museum Refreshment Room, Marx swiftly and forcibly enunciates a political position and a political philosophy, and then, issuing an invitation to Miss Potter to visit her in her bachelor-girl lodgings, disappears from the pages of the Webb journal into

---

[1] Karen Hunt, *Equivocal Feminists. The Social Democratic Federation and the Woman Question, 1884–1911* (Cambridge: Cambridge University Press, 1996); June Hannam, 'Women and the ILP, 1890–1914', in *The Centennial History of the Independent Labour Party*, ed. by David James, Tony Jowitt, Keith Laybourn (Halifax: Ryburn, 1992), pp. 205–8; Carolyn Steedman, *Childhood, Culture and Class in Britain. Margaret McMillan, 1860–1931* (London: Virago, 1990); Christine Colette, 'Socialism and Scandal', *History Workshop*, 23 (1987), 102–11.

[2] For the biographical entry of women into the annals of British socialism see Hunt, *Equivocal Feminists*, pp. 4–7.

[3] See *Writing Lives: Conversations between Women Writers*, ed. by Mary Chamberlain (London: Virago, 1988), pp. 100–117.

some other mysterious political terrain where Miss Potter cannot follow.[4] Webb
was very curious about her, and perhaps envious of her living alone ('exactly the
life and character I should like to study') but she did not go to the rooms in Great
Coram Street, 'for unfortunately one cannot mix with human beings without
becoming more or less *connected* with them'.[5]

What is usually remembered from this account is Miss Potter's belief that she
had taken tea with a drug addict. 'In person she is comely', she recorded early next
morning, though she had been

> dressed in a slovenly picturesque way with curly-black hair flying about in all
> directions ... complexion showing the signs of an unhealthy excited life,
> kept up with stimulants and tempered by narcotics ... should think has
> somewhat 'natural' relations with men! Should fear that the chances were
> against her remaining within the pale of 'respectable' society.

This is the passage that is often extracted from Beatrice Potter's much longer
account – a strange mixture of jealousy, prurience and incomprehension – in
which the *real* problem with Miss Marx was elided by what Kapp noted as her
bizarre rendering of her as a slut and dope-fiend.[6] 'It was useless to disagree with
her,' wrote Potter; 'she refused to recognise the beauty of the Christian religion.'
Indeed,

> she read the Gospels as the Gospels of damnation. Thought that Christ, if he
> had existed, was a weak-headed individual with a good deal of sweetness of
> character but quite lacking in heroism.

Marx's resolute secularism and materialism were a problem for many other late
nineteenth-century British socialists quite as much as they were for Beatrice Potter.
They may have known less about the roots of their belief in Protestant dissent, in
the radical Christianity of the Civil War and the Interregnum than do their late
twentieth-century historians, but they still knew an alien, materialist, Continental
mode of thinking when they saw one.[7] Indeed, Miss Marx told Miss Potter that
her kind of socialist 'wanted to make the working class disregard the mythical next
world and live for *this world* and *insist on having* what will make it pleasant to
them'.[8]

Eleanor Marx appears on the borderlines, in the liminal spaces and places of
the historiography of British socialism because of her political beliefs and her

---

[4]   *The Diary of Beatrice Webb. Vol. 1 1873–1892. Glitter Around and Darkness Within*, ed. by
      Norman and Jeanne MacKenzie (London: Virago, 1982), pp. 86–8.
[5]   *Diary of Beatrice Webb, Vol. 1*, p. 88. For Marx's living arrangements at the time, see Kapp, I,
      283.
[6]   Kapp, I, 284.
[7]   Stephen Yeo, 'A New Life: The Religion of Socialism in Britain, 1883–1896', *History
      Workshop*, 4 (1977), 5–56.
[8]   *Diary of Beatrice Webb, Vol. 1*, p. 87.

political career. In any case, by far the greatest quantity of historical attention has been paid to the ILP, both in its relationship to the trade union movement and to the other major party of the British left, the SDF. The general historical emphasis has been on these parties as the cradle of the Labour Representation Committee (formed in 1900 to support the election of Labour candidates to Parliament) and the Labour Party proper. Marx's political career, on the other hand, traces out a history of split and fraction, of the transmutation of one tiny band of comrades into another one, with a new name. She joined the SDF in 1883 and stayed a member until 1894, when after a very brief period on its Executive she joined William Morris, Edward Aveling and others in breaking away and forming the Socialist League.[9] There were even further splits, and in 1888 the branch to which Marx and Aveling belonged was excluded from the League, and became the Bloomsbury Socialist Society.[10] The 'ceaseless factionalism' of the Socialist League, and Morris's aversion to the grubby practicalities of electioneering and trade union campaigning were among the reasons for Marx's disillusionment with the League.[11] Her biographer understands this split of 1888 as part and parcel of Marx's identification with the working-class movement and the direction of her political activity towards the New Unionism which sought to organize the vast numbers of unskilled and semi-skilled workers of late Victorian Britain.[12] Having devoted much time and propaganda to the National Union of Gasworkers and General Workers' Union, Marx rejoined the SDF two years before her death.

Across all these groupings and regroupings, her great value to her many compatriots lay in her skills a journalist and orator, her personal acquaintance with many European socialists, and her abilities as a translator. Her work of translation, for the socialist press of Germany, France, Italy, Latin America and Russia, was immense. And there was the major work of translating her father's writings, including parts of *Capital* (she did this in collaboration with Edward Aveling in the years after Marx's death, and the death of Engels in 1895). Eleanor was not the only Marx daughter to be bequeathed the task of translation. Laura Lafargue had a long and convoluted relationship with her father's *Communist Manifesto* (1848), turning it into French by way of a obscure English translation of 1850, to appear serially in *Le Socialiste* at the end of 1885, when it replaced the first French translation of 1848.[13]

---

9   See Kapp, I, 211–12, 224; Kapp, II, 1–44, 57–9, 60–68, 92–3; E.P. Thompson, *William Morris. Romantic to Revolutionary* (New York: Pantheon, 1976), pp. 342–65; Hunt, *Equivocal Feminists*, p. 60.

10 Kapp, II, 248–66, 367–71, 374–8, 384–5; Thompson, *Morris*, pp. 564–5.

11 Kapp, II, 264–5; Thompson, *Morris*, pp. 564–5.

12 See David Howell, *British Workers and the Independent Labour Party, 1888–1906* (Manchester: Manchester University Press, 1983) pp. 109–22.

13 The Manifesto was originally published in German, in the headquarters of the exiled German Workers' Educational Association. The first English translation (by Helen MacFarlane) appeared in the short-lived *Red Republican*, and probably languished unread in English, until

Are biographies matters of inheritance? Not so much the inheritance of a parent, who might hand down the endless task of translation, but in the way that you come to live the life (and perhaps tell the story of that life) because the place you are in necessarily gives rise to a particular kind of story? The claim is made for fictional lives of the nineteenth century, as Franco Moretti maps the complex movements across great European cities that structure the plot of numerous contemporary novels.[14] Here, however, we must consider non-fictional lives – lives lived in historical time – the idea of a life, the way it gets told (by she who lives it and her biographers) and the material used in the telling. Cities, the biographical structures that emerge from them and that are their legacy, are then our first topics.

We have a space already mapped out in which to read Marx's story, in the history of British socialism (and a more dimly-perceived European Marxism) sketched above. Then there is a newer backdrop to it, set in place by modern historians who have considered female social action, philanthropy, and the developing field of professional paid work for middle-class women in the period 1870–1910. Further details have been filled in by literary and cultural critics who have seen the fictionalization of lady visitors, rent collectors, settlement workers and health visitors in the figures of New Women, *flâneuses* visible and invisible, City Girls, Shop Girls, insurgent women and wild women in contemporary fiction.[15] This cast of characters (of fictional and historical *engagées*) lived the same kind of story and the same kind of politics as Eleanor Marx (though not exactly the same, which is the point of the story told here). All of them, young men as well as women, mapped the great city of the world in the same structure of time and by their walking of it: by the same hurried passage through its streets to the same kind of meeting, their return from the journey across the bridges to outcast London regulated by tram and overland railway timetable; back to bright, glittering ideas spoken in dim rooms, somewhere in the same fictional and real square mile of Bloomsbury, sometime between the 1870s and the 1890s.

Biography – the telling of a life – crosses generic boundaries at the time of writing and the countless times of reading. Cities might be the place where the passage between the fictional and the real, autobiography and the novel, and one quarter and another, have to take place. Moretti is emphatic that '*each space determines or at least encourages its own kind of story*', that specific stories are the

---

the new version of 1888. See *The Red Republican and the Friend of the People. Edited by G. Julian Harney*, ed. by John Saville, 1:21 (9 November, 1850); Karl Marx and Frederick Engels, *The Communist Manifesto. A Modern Edition*, ed. by Eric Hobsbawm (London: Verso, 1988) and Kapp, II, 119. Hobsbawm's Introduction gives an account of the *Manifesto*'s 'conquest of the world'.

14   Franco Moretti, *Atlas of the European Novel. 1800–1900* (London: Verso, 1999).

15   The literature on this topic is now enormous. For a recent account see Sally Ledger, *The New Woman: Fiction and Feminism at the fin de siècle* (Manchester: Manchester University Press, 1997).

product of specific spaces.[16] If a life (invented or recounted) is an idea as much as it is a chronology of actually once-occurring events, then – though Moretti does not make this point – a particular space will furnish story and plot for any life, whether it be fictional, historical, autobiographical or biographical. All must be imagined before they can be written. Cities then, might have all the power that Moretti gives them in *Atlas of the European Novel* and in his reading of the novels of Dickens and Balzac: they provide the experience that can force us to obey the injunction that Charles Taylor explores in *Sources of the Self* (1989), to *have to* (to be *compelled* to) live life as a story.[17]

London was the setting for a particular kind of heterodox biography that emerged between 1870–1900. A typical life (lived and told) was that of Margaret McMillan (1860–1931), socialist orator and journalist, 'saviour of childhood' and member of the ILP.[18] Kapp points out in her biography of Marx that the Independent Labour Party was the significant development in the working-class movement in the 1890s. She shows Marx in attendance at its founding Conference in Bradford in 1893, but only in attendance, only a visitor. She had another political life back in London, was still charting her course with the Gas and General Labourers' Union, speaking as an 'expositor of Marxism' to the working men and women who 'spontaneously called for her'.[19]

McMillan on the other hand, had left London in 1893, after a period doing the kind of crazy voluntary social work, political oratory and sporadic journalism that shapes many of her fictional contemporaries.[20] She spent ten years in Bradford, returning to the Metropolis in 1902. In her writing, Bradford became another remembered city of light, a place that briefly allowed the inscription of a young woman's personal and political story: 'London is brilliant', she wrote in 1912. 'London is the Brain of the World. But I love to think of Bradford. For there Labour was shorn of all that is ugly and debasing. One saw it as in a morning light, half-freed and giving promise of what it will be one day, when divorced entirely from ignorance and failure.'[21]

The heterodox London that McMillan left in 1893 was reworked in the many pieces of fiction she produced for the labour press, from the early 1890s onwards, but most memorably and enduringly in the biography of her sister Rachel, which she published in 1927. Here she describes the mid-1880s: Rachel has found a job

---

16 Moretti, *Atlas*, pp. 70, 100. Emphasis in the original.
17 Charles Taylor, *Sources of the Self. The Making of the Modern Identity* (Cambridge: Cambridge University Press, 1989), p. 289.
18 See Steedman, *McMillan*.
19 See Kapp, II, 526 and Howell, *British Workers*.
20 See Margaret McMillan, *Life of Rachel McMillan* (London: Dent, 1927). Ledger, *New Woman*, pp. 35–61, gives examples of voluntary social work in novels and in life. See also Ruth Livesey, *Women and Social Action in London, 1880–1914*, PhD, University of Warwick, 1999.
21 Margaret McMillan, 'How I Became a Socialist', *Labour Leader*, 11 July 1912.

in a working-girls' hostel, a tall narrow house in Bloomsbury Square, which stands 'in the midst of eager pulsing life ... streets nearby crowded with artists, adventurers, Bohemians of many lands ... people who lived an anxious, eager and perilous life'.[22] Louise Michel, 'la Vierge Rouge' of the Commune, Prince Kropotkin, and a wonderfully funny patroness, Lady Meux of the brewing dynasty, are figures who move in and out of the London pages of the *Life of Rachel McMillan*. But looked back on, at a distance of fifty years, the working-girls' hostel itself and its inhabitants were McMillan's metaphors for the life-story she had embarked upon. She recalled in 1927 that she and her sister 'lived the lives of adventurers':

> The one thing we had in common (Rachel and I belonged to them now) was that we must take our chance just as the press-gang victims took their chance yesterday ... Outside, and close by, was the roaring, boundless human sea, strewn over with wrecks, some visible, but for the most part hidden and soon forgotten. It was a toss-up what became of any of us[23]

In historical and topographical time, the hostel was actually to be found in what is now Endsleigh Gardens, the birthplace – and in the 1880s still the home – of Montague David Eder, the son of a Lithuanian immigrant who had become a substantially wealthy diamond merchant. Eder was a cousin of Israel Zangwill (who collaborated with Eleanor Marx on 'A Doll's House Repaired' in 1891), Secretary to the Bloomsbury Socialist Society, a member of the ILP (after 1893) and later, much later, when he was a practising psychoanalyst and clinic doctor at Margaret McMillan's open-air schools in Bow and Deptford, the first English translator of Freud (though not the first to do *The Interpretation of Dreams* into English: there was an American translation before Eder's *On Dreams* of 1914).[24]

Eder is the most engaging and surprising of the English ethical socialists, not only because of the biographical yoking of Marxism to Freudian psychoanalysis he allows (Eder's serious involvement with the Bloomsbury Society in the 1880s makes the two bodies of thought appear no further apart than the short step between Endsleigh Gardens and Great Coram Street) but also because of the attractiveness of his socialism, learned in those early years with Eleanor Marx, who wanted the workers 'to live for *this world* and *insist on having* what will make it pleasant to them'. By joining the ILP in 1893, Eder perhaps allied himself with those who believed, like McMillan, that it was their duty to bestow on the proletariat what was pleasant for them, but Eder never forsook the principle of

---

[22] McMillan, *Rachel McMillan*, p. 34.

[23] McMillan, *Rachel McMillan*, pp. 35–6.

[24] See *David Eder: Memoirs of a Modern Pioneer*, ed. by J.B. Hobman (London: Gollancz, 1945). Also see Matthew Thomson, 'Mind in Socialism: Montague David Eder, Socialist, Psycho-analyst and Zionist', in *Socialism in Medicine*, ed. by Roger Cooter and Russell Viner, in preparation.

that pleasure, which was that the working class could, or should, have it in the first place. 'As the son of a Jewish pedlar,' he wrote, 'my opposition to [Karl Pearson's Eugenics Laboratory] is no doubt prompted by personal feelings (since I rebel at being a working man under Pearson's leadership)'.[25] Discussing 'What Reforms Are Most Needed' in 1910, he listed 'Provision of shower baths in all elementary schools ... warm and cold water and soap. Decent boots. Full insides and clean outsides.'[26] Laying out his plans for the state 'Endowment of Motherhood' he wrote of free housing, food, fuel, lighting and clothing for expectant mothers, a kind of 'Grand or National Truck Act' that would also provided women with 'money to spend at [their] own free will'. The state should support a mother, he argued, no matter what her marital status might be, but a woman's life should not be sacrificed to 'the somewhat monotonous calls of infant life'. He knew that 'all human society is moulded by desire'. He sought to 'alter the prevalent views upon ... sex morality ... to restate the Socialist position in biological terms', to devise reasonable ways of living a life.[27] The scandalous paper he read to the 1914 North of England Education Conference in Bradford on 'The "Unconscious" Mind in the Child' was based on 'certain psychological observations taken among some fifty or sixty boys and girls in a recently opened MacMillan [sic] open-air camp at Deptford, to illustrate and confirm the "neurological" conclusions of Freud'. He was among the first to allow working-class children to dream (allowed that they could dream, and that like other, more favoured children, had an unconscious life).[28] His work and writing in the early twentieth century shows very clearly the socialist injunction, learned with Morris and Eleanor Marx, and in and out of the groups they belonged to, to educate desire.[29]

Over the actual streets of 1880s London, the human tide flowing through them, the ardent young men and women on their way to meet and to talk and to understand, we must lay a fictional grid of one square mile, south of Euston Station. It is the square mile in which, in historical and topographical time, Eleanor Marx and Margaret McMillan lived and wrote, and from which they journeyed out: to the East End, to the dock gates during the Great Dock Strike of 1889, to a thousand provincial union and socialist meetings (the main-line

---

25 David Eder, 'Eugenics and Human Sacrifice', *New Age*, 9 September 1909.
26 David Eder, 'What Reforms Are Most Needed', *Christian Commonwealth*, 5 January 1910.
27 David Eder, *The Endowments of Motherhood* (London: New Age Press, 1908), pp. 1–3, 45–49.
28 M.D. Eder and Mrs Eder, 'The Conflicts of the Unconscious in the Child', *Child Study*, 9:6 (1916), 79–83. 'Child Life and Sex Teaching', *Yorkshire Observer*, 3 January 1914. Hobman, *Eder*, p. 77. For a fictional working-class child dreaming, see Steedman, *McMillan*, pp. 68–70. In Hobman's commemorative volume Eder was called a 'modern pioneer': a supporter of 'socialism, Zionism, psycho-analysis and all humane causes'. Here, in the most charming and desirable of epitaphs, Sigmund Freud wrote that 'Eder belonged to the people one loves without having to trouble about them'.
29 On 'the education of desire', particularly in relationship to William Morris's political philosophy, see Thompson, *Morris*, p. 806.

terminals, Euston, St Pancras and King's Cross stations, are the reason for this square mile and not another). In these streets, in its meeting rooms and societies, the campaign for the Eight Hour Day was organized, and that extraordinary series of meetings in Hyde Park in May 1890, when Marx said that she heard 'for the first time since 40 years, the unmistakable voice of the English proletariat'.[30] But it is the space – the square mile – of representation too.

This is the bedsitter land that provides the setting to Isabella Ford's *On the Threshold* (1895) and other novels of the 1890s, novels that take as their theme tremulous young womanhood, on the verge of a social discovery that will lead to a new ordering of life.[31] In fact the chapter entitled 'London' in McMillan's book needs to be read as an item of this genre, especially for the way it evokes the drama of genteel dread that the independent life forced on young women like Rachel: 'The note of anxiety prevailed. Anxiety that sometimes passed into a kind of terror and even into despair. Hundreds of girls were here [in the hostel] who lived from hand to mouth, holding ill-paid jobs precariously, and in constant danger of losing them altogether.'[32]

But the heroines of *On the Threshold* (again, two young women from the North; Yorkshire though, rather than from Scotland as were the McMillan sisters) are in London to study, not to work. Set in a not-too-remote 'then', Kitty Manners, twenty-two years, has 'come up to London ... to study Art', and the narrator, Lucretia Bampfylde, to study Music.[33] It is 'then', not 'now' (perhaps ten or fifteen years before its time of composition) for these are the days before the era of 'ladies' chambers and cheap flats', and Kitty and Lucretia settle in 'three dark small rooms in Bloomsbury', with a stock-type landlady of shop-soiled awfulness, and a maid-of-all-work called Beatrice who, as their very own Domestic Oppressed, allows their first articulation of political principle. 'We were quite sure', remembers Lucretia,

> that the oppressed in this world were the good and the oppressors the bad. We had hitherto only lived with the oppressors ... [We were sure] that children were better than parents, women than men ... [and that] a maid-of-all-work must be on a distinctly higher moral plane than a landlady. This superior goodness on the part of the oppressed was a reason for espousing their cause.[34]

---

[30] Kapp, II, 380–98.

[31] Isabella O. Ford, *On the Threshold* (London and New York: Edward Arnold, 1895). See Ledger, *New Woman*, pp. 35–61.

[32] McMillan, *Rachel McMillan*, p. 34.

[33] For the import of this kind of temporal dissonance – the 'then not now' of the nineteenth-century novel, see Donald Lowe, *A History of Bourgeois Perception* (Brighton: Harvester, 1982).

[34] Ford, *On the Threshold*, pp. 9–12.

Beatrice is a very great disappointment to them, but also and at the same time, functions as a most efficient Domestic Urban Surveyor, bringing into their dingy parlour the tales of domestic wretchedness that illustrate the first volume of Charles Booth's *Life and Labour of the People of London*, and that would, in 1902 and the third edition, furnish the 'Fifty Stories Illustrative of the Causes of Poverty'; or that already, when Ford wrote, framed Arthur Morrison's *Tales of Mean Streets*.[35] And Beatrice's Fall, into Low Life Deeps, into Outcast London and prostitution will lead Kitty and Lucretia into Darkest London itself. 'It was the first time in our lives that we were brought face to face with the great dark side of humanity', recalls the narrator; and she pauses to remember the great tide of London street life, in which Beatrice, briefly glimpsed, was 'swallowed up, lost to us, in the stream of men and women ... spreading itself over the pavement'.[36]

The journey into Low Life Deeps made by these characters was a common one. Lady visitors for the Charity Organisation Society, female rent-collectors, all manner of slum missionary did it; but so did politically engaged socialist (and indeed, revolutionary) young women. McMillan saw and recorded the horrors of working-class domesticity in Bradford (and much later in Deptford, though the means for *seeing* it and writing it remained remarkably consistent across twenty years);[37] Marx 'discovered' the poor in the late 1880s during the Great Dock Strike with a language (and – it seems – a mode of perception) that is strikingly similar to that of the slum visitor: 'Room!' she expostulated to her sister Laura. Not a room at all, but a

> cellar, dark, underground ... [a] woman lying on some sacking and a little straw, her breast half eaten away by cancer ... naked but for an old red handkerchief over her breast and a bit of sail[cloth] over her legs. By her side a baby of three and other children ...[38]

This encounter is written again and again in a very wide variety of late nineteenth-century literature. But the proposition of this essay is that Marx's was not the same record as the slum visitor's, nor even the same as the heart-wrenching socio-fiction that McMillan took away from these terrible encounters, to publish in the *Clarion* and the *Labour Leader*. McMillan and Marx did not take the same thing away from those filthy, broken rooms; and perhaps Marx took nothing away at all.

The passages about London in Isabella Ford's *On the Threshold* are very beautiful – but how could they not be? Raymond Williams showed us a long time

---

35 Charles Booth, *Life and Labour of the People. Volume 1. East London* (London: Macmillan, 1891) pp. 3–27, 131–55, 156–71; Charles Booth, *Life and Labour in London. Second Series. Volume 4* (London: MacMillan, 1902) pp. 350–80; Arthur Morrison, *Tales of Mean Streets* (London: Methuen, 1894).

36 Ford, *On the Threshold*, p. 52.

37 Steedman, *McMillan*, pp. 98–120.

38 Kapp, II, 261, 262, 287.

ago, in the 'Cities of Darkness and of Light' chapter of *The Country and the City*, the voluptuous and fluid (and always slightly greasy) material from which you must cut your cloth when you describe the Great City of the World, from at least the early 1800s.[39] You cut it thus then; and you must cut it this way now, a century, or a century and a half later. You will always hear, and make your reader hear 'the wonderful, ceaseless beating of feet and the tread of hoofs, beating and echoing from long, far-stretching miles of pavement'.[40] This is how Kitty and Lucretia experience London when they return from their first vacation in the North, and Lucretia recalls being

> thrilled by that deep and mysterious emotion which the first glimpse of London always produced within us ... The sound awed us, and yet invigorated us, for in its very immensity it seemed somehow akin to our own strong youth and ardour[41]

'Even now,' she says, 'the sound still thrills us with the same mysterious feeling of kinship, for the footsteps seem laden with all the weariness, all the sadness which the world holds, and which is therefore part of our own lives'.

Their search for Beatrice leads them to a Common Lodgings House, peopled with characters at least 150 years old in generic terms, though bearing the particular marks of Modern Low Life, inscribed in the works of the 1870s and 1880s that have just been evoked.[42] In particular, as representational development of the late nineteenth century, we should note the stunned prurience with which the sexual mores of the poor and the sexuality of working-class women is explored.[43]

---

[39]   Raymond Williams, *The Country and the City* (St Albans: Paladin, 1973), pp. 259–79.

[40]   In 1991 John Barrell condemns the racist 'infection' of Thomas de Quincey, holds up for condemnation his rabid superimposing of an imagined and engulfing East on the Saturday crowds of London poor, making their quite ordinary weekend purchases at the green-markets, but experienced by the observer in that moment as the limitless and teeming hordes of Asia; and even as Barrell points this out, we hear from de Quincey that evocation of London. John Barrell, *The Infection of Thomas de Quincey: A Psychotherapy of Imperialism* (New Haven and London: Yale University Press, 1991), pp. 1–6.

[41]   Ford, *On the Threshold*, p. 87.

[42]   There is much modern commentary on the eighteenth-century establishment of the 'characters' of low life. See for example Janet Thaddeus, 'Swift's Directions to Servants', *Studies in Eighteenth Century Culture*, 16 (1986), 107–23, for the development of 'Mollspeak'. L.B. Faller, *Turned to Account. The Form and Functions of Criminal Biography in late Seventeenth and early Eighteenth Century England* (Cambridge: Cambridge University Press, 1982). Also see Juliet Mitchell, '*Moll Flanders*. The Rise of Capitalist Woman' (1978) in *Women: The Longest Revolution* (Harmondsworth: Penguin, 1984) pp. 195–218. Much of this work makes reference to J.L. Rayner, *The Complete Newgate Calender*, 5 vols (privately printed, 1826).

[43]   The haunting epitome of this prurience is Rudyard Kipling's 'The Record of Badalia Herodsfoot' (1890) in *Many Inventions* (London: Macmillan, 1893). For the established convention of the working-class woman with the bruised face explaining to the lady visitor that ' 'e's like that Miss', see Livesey, *Women and Social Action*.

To indicate Ford's employment of the Working-class Stereotypical like this is to make two points. The first is an obvious one, and not very interesting: that Isabella Ford, daughter of the Leeds Quaker gentry, who transmuted her family's tradition of philanthropy into hard practical organizational work for the Tailoresses' Union, into lifelong membership of the ILP and the struggle – political and ideological – for women's suffrage, need have done no more than read extensively in 'Slice of Life' fiction and the urban social survey to produce these very professionally-done scenes.[44] The second and more interesting point is to do with how knowing the text is, about its own origins, and its own gentle fun, which is consistently had at the expense of its middle-class protagonists. This is one of the first Biscuits in Bloomsbury/Cocoa Communion sagas produced by modern print capitalism. The young women's vibrant friendship connects them to the world of social and political thought, which they debate enchanted, late into the night. The narrator is indeed charmed and touched by her younger self, as it is clear Ford was with her creation. After their first encounter with Horrible London, Kitty and Lucretia are too excited to sleep, and sit up all night eating biscuits and whispering that 'we must swear to one another, our love for each other, that we will set about changing all this. Let us solemnly swear it now, Lucretia dear'.[45] There are many other meetings of minds and hearts over the cocoa. The tender amusement with which Ford writes these scenes suggests that they already exist, in other texts, to be reworked by her as a comedy of political awakening.

The threshold on which the girls hover is certainly that of Life – a new woman's life – but also that of political understanding. Again, the wry and indulgent voice follows Lucretia and Kitty through Bloomsbury squares and terraces, to reform meetings and discussion groups. The very first time they venture out of their rooms is to the inaugural meeting of a reforming society to be held in one of the grander Bloomsbury squares. These scenes, where revolution is debated in drawing rooms, are truly funny, partly because they recognize themselves – and the opinions they have their protagonists rehearse – as formulaic. There is a particularly delicious scene in which Lucretia's aunt becomes quite pink and girlish on hearing about the socialist revolution from a young poet with 'a very pleasant power of at once establishing friendly understanding – a kind of comradeship – between himself and the person to whom he was talking; a power which made discussion with him of one's most cherished or most heterodox opinions not only possible, but pleasant'. In a Gordon Square drawing room the orthodoxies of social intercourse lead Aunt Henrietta to outdo him in revolutionary determination, expressing sentiments which pursued logically, could only lead to the barricades and the tri-coloured cap. 'I began at last to see a picture

---

44 See June Hannam, *Isabella Ford, 1855–1924* (Oxford: Blackwell, 1989). For 'Slice of Life' fiction see Williams, *Country and City*, pp. 271–2.

45 Ford, *On the Threshold*, p. 52.

of her mounting a barricade in the Euston Road, wearing the cap of Liberty, and carrying a scarlet banner'.[46]

'All of us', remembers Lucretia, 'were Socialists more or less, and any disagreement among us concerned merely the particular manner in which we believed our ideal future would be realized.' Kitty believed that the awakening of women was the key to the problem, whilst Estcourt (the young Socialist and poet, of impeccable manners and persuasive conversation, who becomes Kitty's suitor) 'believed that the future lay with the people, the wage-earners of the country'.

These oppositions, between two socialisms, one demanding the liberation of women, one seeking first the freedom of the people, shape the very histories of British socialism that we are still producing. Here they are ironically laid out for the reader.[47] On their first night in lodgings, Kitty presses a sprig of watercress between the pages of Mazzini's *Faith and the Future*: 'I read that so that I may be ready when the revolution comes'.[48] (The watercress is because they have determined that in their new freedom they will eat the fast food of late Victorian London – shrimps, watercresses and sprats).[49] At the beginning of it all, Kitty's personal and political Bible is Mill's *Subjection of Women*, and Lucretia's 'a volume of Shelley'.[50] Their taste in political literature changes with their progress, and halfway through the story 'Ruskin was superseding Stuart Mill with Kitty, and "When lilacs last in the door-yard bloom'd" was now my favourite poem.' Ford lays out plainly the history of political ideas and theory that late twentieth-century historians of British socialism describe, using the same markers of literature to map the traditions of revolutionary radicalism, equal-rights Liberalism, many feminisms, the deep interior pleasures of Ruskinian anti-industrialism and the promises offered by Whitman's 'comradeship', all of which contributed to late nineteenth-century socialist thinking. Ford clearly expected her audience of 1895 to know what the move from Mill to Ruskin, from Shelley to Whitman, actually meant, so that we are forced to wonder whether David Howell, Stanley Pierson and Kenneth Morgan really needed to do their work on the intellectual origins of British socialism, or at least, to express surprise at the perceptions of historians being the taken-for-granted of novelists and their readers in the 1890s.[51]

---

[46] Ford, *On the Threshold*, pp. 175–82.

[47] See Stanley Pierson, *Marxism and the Origins of British Socialism* (New York: Cornell University Press, 1973); Howell, *British Workers*; Kenneth O. Morgan, *Labour People. Leaders and Lieutenants. Hardie to Kinnock* (Oxford: Oxford University Press, 1987); Hunt, *Equivocal Feminists*.

[48] Ford, *On the Threshold*, pp. 16, 202.

[49] Ford, *On the Threshold*, p. 12.

[50] Ford, *On the Threshold*, p. 16.

[51] For similar accounts of the intellectual and aesthetic trajectories of British socialism see Pierson, *Marxism*; Howell, *British Workers*, pp. 352–62; Yeo, 'Religion of Socialism in Britain'. For the Labour Party's understanding of formative influence see W.T. Stead, 'The Labour Party and the Books that Helped Make It', *Review of Reviews*, 33 (1906), 568–82. For one account – among many – of Giuseppe Mazzini's importance see Margaret McMillan, 'A

These vibrant young women's lives – Kitty's and Lucretia's – are told contrapuntally with a terrible detailing of 'A Woman's Life', lived on both sides of the class borderline. There is a rewritten 'Lizerunt' who in *On the Threshold* picks up a young man in a Tottenham Court Road pub, goes off to live with him and to sport a 'crushed and discoloured' face a page or so later;[52] and there are the ladies of Bloomsbury, who make Lucretia cry out for an answer as she stares out across Gordon Square from her aunt's first-floor window:

> 'Tell me why women's lives are – like these' – I pointed vaguely out the window towards the houses of her friends; ... 'Tell me if there is not in your lowest, most secret soul, a longing, a great burning longing, for a real life, with real people in it.'[53]

Her aunt's friends can only point to a future that is 'nothing so much as a monotonous journey along a dusty, shadeless high-road'. At one point Kitty declaims that

> 'all the sorrows of all the women everywhere were born in me ... Lucretia, there is an idea, a knowledge, growing within me like a flood, that I shall find out a way, a meaning, if I listen to those voices that are always crying out.'[54]

Kitty's answer to the Woman Question is that a woman's life must be an attempt 'to live in these narrow spaces, and yet be free',[55] and it is reiterated by the end-stop of *On the Threshold*, which is Kitty's betrothal to Estcourt. She announces her engagement to Lucretia in the surprising Arcadia of a City of London tea room, a piece of preserved rural England with roses round the door; a fragment of the countryside, the place where nothing happens, preserved in the depths of the great city, which is the place where something always might.[56]

It seems scarcely worth making the point that Isabella Ford's lifelong devotion to trade unionism, socialism and suffrage all quite belie the plot she concluded in 1895. Or, it is a point worth making, in order to say this: that heterodox London produced its own fictions and its own fictional histories, in this particular case to make a young woman's life emblem of much wider political debates and processes. In the historical time in which this novel was written, and to which it makes reference, it is deeply satisfying to the historian of the labour movement to find more evidence for the proposition that the Independent Labour Party was the strand of English socialism that first inscribed the personal as political, and that

Calendar of Socialist Saints. Biographies in Brief. Mazzini', *Young Socialist* (June 1909).

52   Ford, *On the Threshold*, p. 154. Arthur Morrison, 'Lizerunt', in *Tales of Mean Streets* (London: Methuen, 1903), pp. 31–62.
53   Ford, *On the Threshold*, pp. 134–5.
54   Ford, *On the Threshold*, p. 124.
55   Ford, *On the Threshold*, p. 190.
56   Ford, *On the Threshold*, p. 202.

was able – in the biography of its members at least – to wed Marxism to feminism, and both of them to psychoanalysis. We have seen David Eder's trajectory show these radical, surprising conjunctions most clearly; but they are present in all the literature, fictional and otherwise, that has been mentioned. Ten years ago, describing his involvement with the Bloomsbury Socialist Society and the Independent Labour Party allowed me to write about a form of socialism that, in its evolution between the late 1880s and the formation of the Labour Representation Committee in 1900, transcribed working-class experience in the private sphere as well as the sphere of labour, and made that experience into political analysis and political understanding. In my account of Margaret McMillan, I was able to give a detailed account of the way in which the ILP and its party workers did this, because it did actually happen; and of course, mine was not the sole endeavour of fifteen years ago, to assess the forms of political representation and action in the past that had allowed the personal to become political, long before second-wave feminism produced that transition as a political slogan in the 1960s and 1970s. The difference between then and now is that then I did not have an opinion on this (I was interested in saying 'No, not quite like that'; or 'It happened earlier than you think'); or I might even have thought that it was a good thing. Now I think it was a disastrous thing.

For Ford's novel of heterodox London points to the compulsions of the comic mode, the dreadful self-indulgent wryness that we are bound to employ when – in which we *go on* – representing English socialism. We may, by reading it, be alerted to the tragedy of making stories about it, perhaps see the dangers of making stories for, or out of, any form of politics. The young women discussed here – fictional and real; characters in books and their creators – took *themselves* away from those cellars, attics and greasy lodging houses; they took away a new story of themselves, a form of subjectivity, an experience embodied in a narrative that linked their own life to the working-class tragedy. This enhanced sense of self made out of the tiny fragments of other people's stories allowed them to exercise a political philanthropy that was probably less damaging than that exercised by the Charity Organisation Society worker (and was almost certainly less unpleasant to be the recipient of), but which did the same thing with the story in the end, that is, fashion a bourgeois subjectivity out of it. Marx did not do this – perhaps – because the woman with the cancerous breast was, in her vision, no more than, or as much as, a poorly-paid, unrepresented worker, who needed shorter working hours, not an item of the slum visitor's own identity.

These relationships of identity and class, the ways in which young women and men made themselves in the course of political action, are also questions of narrative: of how a story of the self is found, and how it might be changed in the telling. Among all the hurried movement through fraction, split and regrouping that was the experience of Eleanor Marx, David Eder and many others during the 1880s and early 1890s, there is an important reflection on these questions to be found in William Morris's *News from Nowhere* of 1891.[57] It is important partly because it is famous, and response and analysis to it has formed the multi-layered biographical inheritance with which late twentieth-century historians, biographers and literary critics are bound to approach lives like these. *News from Nowhere* was in part a response to *The Communist Manifesto*, which received its second translation into English, the one that enabled its 'conquest of the world', in 1888.[58] Like most adherents of the emergent British socialist and workers' parties of the later nineteenth century, William Morris found that there were 'two main sources of dispute' with its proposals and implications. They were that 'we cannot agree as to what is likely to be the precise socialist system of the future, and we cannot agree as to the best means of attaining it'. His solution, and it is famous, was to find an answer in narrative terms; to find a plot.

News from Nowhere starts with someone recounting how 'Up at the League' (which for the purposes of the real square mile with which this chapter deals, we should remember *was* the Socialist League, with Morris and Marx and Aveling as members, and David Eder waiting in Endsleigh Gardens for the next split, which will make him Secretary of the breakaway Bloomsbury Society...):

> There had been one night a brisk conversational discussion, as to what would happen on the Morrow of the Revolution, finally shading off into a vigorous statement by various friends of their views on the future of the fully-developed new society.

One man leaves the group, and muses, on the train journey home: 'If I could but see a day of it ... if I could but see it.'[59] Morris allows him to do so, in the dream he has his character have, and that forms the text of the romance; the dream of the days after the Revolution. This is the same compulsion of narrative that shapes *A Dream of John Ball* (1886), when Morris wrote that 'Men fight and lose the battle, and the thing they fought for comes about in spite of their defeat, and when it comes, it turns out not to be what they meant.'[60]

Morris was not the only socialist of the period to find in narrative some kind of solution to the problem posed by revolutionary Marxism. The solution was to tell it *as if it has already happened*, which of course quite prevented it ever happening at all.

As we disinter the biographies of these young socialist men and women of a century ago, we enter the maze of many other stories that they made for

---

[57] William Morris, *News from Nowhere, or, An Epoch of Rest, Being Some Chapters from a Utopian Romance* (London: Reeves & Turner, 1891).

[58] Karl Marx, *The Communist Manifesto*, trans. by Samuel Moore (London: William Reeves, 1888). See Kapp, II, 119 and Francis Wheen, *Karl Marx* (London: Fourth Estate, 1999), p. 124. This translation is used for *The Communist Manifesto: A Modern Edition*, ed. by Eric Hobsbawm (1998).

[59] Morris, *News from Nowhere*, pp. 1, 2.

[60] Kapp, II, 53.

themselves out of the lives of others, and from which they made characters for others to read, in many types of writing. To add to these accreted narratives there is the work of the many historians of late nineteenth-century socialism, who have laid down another layer of biographical convention, in modern tellings of these lives. In *Atlas of the European Novel*, it is not Franco Moretti's purpose to deal with these weird borderlines between literature and life, between the autobiography of the writer and the one she gives to the characters she invents. Specific spaces are the determinant of specific stories – the 'tales of two cities', London and Paris – that Moretti discusses, and the stories remain firmly literary. Yet autobiographies of London women of the left at the end of the last century were mapped by the same exact topographies that Moretti deals in: a charted and timetabled movement from West to East, across the bridges, and back again, past all the houses in between. But their stories were made on the vertical plane as well as on the horizontal: there were old stories of low life, reformulated for the 1890s, the modern comic turns of working-class life, the existing literature of the endless streets, all of which are fashioned into the biography told. 'Autobiography is to do with time, with sequence, and with what makes up the continuous flow of life', wrote Walter Benjamin. What he wanted to do, on the other hand, was to write of 'space, of moments and discontinuities'.[61] In *On the Threshold* there are certainly these moments, when the protagonists are moved, so fast that you scarcely see it, to quite different temporalities, into fragments of another space. As Kitty and Lucretia cross Russell Square, 'the blackbirds were whistling among the bushes, and the trees were clad in light green, that light green which in London seems particularly brilliant. Down a long street we caught a glimpse of a young moon.'[62] But in the novel as a whole narrative cannot be gainsaid: this – even this moment – must be fashioned into biography. Because there is the long street, which always goes somewhere, even though it appears endless. It is this purposefulness, this time, with sequence, that makes up the continuous flow of biography, and which may turn out to be the narrative legacy of the space of the city.

***

Eleanor Marx and the authors of a political woman's life that have been discussed must make us wonder yet again, about the comedy, the gentle and terrible fondness of Ford's and McMillan's evocation of the 'then' (1870s? 1880s? 1890s?) that made them political women. And we might note this: that Eleanor Marx has

---

[61] Walter Benjamin, 'A Berlin Chronicle' (1932), *One Way Street* (London: Verso, 1979), p. 316. Benjamin is to be encountered in Elizabeth Wilson, *The Sphinx in the City. Urban Life, the Control of Disorder, and Women* (London: Virago, 1991), pp. 133–59. As well as the extraordinarily felicitous encounter with Benjamin, here are also to be found here young women of the late nineteenth-century metropolis moving through the city as if it were their home.

[62] Ford, *On the Threshold*, p. 87.

escaped this terrible and sentimental trap. She died in the most conventional of female melodramas. She took her own life because of a final and unbearable betrayal by a man who was simply not worthy of her, a discourse of desire that can be shown – as Linda Kauffman has shown it – worked upon and reused, transmuted yet insistent, from the time of Classical Antiquity.[63]

And yet: there is absolutely no room in Marx's story for the diminishing, subordinating gaze of benevolent sympathy, nor for the contemplation of a girlish silliness, to provoke laughter and tears, both at the same time. Marx's nobility and dignity owe much to the efforts of her biographer, and the decorum and gravity with which her life has been told. But Yvonne Kapp would not have been able to do that, fine writer though she was, without a central truth of Marx's life, and the story we must tell out of it: that she worked with a politics that did not have a space for the interiority that the Independent Labour Party moved into the public arena; that other people's lives – working-class lives – were not, within her understanding, items for the art of self-fashioning. She did not have to see her relationship with Aveling and the end she made of it as emblem of the history of the world, nor as metaphor for the social tragedy. She could not use desperate and poverty-stricken lives, told at third hand, to articulate her own. Her suicide was not an emblem of the social, nor of a woman's life. She quite escaped the Poor Sad Woman's Story (which, I regret to say, received its most detailed fashioning by my political generation, in the 1970s and early 1980s). So against the grain of everything that I – and many others – have so lovingly described, the pleasure of finding the personal made political, so early, so clearly, I think I want to venture this: that those connections turn out to be no radical legacy at all; and that Eleanor Marx, who did not live within the twined and muffling embrace of the personal as political, was in some small measure, free.

---

63 Linda S. Kauffman, *Discourses of Desire Gender Genre and Epistolary Fiction* (Ithaca: Cornell University Press, 1986), pp. 30–61. See also Peggy Kamuff, 'Writing Like a Woman', in *Women and Language in Literature and Society*, ed. by Sally McConnell-Ginet, et al. (New York: Praager, 1980); Nancy K. Miller, '"I"s in Drag. The Sex of Recollection', *The Eighteenth Century. Theory and Interpretation*, 22 (1981), 47–57.

Chapter 3

Revisiting Edward Aveling

William Greenslade

I

Who, we might ask, either needs or wants to dwell for long on the appalling Edward Aveling, to whom Eleanor Marx sacrificed herself so disastrously? There can be few men of his time for whom the record is so recurrently one of distaste – particularly as it has come down to us through the reactions of those who knew him well. His physical appearance prompted extreme reactions. For the leader of the Social Democratic Federation, H.M. Hyndman, he had 'a forbidding face – ugly and even repulsive, nobody can be as bad as Aveling looks'. For G.B. Shaw 'he had no physical charm except a voice like a euphonium'. Eleanor Marx's friend Olive Schreiner found him morally as well as physically repellent – 'the real criminal type'.[1] For Shaw, to the question 'what sort of a man was Edward Aveling?', the answer from anyone who knew him was a shriek of laughter and the question: 'how much have you lent him?'[2] Aveling was always hard up and on the lookout for a loan.

Yet Aveling's serial sponging provided Shaw with a model for his clever and not unattractive cad, Dubedat, in *The Doctor's Dilemma* (1906). Despite his callowness in personal relations, he had an undoubted intellectual and sexual energy which attracted some as it repelled others. No one was more drawn to this than Eleanor Marx herself, who saw in Aveling something of her own father's 'energy and sexuality', and felt that here was a man who would 'give her the confidence to work'.[3]

If evidence were needed of the extent to which Aveling has become *persona non grata* for scholarship on late nineteenth-century British socialism, the absence of a critical study helps to supply it. It was perhaps not surprising that he did not make it to the *DNB*, but he also failed to reach *DNB Missing Persons* (1993); on the other hand he was admitted to Frederic Boase's *Modern English Biography*

---

[1] Cited in Kapp, I, 265
[2] Michael Holroyd, *Bernard Shaw: Vol 1: The Search for Love* (London: Chatto & Windus, 1988; London: Penguin, 1990), pp. 153–5. He had accumulated £400 of debt – over £30,000 in today's terms – by the age of thirty-two.
[3] Faith Evans, 'The Daughter of Modern Socialism', *Independent (Review Section)*, 1 April 1998; Kapp, II, 204.

(1908), and attracted an excellent entry in J.O. Baylen and Grossman's *Biographical Dictionary of Modern British Radicals* (1988).

Aveling was born in North London in 1848, the son of a congregational minister. A precocious scholar, he passed exams and picked up prizes at an early age, graduating in Biological and Zoological Science at University College, London in 1870, receiving a doctorate in Science in 1876. He got a foothold in the academic world as a lecturer at the London Hospital and at King's College, but was marginalized by his militant atheism and spent the rest of his life as a freelance teacher, coach, public speaker, journalist, editor, translator, textbook writer, dramatist and actor. He was a prolific and successful speaker all over Britain, an effective political organizer, an energetic editor of at least three leading secularist and socialist papers, dramatic critic and, according to Sidney Webb and Annie Besant, a brilliant teacher. He translated Marx's *Capital*, Engels's *Socialism, Utopian and Scientific*, and wrote extensively on Darwinism.

So the Edward Aveling story, and, in particular, the Aveling–Marx story, is complex. The man has to be reckoned with, in his own terms, as a significant element in the political and cultural history of late Victorian radicalism and socialism, in which from the late 1870s to the mid-1890s he figured prominently until his death in 1898. This essay examines, in particular, his career as secularist and Darwinist, his role in steering the secularists towards socialism and the uncertain interplay of Darwinism and socialism in his work, together with some observations about his equivocal writerly achievement and identity.

II

In the secular movement of the late 1870s, Aveling found a natural ideological home. For an anti-establishment, anti-religious materialist it was the natural place for him to be. Yvonne Kapp memorably writes that 'the path leading from non-conformity to Freethinking and from there to Socialism was ... a public highway along which marched many of the founders of the British working class movement'.[4] Nevertheless both Kapp and Edward Thompson tend to underplay the significant work that Aveling did for the *National Reformer* and the National Secular Society (NSS), the radicalizing formation of the NSS and the extent to which the socialist movement both learned and benefited from it in the pivotal period of its formation in which Aveling, I will argue, played a key role.

Nineteenth-century secularism was a well-established counter-movement in British society. In its early days, in the 1850s, it had stood for a secular state free from privilege, for a free press, free assembly and abolition of the monarchy. Philosophically it was rationalist and materialist. But under Charles Bradlaugh and

---

4   Kapp, I, 267.

(latterly) Annie Besant, the NSS had both accentuated its atheistic line and broadened its agenda to include support for land reform, birth control and women's rights. Bradlaugh's effective, if domineering leadership had seen its membership grow sixfold through the 1870s. By the time Aveling joined the organization, the NSS had all the 'appurtenances of a great organisation – leaders, apostles, newspapers, lecture halls and internal disputes'.[5]

Here was a ready-made system of publicity and dissemination. Speeches by the leading apostles of the movement were reported in the *National Reformer* and other secularist papers, published in full in papers like the *Freethinker* (founded in 1881) and *Progress* (founded in 1883) and sold separately as pamphlets which were, in turn, advertised in these papers. It was a system of circulation which secured the most effective momentum of intellectual capital, and ensured that a leading apostle like Aveling was given maximum exposure. Aveling's publicity-seeking temperament was perfectly attuned to, and indeed thrived on, such a system; it helped, too, to shape his rhetorical practice, so crucial to his 'effect' as a propagandist.

His writings for the NSS were formidably various, the topics he addressed numerous. In a little over nine months, in 1879–80, he wrote a hundred articles and speeches. For the secularists, Aveling's work was notable for its attention to scientific materialism in a context of an explicit evolutionism, eventually to be expounded in full in Aveling's all-purpose 'gospel of evolution'. And in the monism of the German embryologist Ernst Haeckel, with whom he had corresponded and whose *The Pedigree of Man* he translated,[6] Aveling found an idea which served him effectively throughout his Secularist phase.

Haeckel posited that mind and matter were aspects of the same universal substance, and that only by the 'rational activity of genuine science', rather than by the mystic fruits of so-called revelations which underpins Judaeo-Christian religion, 'shall we attain to a knowledge of the truth'.[7] Aveling reiterated this kind of universalism time and time again in his writings: 'Matter and motion are all in all', Christianity has 'no scientific … no natural basis', whereas evolution is founded on a 'natural and scientific basis'.[8]

Aveling frequently turns, rhetorically, to the celebration and observation of nature as an all-purpose category. In his secularist credo of July 1879 he announced his desire to 'labour for freedom of thought, of word, of act, for all men and women. Beautiful Nature, the eternal comforter, is with us'.[9] In secularist tracts like 'Why I Dare Not Be A Christian' he assimilates Christianity to nature as

---

5   Warren Sylvester-Smith, *The London Heretics 1870–1914* (London: Constable, 1967), p. 34.
6   Tsuzuki, p. 87.
7   Ernst Haeckel, *The Riddle of the Universe* (1899; London: Watts & Co., 1929), p. 275.
8   Edward Aveling, *The Gospel of Evolution* (London: Freethought Publishing Co., 1884), pp. 37, 36.
9   Cited by Tsuzuki, p. 81.

evolutionary process – with its laws of inevitable progress and decay. Christianity is a form of thought 'now slowly falling to its death ... the great trees rise giant-like and stretch forth mighty arms to all the winds of heaven year after year. They would seem as eternal. But upon these also slow decay takes hold ... crash after crash resounds through the forests untrodden of man'.[10] And Aveling adopts nature worship of another kind, the fashionable paganism of the period shared by other iconoclastic writers on the rebound from congregationalism, like R.L. Stevenson. This connects with his enthusiasm for Ibsen – especially *Ghosts*. He condemns Christianity as 'cold, passionless, songless', its 'icy breath withering the 'old, beautiful pagan creed'.[11]

For his secularist audiences Aveling's principal achievement was to instil the idea that with their traditional commitment to materialism and rational and free enquiry, they were in the best possible position to hasten the extinction of Christianity and to drive the engine of progressive evolutionary development in a secular state: 'The preachers of this new gospel are nature herself and all her children ... its temples ... are the halls of universities, the state schools, the science classes for our young men and maidens, the laboratories and the studies of the philosophers, the hearts of all that seek for truth'.[12] By the time Aveling made this claim in 1885, he had committed himself to socialism, but it was his experience in the secular movement as a teacher, coach and propagandist that earned him the right to make it.

III

Bradlaugh and Besant always believed that Aveling's main contribution to secularism had been to infuse it with scientific rigour and knowledge; his very first contribution to the *National Reformer* had been an essay on 'Darwin and His Views' (January 1879). And Aveling had been industrious in positioning the topic of scientific education within a wider social agenda. Annie Besant had a high regard for this talent of Aveling's as well as for his teaching ability (she had been one of his star pupils). Now, when shifts in political allegiance were under intense scrutiny, Besant, who almost certainly had an affair with Aveling, spotted his interest from late 1882 in the bohemian socialists Shaw, Havelock Ellis, Olive Schreiner and Eleanor Marx who met in and around the British Museum.[13] She went public in the *National Reformer* (just before Marx and Aveling themselves went public) in the summer of 1884 with a scathing attack on Aveling's ignorance

---

[10] Edward Aveling, *Why I Dare Not Be A Christian* (London: Freethought Publishing Co., 1881), p. 7.

[11] Edward Aveling, *God Dies, Nature Remains* (London: Freethought Publishing Co., 1881), p. 1.

[12] Aveling, *The Gospel of Evolution*, p. 48.

[13] Tsuzuki, p. 104.

of socialism, before 1882.[14] The legacy of bitterness gave way, in time, to Besant's determination not to allow Aveling to take the credit for moving secularist opinion in the direction of Socialism. It was she, not Aveling, who leavened 'London Radicalism' with 'Socialist thought': by 'treating the Radical as the unevolved Socialist rather than as the anti-Socialist we gradually won him over to Socialist views'.[15]

Besant was surely right to claim this privilege, but Aveling, as an influential figure near the top of the secularist movement, must also take much of the credit. The same year, 1882, in which he was casting his eyes round the Reading Room, he was breaking new political ground in London politics by securing election to the Westminster Board of Education. Aveling was supported not only by Secularists but also by Hyndman's Democratic Federation, and in return he made a point of declaring that he had been elected to help not the residents of Mayfair or Belgravia but the poor of Soho and Seven Dials. However, Aveling did very little for the Board once elected – whether because his other formidable writing commitments at this time made this difficult, or because he viewed the move instrumentally as a stepping-stone to the wider socialist politics of London. In any event, Tsuzuki is probably right to claim that 'through his campaign he was initiated into the organised socialistic movement'.[16]

Annie Besant was only one of several important political figures who switched to Socialism from secular or radical organizations at this period; others included prominent working-class figures like Tom Maguire, John Burns, John Bruce Glasier, J.L. Mahon, Tom Mann, George Lansbury and Robert Banner, all of whom joined the Hyndman's SDF.[17] Contacts between secularists and socialists in this very fluid period of shifting allegiances, were numerous and the boundaries which separated them were indistinct. There was considerable permeation by both sides, and here Aveling's role was certainly pivotal.

But he also had a stroke of luck. In 1882 the founder and editor of *Progress*, G.W. Foote, was imprisoned for blasphemy for printing anti-religious cartoons in the *Freethinker* and Aveling became interim editor of both papers. While Foote served out his one-year prison term, Aveling saw an opportunity to push ahead with his strategy. He commissioned Eleanor Marx to write an obituary of her father[18] and secured an article from Edward Carpenter on 'Desirable Mansions'.[19] Only three months after taking up the editorship both Aveling and Marx joined Hyndman's Democratic Federation.

---

[14] *National Reformer*, 4 May 1884.

[15] Annie Besant, *An Autobiography* (London: T. Fisher Unwin), p. 311.

[16] Tsuzuki, p. 90.

[17] Stanley Pierson, *Marxism and the Origins of British Socialism* (Ithaca: Cornell University Press., 1973), pp. 70–71; W. Wolfe, *From Radicalism to Socialism* (New Haven, Conn.: Yale University Press, 1975), p. 302.

[18] Eleanor Marx, 'Karl Marx', *Progress* (May 1883), 288–94.

[19] Edward Carpenter, 'Desirable Mansions', *Progress* (June 1883).

Then in January 1884 a new socialist paper, *To-Day*, was set up by the Democratic Federation, with an article by Aveling in its opening number on 'Christianity and Capitalism'.[20] The editors of *To-Day* were the socialists J.L. Joynes and Belfort Bax; Aveling, in the same month, had managed to get both of them to write on socialist topics for the still ostensibly secular *Progress*. Back in *To-Day* Marx launched an offensive on the doctrine of 'Parson Malthus', so dear to the hearts of the secularists.[21] Marx and Aveling ceased to write for *To-Day* in summer 1884, after Hyndman replaced Bax with the more pliant Henry Champion.

A striking case of Aveling's permeation strategy at work was a lecture which he delivered as President of the North-West London branch in early 1884, to the NSS, later published in the Freethought *Atheistic Platform* series. Aveling admits to his audience that the content will prove unpopular, since to 'The Curse of Christianity', on which he had lectured the previous week, he now wishes to link the 'The Curse of Capital'. He is now 'an Evolutionist, an Atheist, and a Socialist'.[22] This speech was cleverly aimed at his audience of 'radicals', rather than merely 'secularists'. An attack on Christian ethics, pitched well within the horizon of secularist expectations, lays the ground for the assimilation of decidedly unpalatable socialist imports: the concept of 'labour power', the facts of 'production' and the warning that the secularist quest for the extension of the franchise could only be a 'transition' remedy. Aveling urges the radicals in his audience to learn from 'evolution' and adopt policies which will change 'not only the future of the individual', but 'his environment': 'you that are students of Darwin ... must alter the condition of society as it is at the present time, and then you will get a reaction against the individual'. He ends by inviting the secularists not to ignore how rapidly Socialism is currently spreading in Germany and France. 'Do you intend to ignore a movement like that?'[23]

Aveling clearly relished the editorial opportunity. Actively assisted by Marx, in Foote's absence, he was playing an effective game by drawing the teeth of radicalism and assisting the transition to a socialist point of view.

Foote became available to edit *Progress* from March 1884 but it was not until December of that year that he finally took the paper back: it is possible that he believed that Aveling's success in raising the profile of paper[24] needed to be weighed against the evidence of his departure from the faith. As early as September 1883 Eleanor had noted with satisfaction that under Aveling's leadership 'this little magazine is beginning – to the great annoyance of Bradlaugh

---

20 Edward Aveling, *Christianity and Capitalism* (London: Modern Press, 1884, pp. 1–12; repr. from *To-Day* [January 1884]), generally regarded as Aveling's first socialist article.
21 See Tsuzuki, p. 102.
22 Aveling, 'The Curse of Capital', *Atheistic Platform*, 11 (1884), 164–76 (p. 164).
23 'The Curse of Capital', pp. 165–6, 168–9, 175.
24 Aveling had himself contributed no fewer than thirty-six reviews, articles and poems between 1883 and 1886.

to have a really good circulation'.[25] While in private the Avelings might be dismissive of the secularist leadership, in public it was politic to maintain, as far as possible, cordial relations. On the eve of Foote's release from prison in February 1884, Marx, perhaps strategically, urged the readers of Hyndman's *To-Day* to gather outside Holloway gaol and to extend to Foote a 'hearty welcome'.[26]

Aveling's 'Christianity and Capitalism' is amongst his most vitriolic efforts. The prospect of the established church in one of its 'spasms of sympathy'[27] provoked him as few other subjects could. There is an Oedipal violence in his aim to slay the twin-headed monster of Christianity and Capital, to expose the 'false basis of our ethical ... and our commercial system'.[28] Aveling brackets Christianity with Capitalism by mounting an assault on the recent publicity which Christian philanthropists had been giving to the social question, especially in the single most influential pamphlet of the decade, 'The Bitter Cry of Outcast London' (1883) by the congregationalist minister Andrew Mearns. Aveling turns on Mearns, on the journalist George Sims and on other outspoken Christians who believe that 'a heaven waits' for 'the most miserable'.[29] But it was the prospect that radical Christians might not only write powerfully but demonstrate ideological sophistication that particularly provoked Aveling's scorn. One such Christian spokesman, the Reverend Dawson Burns, points up the 'ghastly mockery' of a situation in which 'the existence of ... colonies of heathens and savages in the heart of our capital should attract such little attention'.[30] Aveling answers: 'How dare any man speak of a merciful father to the dwellers in ... fever-haunted charnel-houses for which they pay more weekly than their graves will cost once for all?'[31] That Christian writers had temporarily stolen the limelight rankled: the clinching point, designed to highlight the condescending ignorance of churchmen about the poor, is incoherently expressed, the argument botched.

IV

While Aveling's Darwinism provided him with a basis for putting the secularist message on a scientific footing, it also posed him some difficulties, since his social philosophy of progressive Darwinism and his socialist materialism were not always compatible. Aveling, following Herbert Spencer, applied the central tenets of Darwinism, in Lamarckian terms, to contemporary society. Natural selection, he wrote, 'must lead to the improvement of the species', the 'steady advance in

---

[25] Eleanor Marx to Laura Lafargue, 14 September 1883, in *Letters*, p. 170; Tsuzuki, p. 98.
[26] Kapp, II, 36.
[27] *Christianity and Capitalism*, p. 1.
[28] *Christianity and Capitalism*, p. 3.
[29] *Christianity and Capitalism*, p. 9.
[30] *Christianity and Capitalism*, p. 10.
[31] *Christianity and Capitalism*, p. 12.

organisation', the 'ever-increasing adaptation of the structure and function of the living thing to the condition of its environment'.[32] Sexual selection and the criteria which impel it emerges as the key test of how far man has evolved: 'In man, sexual selection has played no small part in the determining of the characteristics of particular individuals, and through them of the race.'[33] 'Today the choice is a very complex matter', he warns, and 'infinite care' needs to be 'exercised'. Education will enable people to make progressively wiser choices. The suspicion that those who do not make rational choices operate at a lower level of development is confirmed by Aveling's degenerationist distaste for those who have not bred with these choices in mind:

> Large families ... point to a coarseness of intellect on the part of the parents that goes as far down as wickedness ... a glance at the wretched progeny ... shows us that repetition of similar parts mean lowness of organisation ... The same poor faces, the same weak limbs, the same tendency to disease, the same low intellectual stamp. You will see it if you look into the thousands of cottages, or into the foul, stifling dens of town courts ... today.[34]

Who can these beings be? Possibly the same brutish exemplars of biological reversion which Aveling's 'courageous' or 'idealist' reader observes sheltering under the Adelphi arches – the 'huddled-up forms, whose limbs are often interwoven in a horrible embrace, something akin to the linked arms and legs, the intertwined bodies of a colony of gibbons asleep in the Asiatic night'. This was from an 1884 essay, 'Brute Habits of Man', which post-dated by three months the inception of his so-called Socialist phase.[35] There is also the thoroughly conventional invitation to the reader to inspect the *paysage moralisé* of outcast London, 'which you will take' for the 'first circle' of Dante's *Inferno*.[36] Aveling seemed to have few inhibitions about slipping into this fashionable anthropology disguised as analysis, and was prepared to run with biological determinism for the sake of producing good copy; all the talk about reversion is no more than the higher showing-off.

A more authentic 'inferno' was addressed in Marx and Aveling's 1885 *The Factory-Hell* pamphlet, published by the Socialist League a year after 'Brute Habits', and three years after *Darwinism and Small Families*. For now we see a different use of the metaphor and a different mode of seeing. Rooted in a detailed observation of factory practice, enumerating the failures of the Factory Acts and the consequences for the lives of factory workers, including children, the essay builds an impressive case from a powerful empirical base, in the best tradition of

---

[32] Edward Aveling, *The Student's Darwin* (London: Freethought Publishing Co., 1881), pp. 248–9.

[33] Aveling, *Darwinism and Small Families* (London: Besant & Bradlaugh, 1882), p. 6.

[34] *Darwinism and Small Families*, p. 4.

[35] *Progress* (April 1884), 325–31 (p. 331).

[36] 'Brute Habits of Man', p. 325.

Marx's study of Blue Books and the operation of the Factory Acts for *Capital*; indeed, the essay has the stamp of Eleanor Marx about it, precisely in its determined refusal to objectify the victims of the factory system other than those of the system and conditions of production. The hell of the factory system is that it will blast the 'lives of the workers as long as the capitalistic system of production lasts'.[37] The alienated condition of labour determines the quality of the whole life of the worker:

> No one has heart in the work done in our hideous factories whose chimneys rise up like curses from earth to heaven. The sooner it is over, the sooner to sleep or drink, or the low form of amusement for which their degrading toil leaves them fit.[38]

There is lowness and degradation here, but not a hint of the objectification by biological determinism; the mode of seeing is simply too well informed and too sympathetically engaged in the actual struggle of existence to admit the patronage of Aveling's degenerationism. Given Marx and Aveling's well-known hostility to Malthusianism, the legacy Aveling inherited from secularism had, throughout 1884, to be displaced into a discourse possibly less offensive to Eleanor and Engels. Yet is it is far from clear how she could have taken up with a man who only a year before had written the pro-Malthusian *Darwinism and Small Families*. Might Aveling have disavowed the piece, or claimed that it was written by someone else – Annie Besant perhaps?[39]

V

An evaluation of Aveling's achievements must indirectly influence our view of Eleanor Marx: quite how may be left to others to judge. The various 'lives' and roles that he plays out – dandy and man of the theatre, earnest evolutionist, romantic visionary, fearless freethinker – seem to be bound up with the improvised nature of his position in the cultural and political life of the period. His financial and sexual opportunism was informed by an instability which had social as well as psychological origins.

In 1885 Aveling argued that, like the young prostitutes in W.T. Stead's sensational *Pall Mall Gazette* revelations, he too was forced to prostitute himself to the market as a 'middle-class man who writes for his livelihood ... of necessity in journals of which ... he does not approve';[40] the issue of prostitution for mid-1880s socialism was, of course, one of class exploitation: the cause of prostitution

---

[37] *The Factory Hell*, p. 56.
[38] *The Factory Hell*, p. 52.
[39] I am grateful to Deborah Lavin for this point.
[40] Edward Aveling, 'The Recent Revelations', *Progress* (September 1885), 417–22 (p. 420).

was 'the economic condition of society ... the whole of the proletariat, men and women alike, are prostitutes'.[41] This was a standard socialist tactic for outflanking the radicals, recently employed by Eleanor Marx in *The Woman Question*, and Aveling borrows from it. But then the necessity of the writer faking it, the implied bad faith, was the guarantor of Aveling's identity, shaped precisely by contradictions he sloughed off as systemic. That he was so consistently on the make was a part-consequence of the freelance vocation, but there was clearly a decisive psychological drive at work. His ventriloquism, his improvised strategies of borrowing, of fabrication, his bucking the system (playing the ends off against the middle) were psychological necessities. Aveling could never have been comfortable with or fulfilled by the academic career for which he appeared so suited in his early twenties: to a quite unusual degree he was sustained by the heat of public controversy and ideological conflict which a university environment was unlikely to offer him.

This meant that principle and self-interest were always entangled in Aveling's career; he certainly could not tell the two apart. Fired by a virulent atheism, Aveling identified his interests with Bradlaugh and Besant; he then shifted his radical secularism onto the terrain of the coming socialist movement with its competing leaders, Hyndman, Morris and Engels. It was always vital for him to align himself with a dependably principled but iconoclastic and radical leading figurehead such as Bradlaugh, Hyndman, Morris and, pre-eminently, Engels. In the febrile, fiercely ideological milieu which dominated the 1880s, respect could too easily be earned through public vilification by the enemy. First Bradlaugh and later Engels were persuaded that faults attributed to Aveling were being invented by political and ideological opponents. Campaigns mounted against his secular activities by Sir Henry Tyler, or against his socialist probity by Hyndman, only confirmed for both Bradlaugh and Engels the destructive power of sectarianism, and so conferred on Aveling a glamour associated with political martyrdom. The belief that victimization was rife came all too easily to Engels, as it did to Eleanor Marx, and this habit goes some way to explain the blind spot each had for Aveling.

Yet Engels observed that Aveling had the 'remarkable knack of giving London what London requires'.[42] Since he was referring here to the prospects of his success as a playwright (which were negligible) we should not give much weight to the comment, but it does contain more than a grain of truth. It may be no accident that Aveling never ceased to revere Sir Henry Irving, the greatest living ventriloquist of them all, who at one point he had attempted to pass off as his own brother.[43] Did the theatre and its cult of image offer a kind of permission to invent the persona of 'Alec Nelson' – man-about-town dramatic critic, actor and

---

[41] Aveling, 'The Recent Revelations', p. 420.
[42] Kapp, II, 254.
[43] Laurence Irving, *Henry Irving: The Actor and His World* (London: Faber & Faber, 1951), p. 257.

author of one-act matinées (author of the Jerome K. Jerome-like *Comic Cricket* in 1891)? When Aveling and Marx's *The Woman Question* was turned into an essay for the *Westminster Review*, Marx's original article for *Commonweal* was infused by Aveling with orotund phrasing and classical allusion designed to produce an effect of the literary, so as to make the socio-political challenge of the material more acceptable.

Such a strategy has all the hallmarks of a writer who is overconditioned by what he takes to be an idiom to which he should conform, by a compulsion to adapt the medium to the message. A man who could turn his hand to a variety of styles of writing, whether of Shelley-esque lyricism or dogged, unashamedly prosaic rationalism and then, adding to the embarrassment, attempt to blend the two, is a man who never found his own voice. Perhaps he could only bear to be T.R. Ernest/E.D./Alec Nelson/Edward Aveling. He could not bring himself to call Eleanor by the familiar name which her family had always affectionately used, 'Tussy'. To do so would have been to face up to what had to be at all times repressed: that there was not and could not be an equivalent nickname – no single defining term of endearment.

Aveling could never love Eleanor Marx, since the man who the year before the end changed his name, his date of birth and merged his handwriting style with hers,[44] never actually knew who he was. Only the name on the cover could tell him that. And if this sounds as if Aveling conforms to the type of the self-reflexive, self-fashioning late Victorian aesthete, we should not be fooled. In producing himself through acts of 'commodification, or commercial exploitation of the dandiacal self', Oscar Wilde always knew that this was the name of the game.[45] Aveling never did.

---

[44] H.M. Hyndman, *Further Reminiscences* (London: Macmillan, 1912), p. 145.
[45] Regenia Gagnier, *Idylls of the Marketplace* (London: Scolar Press, 1987), p. 7.

Chapter 4

Eleanor Marx and Henrik Ibsen

Sally Ledger

Eleanor Marx wrote to her friend Havelock Ellis in December 1885: 'I feel I *must* do something to make people understand our Ibsen a little more than they do, and I know by experience that a play read to them often affects people more than when read by themselves.'[1] Marx subsequently sent out invitations to a 'few people worth reading *Nora* to', and on 15 January 1886, in their flat in Great Russell Street, Marx and her common-law husband, Edward Aveling, hosted a reading of *A Doll's House* in the reliable Henrietta Frances Lord translation. George Bernard Shaw took the role of the blackmailing bank clerk, Krogstad, and William Morris's daughter May played the long-suffering Christine Linde; Eleanor Marx took the lead as Nora Helmer, whilst Edward Aveling played the chauvinistic and hypocritical husband, Torvald Helmer. This private performance of *A Doll's House* heralded the emergence of 'Ibsenism', a political and cultural formation of the 1880s and 1890s consisting of Marxists, socialists, Fabians and feminists, who jointly hailed Ibsen as spokesman for their various causes.

Marx had been introduced to Ibsen's work by her friend Olive Schreiner, the South African novelist whose *The Story of an African Farm* (1883) had announced her as the first of the New Woman novelists living and writing in England. A few months before Marx and Aveling spent a holiday with Schreiner and Havelock Ellis in the summer of 1884, Olive had enthused to Ellis about the Norwegian's plays:

> Have you read a little work called *Nora* by Ibsen, translated from the Swedish [sic] by Frances Lord? It is a most wonderful little work ... It shows some sides of a woman's nature that are not often spoken of, and that some people do not believe exist – but they do.[2]

The Frances Lord translation of *A Doll's House* was first published in *To-Day*, edited by John Foulger, which Ellis later described as 'a monthly magazine to which brilliant representatives of the new social movements, shut out from other

---

1 Kapp, II, 103.
2 Letter to Havelock Ellis, 28 March 1884, in *Olive Schreiner, Letters 1871–9*, ed. by Richard Rive (Oxford: Oxford University Press, 1987), p. 36.

avenues to publicity, were always welcomed'.[3] Mediated as it was through the radical press, Ibsen's work immediately acquired an anti-establishment cachet.

Introduced to *A Doll's House* by Schreiner, Marx in turn brought the attention of Shaw to Ibsen's work, an intellectual encounter which was to have a profound impact on his writing for the theatre. Marx, Aveling and Shaw organized a number of readings of Ibsen's plays at a time when the Norwegian's work was quite unknown in England, and thereby played no inconsiderable role in promoting him as the progenitor of 'modern' drama on the European stage.[4]

The political and cultural impact of the arrival of Ibsen's work on the London stage cannot be overstated. Writing thirty years after the 1889 London premier of *A Doll's House* at the Novelty Theatre, the writer Edith Lees Ellis recalled the moment:

> A few of us collected outside the theatre breathless with excitement. Olive Schreiner was there and Dolly Radford the poetess ... Emma Brooke ... and Eleanor Marx. We were restive and almost savage in our arguments. What did it mean? Was it life or death for women? ... Was it joy or sorrow for men? That a woman should demand her own emancipation and leave her husband and children in order to get it, savoured less of sacrifice than sorcery.[5]

This first unbowdlerized public production of *A Doll's House* was attended by a dazzling array of bohemians and intellectuals, some of whom – such as Shaw and Marx – were to become London's leading Ibsenites. This was not the usual London theatre audience attending the mainstream productions of comedies, romances and melodramas which had dominated the English theatre throughout much of the Victorian period; Ibsen's drama, engaging as it did with pressing social issues, drew what we might now refer to as an 'alternative' and highly politicized audience.

The exhilarating promise of freedom dramatized in Ibsen's *A Doll's House* made a huge impact on the left-leaning *literati*. The radical novelist 'Mark Rutherford' reflected that: 'It greatly excited me, and as the house was crammed with people who proved to be excitable too, their laughter and tears wrought upon me with almost too much power.'[6] Ibsen's most antagonistic reviewer, Clement Scott, was none the less impressed by the quality of the audience at this inauguration of the playwright's reign amongst socialists and feminists in England,

3   Havelock Ellis, *My Life: Autobiography of Havelock Ellis* (Cambridge, Mass.: Riverside Press, 1939), pp. 195–6. Bernard Shaw's fiction also first appeared in *To-Day*, and Ellis himself was a regular contributor.
4   Ruth Brandon, *The New Women and the Old Men: Love, Sex and the Woman Question* (London: Secker & Warburg, 1990), p. 30.
5   Edith Lees Ellis, *Stories and Essays* (Berkeley Heights: Free Spirit Press, 1924), p. 128.
6   William Hale White ('Mark Rutherford'), *Letters to Three Friends* (London: Oxford University Press, 1924), pp. 45–6.

noting that 'the interest was so intense last night that a pin might have been heard to drop'.[7]

Ibsen's appeal to London's leading socialist figures in the late nineteenth century can be readily explained.[8] Though he was politically uncommitted – it would be fair to say that he loathed both politicians and the political process itself – the Norwegian shared with socialism's more bohemian wing a profoundly critical stance towards the most hallowed of bourgeois social institutions and conventions.[9] The issues raised in his plays – free love, marriage, women's role in society, women's sexuality, bourgeois morality – were fiercely debated amongst socialists and feminists in the 1880s and 1890s. The Men and Women's Club – of which Marx was an associate – was a prominent forum for such issues; but they were a general focus of concern in the wider culture as well.[10] The rise of the New Woman fiction in the 1880s and 1890s, the development of a socialist poetics in the work of William Morris, and the proliferation of novels from the Zolaesque school of naturalism, all meant that the theatre – and cultural life more generally – were ripe for the arrival of Ibsen's plays on the London stage. Most of Ibsen's followers in England were from a middle-class background, and as Shaw put it so succinctly:

> It is in the middle class itself that the revolt against middle-class ideals breaks out ... Neither peer not labourer has ever hated the bourgeoisie as Marx hated it, nor despised its ideals as Swift, Ibsen and Strindberg despised them.[11]

Marx had hoped at one stage to become an actress, and her interest in Ibsen brought together her political and cultural interests. She was friendly with the great Ibsen actress Mrs Theodore Wright, who played the role of Mrs Alving in the 1891 London Premier of *Ghosts*, and she wrote glowingly of Elizabeth Robins's performance of *Hedda Gabler* at the Vaudeville Theatre in April 1891, referring to

---

7   Clement Scott, unsigned notice of *A Doll's House* in the *Daily Telegraph*, 8 June 1889, p. 3.

8   For a full exploration of Ibsen's contemporary political appeal in England, see Ian Britain's excellent essay, 'A Transplanted Doll's House: Ibsenism, Feminism and Socialism in Late-Victorian and Edwardian England', in *Transformations in Modern European Drama*, ed. by Ian Donaldson (London and Basingstoke: Macmillan Press, 1983), pp. 14–54.

9   The fullest, most reliable biography of Ibsen is by Michael Meyer, *Ibsen: A Biography*, 3 vols (London: Rupert Hart-Davis, 1967–70); a subsequent biography by Robert Ferguson, *Henrik Ibsen: A New Biography* (London: Richard Cohen, 1996) is less sympathetic and adds little to Meyer's account.

10 For an account of the Men and Women's Club see Lucy Bland, *Banishing the Beast: English Feminism and Sexual Morality 1885–1914* (London and New York: Penguin Books, 1995), Chapter 1. Marx was a guest speaker at the club, but feminist Maria Sharpe objected to her becoming a full member because of her unmarried status as Edward Aveling's lover. See Bland, pp. 6, 173.

11 George Bernard Shaw, 'What About the Middle Class...?', Pt. II, *Daily Citizen* (Manchester), 19 October 1912.

the actress as 'simply magnificent' in that 'wonderful play'.[12] As well as playing an important role in the dissemination of *A Doll's House* in England, Marx translated two of Ibsen's plays – *An Enemy of the People* and *The Lady from the Sea* – and greatly admired *Hedda Gabler*. The significance of these four works to her life and writings, and the ways in which they resonate with the conflicts and contradictions in her *modus vivendi*, will form a focus for the remainder of this essay.

That *A Doll's House* would seem to have been one of Marx's favourite Ibsen plays is suggested by her expression of disappointment to Havelock Ellis that he did not include it in the first selection of Ibsen's plays to be published in English: 'I am sorry *Nora* was not included in the volume. It should have been, I think, in any *first* volume of Ibsen.'[13] The appeal of *A Doll's House* for a woman such as Marx is clear, dealing as it does with a young middle-class woman's troubled negotiation of bourgeois domestic relationships, and her refusal to accept marriage as a moral holy cow. And yet Marx's own private performance of *A Doll's House*, with her lover Edward Aveling playing the narrow, hypocritical Torvald Helmer to her Nora, is with hindsight painfully ironic. For what appealed to Ibsen's enthusiastic following of women in late nineteenth-century England was Nora's confidence in walking out of an unsatisfactory relationship with a man not worthy of her. Drawn as she was to the play, Marx herself none the less seemed to lack Nora's ability to act in her own best interests when it came to the relationship with the man to whom she had attached herself. Nor did she share Nora's defiance in the face of social convention, revealing in her letters a certain social timidity concerning her courageous decision to live with Aveling as his wife. Breaking the news of her imminent cohabitation to her friend Dollie Radford in the summer of 1884, Marx explained her position thus:

> I had half intended to tell you this morning what my 'plans' I spoke of are – but somehow it is easier to write – and it is perhaps fairer to you, because you can think over what I am going to tell you. Well then this is it – I am going to live with Edward Aveling as his wife. You know he is married, and that I cannot be his wife *legally*, but it will be a *true* marriage to me – just as much as if a dozen registrar's [sic] had officiated … E. had not *seen* his wife for many, many years when I met him, and that he was not unjustified in leaving her you will best understand when I tell you that Mr Engels, my father's oldest friend, and Helen [Demuth] who has been as a mother to us, approve of what I am about to do – and are *perfectly* satisfied.
>
> I shall *quite* understand if you think the position one you cannot accept, and I shall think of you both with no less affection if we do not any longer count you among our immediate friends.[14]

---

[12] Quoted in Kapp, II, 476.
[13] Quoted in Havelock Ellis, 'Eleanor Marx – II', *Adelphi*, 11 (1935), 33–41.
[14] 30 June 1884. Radford Family Papers. Quoted in Kapp, II, 16.

This was written in the very year that Marx first encountered Ibsen's *A Doll's House*; the Norwegian's dramatic challenge to conventional morality must have boosted her in her decision deliberately to contravene the social laws of her time.

It is likely that Nora's abandonment of her marriage on the grounds that she and her husband have nothing in common and barely even know one another provided Marx with a rationale for Aveling having walked away from his first wife many years before.[15] But, with hindsight, Marx was no Nora. It is almost as if in acting out the role of Nora, Marx was compensating for her own compromised and unsatisfactory relationship with Aveling. After playing the part of an adoring, uncritical wife for eight years, Nora finally decides that she has a duty to herself as a responsible adult to consider her own personal needs, and not to subjugate herself any longer to the needs of others:

> NORA: I must educate myself. And you can't help me with that. It's
> something I must do by myself. That's why I'm leaving you.
> HELMER (jumping up): What did you say?
> NORA: I must stand on my own feet if I am to find out the truth about
> myself and about life. So I can't go on living here with you any longer.
> HELMER: You're out of your mind! You can't do this.[16]

One important difference between Ibsen's Nora Helmer and Eleanor Marx is the fact that Marx was a mature, well-educated and in some ways at least an experienced woman when she set up home with Aveling. In her thirtieth year, she was already something of a political activist, joining Hyndman's Social Democratic Federation, associating with Helen Taylor and Joseph Cowen, and keeping abreast of all the significant social and political issues in Britain and on the Continent through visitors at her parents' supper table such as August Bebel and Eduard Bernstein.[17] What she lacked was a fulfilling personal life, and she appears to have been willing to settle for a less than ideal intimate relationship with Aveling rather than no relationship at all. Marx, unlike the fictional Nora, did not lack a wider field of action beyond the domestic sphere: what was missing was a secure domestic haven of her own. In this she resembles Ibsen's Christine Linde rather than Nora Helmer: having had to fend for herself for many years, Linde settles for a 'second best' relationship with the reformed blackmailer Krogstad, rather than continue to make her way through life alone.

Clearly *A Doll's House* had a personal significance for Marx; it also, though, was important to her politically and intellectually. She and Aveling quote the play in their 1886 pamphlet, *The Woman Question*, an essay in which Ibsen is regarded

---

[15] Edward Aveling had married Isabel Campbell Frank, the wealthy daughter of a poulterer, on 30 July 1872; the marriage foundered two years later. The reason for the split remains unclear: see Kapp, I, 256–9.

[16] *Ibsen: Plays Two (A Doll's House, An Enemy of the People, Hedda Gabler)*, trans. by Michael Meyer (London: Methuen, 1991), p. 99.

[17] Kapp, I, 211–12.

as a herald of change, both recording and contributing to what the socialist writers hoped would be a catastrophic implosion of the bourgeois social fabric. Inspired by August Bebel's *Woman in the Past, the Present and the Future* (1883), Marx and Aveling's pamphlet throws light on Marx's engagement with *A Doll's House*. For Marx, Nora's domestic oppression was analogous to the exploitation of labour: she argued in *The Woman Question* that 'The position of women rests, as everything in our complex modern society rests, on an economic basis ... Women are the creatures of an organized tyranny of men, as the workers are the creatures of an organized tyranny of idlers.'[18] Towards the end of the essay a future is imagined in which women will have equal access to education and employment, and in which the marriage tie will be replaced by a freer form of union between men and women:

> Thus, woman will be independent: her education and all other opportunities as those of men. The contract between man and woman will be of a purely private nature, without the intervention of any public functionary. The woman will no longer be the man's slave, but his equal. For divorce there will be no need. There will no longer be one law for the woman and one for the man.[19]

Many of Ibsen's concerns in *A Doll's House* are re-articulated here: written shortly after that first private performance of *Nora* in the Marx–Aveling's Great Russell Street flat, it would seem that *The Woman Question* owed an intellectual debt to Ibsen as well as to Bebel.

In an important way, though, Ibsen's vision differs from both Bebel's and Eleanor Marx's, in that the commitment to women's emancipation dramatized in *A Doll's House* appears to apply only to the women of the middle class, and in this particular respect Marx's apparently unqualified enthusiasm for the play is rather surprising. Part of Marx and Aveling's essay on *The Woman Question* is taken up with an attack on the Victorian women's movement for its narrow focus on the needs of middle-class women. Virtually all those concerned with the women's movement in Britain are, Marx complains,

> of the well-to-do classes ... scarcely any of the women taking part in these various movements belong to the working class ... all these ideas of the 'advanced' women are based either on property, or on sentimental or professional questions. Not one of them gets down through them to the bed-rock of the economic basis.[20]

If the Victorian women's movement in Britain was preoccupied with the disabilities of middle-class women specifically, then so were Ibsen's plays. The class

---

[18] *Woman Question*, pp. 4–6.
[19] *Woman Question*, pp. 15–16.
[20] *Woman Question*, p. 6.

orientation of *A Doll's House* is dramatically revealed in a parodic rewriting of the play's final act by Marx and Israel Zangwill, and this suggests that by 1890 at least, Marx had become conscious of the social parameters of Ibsen's vision. Marx and Zangwill's comic spoof, '*A Doll's House* Repaired', is one of a series of 'sequels', serious and satirical, which followed the first public performance of *A Doll's House* in England. The sequel-mania had begun with Walter Besant's 'The Doll's House – and After', in which he imagines the plight of Nora's family twenty-five years after she has walked out on them. Torvald Helmer, Nora's abandoned husband, is now drunk, dissolute and unemployed, and of their two sons one is also an alcoholic and the other is an embezzler. Their daughter is a pure young girl who commits suicide when her mother's shame prevents her from marrying a banker's son. Nora herself has become a cold and hard New Woman writer who 'wrote novels ... which the old-fashioned regarded with horror'.[21]

Walter Besant's moralistic condemnation of Nora's actions provoked a sharp rejoinder from Shaw, who wrote a much more radical response to Nora's abandonment of her marriage in his 'Still After the Doll's House: A Sequel to Mr Besant's Sequel to Henrik Ibsen's Play'.[22] In a prefatory note to their own heavily satirical sequel, '*A Doll's House* Repaired', Marx and Zangwill explain that the 'repairs' they have made to the original were intended to rectify some of Ibsen's 'shortcomings' out of respect for those critics 'whose sound English common sense revolts at the manifestly impossible, nay immoral, conclusion' to the play.[23] Their comic version of the play's third act has Nora begging to stay with her husband, melodramatically overacting the part of sweetly repentant errant wife. Instead of Nora slamming the front door at the end, Torvald flounces out of the room and huffily slams the bedroom door. It is in an invented exchange between Torvald and the blackmailing bank clerk, Krogstad, that Marx and Zangwill begin to bring out the submerged class politics of Ibsen's play. In Ibsen's play, Krogstad sends a letter to Torvald in which he apologizes for having attempted to blackmail Nora, and returns the IOU which he had planned to use as evidence that Nora had committed forgery to borrow money. His generosity is born of his new-found happiness with Nora's friend, Christine Linde. In the Marx and Zangwill version, Helmer and Krogstad have the following exchange:

> HELMER: How much do you want?
> KROGSTAD: There was a time when I wanted merely revenge – and rescue from the mud for myself. But now a happy turn in my life – however, this happy turn brings with it a need of money. In a word, I'm going to be married.

---

21 Walter Besant, 'The Doll's House – and After', *English Illustrated Magazine* (January 1890), 315–25 (p. 320).
22 George Bernard Shaw, 'Still After the Doll's House: A Sequel to Mr. Besant's Sequel to Henrik Ibsen's Play', *Time* (February 1890), 197–207.
23 Israel Zangwill and Eleanor Marx Aveling, '*A Doll's House* Repaired', *Time* (March 1891), 239–53.

HELMER: *You* married! Why, who would marry you?

KROGSTAD: Mrs Linden.

HELMER: What! How could you dare to ask my wife's friend?

KROGSTAD: I didn't. She proposed to me.

HELMER: *She* proposed! Well! I always suspected she was no better than she should be. What can one expect from a woman who has earned her own living?

KROGSTAD: But suppose she had to earn her own living?

HELMER: Women of our class should never have to. In women of the lower classes it may be a necessity, and even very laudable. But for ours! It is a degradation, a destroying of all that is sweetest and most womanly. It makes them flat-chested and flat-footed. The women of our class should be the guardians of the hearth, the spirit of beauty and holiness sanctifying home life. And then it is so ugly to see a woman work. It shocks one's sense of ideal womanliness. And what is worse, it makes the wife independent of her husband. What happiness can you hope for in a union with such a woman? ...

KROGSTAD: Well, I've got as good a chance of domestic felicity as you.

HELMER: What do you mean?

KROGSTAD: Your wife has worked to earn money this long while.

HELMER (*overwhelmed*): Worked! To earn money! What new blow is this?

NORA (*peeping in at door*): Heavens! Lost![24]

One of the major demands of the bourgeois women's movement in the nineteenth century was the right to work outside of the home. This was not, of course, a problem encountered by working-class women, who had all too much work outside of the home, a fact recognized by Marx in the part she played in the campaign (which many feminists opposed) in support of a series of Factory Acts in the 1880s and 1890s.[25] Her ironic understanding of the class-specific bid for freedom which Nora makes in *A Doll's House* is confirmed in a final exchange between Nora and Torvald where, in a reversal of Ibsen's lines in which Torvald reminds his wife of her most sacred duties as wife and mother, Nora begs her husband to allow her to stay at home with her children:

NORA: Oh, Torvald! I must go to the children. I know they're in better hands than mine [i.e. the maidservant's], but still I am their mother.

HELMER (*interrupting*): As you now are, you can be nothing to them. They must be sent to a boarding school.

NORA: Oh! never, never! No mother could ever leave her little ones. Nature, society, religion, all forbid you to separate a mother from her children. You cannot! You dare not!

HELMER: Cannot? Dare not? I both can and dare do what is my duty towards my children.

---

[24] '*A Doll's House* Repaired', p. 247.

[25] One of many discussions of feminism's opposition to the Factory Acts of the 1890s can be found in David Rubenstein, *Before the Suffragettes: Women's Emancipation in the 1890s* (Brighton: Harvester, 1986).

NORA (*hysterically*): But this is monstrous, unnatural, unheard of!
HELMER: Unheard of? Supposing I had not saved you from Krogstad, you would have been condemned as a forger. Do you think you would have your children with you in a prison cell? And what the law would have done on legal grounds, I must do on moral grounds. Unnatural? It is the law of nature in the working classes, and you have debased yourself to their level. Didn't the three nurses you engaged for the children, because I was afraid nursing them yourself would spoil your figure, have to send their own babes to baby farms? And as for monstrous, supposing you had committed suicide, as you selfishly thought of doing, would you not have been separated from the children – and for ever?[26]

In a play which is dominated by its female lead, the figure of Anne-Marie, Nora's maidservant and her children's nurse, is altogether marginalized. Marx and Zangwill's parody suggests, however, that she had not escaped their notice. We learn in passing, in Ibsen's play, that many years before Anne-Marie had to relinquish her baby in order to act as a nanny to Nora when she was a child. As an adult, the infantilized, decorous Nora, naughtily munching macaroons, needs the marginalized maidservant to oil the cogs of her bourgeois domestic world. Nor, presumably, will the need for Anne-Marie's services disappear once Nora has renounced her marriage; the maidservant will presumably be left 'holding the baby', when Nora leaves the marital home and her children in a quest for freedom and her 'self'. Anne-Marie's marginalization in the play (and that of others like her – Bertha, for example, in *Hedda Gabler*) reveals the limitations of the liberal individualism on which this and other of Ibsen's plays are predicated, and which Victorian feminists eagerly embraced.

It is likely that it is the extreme liberal individualism, as well as the suggestion of political anarchism underpinning Ibsen's *An Enemy of the People*, which led Marx to regard her translation of this particular play as, in her own words, mere 'literary hackwork'.[27] In a general way Marx was certainly not a hack translator: she was sufficiently inspired by and committed to Ibsen's plays to learn Norwegian with the sole purpose of translating his works into English. Her rendering of *An Enemy of Society*, as she titled it, was the first English version, and she was paid the princely sum of £5 for it. It was published alongside *The Pillars of Society* and *Ghosts* in the first English-language selection of Ibsen's plays, selected and introduced by Havelock Ellis.[28] Eleanor complained to her sister Laura that she thought it 'a very unwise selection for a *first* volume in English'.[29] Whether or not she actively disliked *An Enemy of the People* is unclear, but it does seem likely that this of all Ibsen's plays would have been antipathetic to Marx's socialism.

---

26 '*A Doll's House* Repaired', p. 252.
27 Letter to her sister, Laura Lafargue, 25 June 1888, quoted in Kapp, II, 248.
28 *The Pillars of Society, and other plays*, ed. with an introduction by Havelock Ellis (London: Walter Scott, 1888). *An Enemy of Society* is the final play in the volume.
29 Kapp, II, 249.

In this 1882 play, Dr Stockmann, the public health officer in a small Norwegian spa town, discovers that the town's water supply has been contaminated by typhus because, in a cost-cutting exercise, the town council, led by his own brother, has not laid the water mains deeply enough. Stockmann expects the local leaders – property owners, journalists and tradesmen – to support him in his determination to publicize the health threat, whatever the economic consequences for the town; and initially they do. But as soon as they realize that they will have to pay extra taxes in order for the water mains to be relaid, they turn against the doctor and denounce him as an enemy of the people, bent on destroying the town's source of income (the new, elegant Spa Baths), as well as its reputation. The lumpenproletariat of the town – this is how Ibsen characterizes them – are easily persuaded to turn against Stockmann: they stone his house, prevent him from speaking the truth in public, and try to drive him out of the town. Stockmann rounds on them, and in a series of impassioned tirades which dominate most of the play's fourth act, he condemns the mass of the people as an ignorant mob, bestial and sheep-like:

> STOCKMANN: For this is the great discovery I made yesterday! The most dangerous enemies of truth and freedom in our midst are the compact majority. The majority is never right. Never, I say. That is one of those conventional lies against which a free, thoughtful man must rebel. Who are they that make up the majority of a country? Is it the wise men or the foolish? I think we must agree that the foolish folk are, at present, in a terribly overwhelming majority all around and about us the wide world over. But, devil take it, it can surely never be right that the foolish should rule over the wise! The majority has might – unhappily – but right it has not. I and a few others are right. The minority is always right.[30]

He goes on to warn that unless he is given liberty to cleanse the town of the filth and lies upon which its institutions are based then it will perish:

> STOCKMANN: You'll poison the whole country in time; you'll bring it to such a pass that the whole country will deserve to perish. And should it come to this, I say, from the bottom of my heart: Perish the country! Perish all its people![31]

Interestingly, other translators have glossed these last lines rather more forcefully as, for example, 'Let the whole people be exterminated!'[32] Marx's more passive formulation has the effect of toning down Stockmann's Kurtz-like desire to 'exterminate' the people. Marx's translation of the title of the play is similarly revealing: to be an enemy of society could be a politically radical position to take

---

[30] *Enemy of Society*, pp. 280–81.

[31] *Enemy of Society*, p. 288.

[32] *Ibsen: Plays Two (A Doll's House, An Enemy of the People, Hedda Gabler)*, trans. by Michael Meyer (London: Methuen Drama, 1991), p. 222.

up if by 'society' is meant its corrupt institutions and stale moral conventions; but to be an enemy of 'the people' (and this is how the play's title is usually translated) is, for any radical reader, far more problematic. Marx, of course, devoted much of her political life to the cause of 'the people'.

In the context of the play's action, Dr Stockmann is morally in the right concerning the town's sewers – the public health of the community should not be put at risk in order to protect commercial interests and the taxpayer's pocket. But the contaminating sewers, the cesspit on which the spa town has been built, acts in the play as a metaphor for *all* civil and political institutions. In his valorization of Dr Stockmann, Ibsen reacts against the petty politics of town councils, and against the political power of petty capitalist tradesmen; but he attacks at the same time the democratic process itself, and sets himself against the mob – the mass of the people – whom that process represents. A contempt for the majority – a contempt which was expressed with rather more in the way of moderation by other nineteenth-century liberals such as Mill, Arnold and George Eliot – would have jarred with Eleanor Marx's commitment to the 'people'.

Added to this there is an incipiently anarchist current running through the play which emerges most intriguingly at the close. Ostracized by the townspeople and refused employment, Dr Stockmann proposes to set up a free school for 'street urchins – real guttersnipes – mongrels. They have good heads on them sometimes.'[33] He aims to educate his pupils as a new radical force, as free, liberated individuals and, despite his (and Ibsen's) ostensible contempt for the lowest echelons of society, there is a recognition here – shared by London's late Victorian socialists – that a 'new' radical politics will emerge from the most oppressed social groups. At the same time, as far as Stockmann is concerned, the new politics will sweep away all existing political institutions: once he has educated his 'guttersnipes' he will get them to 'chase all these damned politicians into the Atlantic Ocean!'[34] The insistence on untrammelled individual freedom and the refusal to countenance existing political institutions and processes does have something in common with anarchism's political project at the turn of the century, and arguably Max Nordau, one of Ibsen's bitterest critical enemies, was not so very much wide of the mark when he characterized the Norwegian as an 'egomaniacal anarchist'.[35] It is significant in this respect that it was in 1888, the year that Marx translated *An Enemy of the People*, that she and Aveling's faction

---

[33] *Enemy of the People*, trans. by Meyer, Act 5, p. 221. Again, Eleanor modifies Stockmann's contempt for the common people by translating this line as: 'street-boys – some regular ragamuffins – ... there may be some good heads amongst them', *Enemy of Society*, p. 314.

[34] *Enemy of the People*, p. 222. Eleanor translates this less contentiously as 'Drive all the wolves out to the far west'. Ibsen is clearly referring here to the politicians who have obstructed Stockmann, so that Meyer's translation is the more helpful and accurate for an English reader even though it is a less literal translation of the original.

[35] Max Nordau, *Degeneration* (1892; Lincoln and London: University of Nebraska Press, 1993), p. 357.

within Morris's Socialist League was excluded, breaking away to form the Bloomsbury Socialist Society after a series of vehement disagreements with the anti-parliamentary anarchist wing of the League. It is very probable then that in 1888, of all years, Marx would have found this an uncomfortable play to translate and promote.

She was evidently much more comfortable with the other Ibsen play she translated, *The Lady from the Sea*. This was published as a separate volume by T. Fisher Unwin in 1890, and Marx and Aveling co-produced the play at Terry's Theatre in May 1891. It is generally agreed that Marx's *The Lady from the Sea* is a rather better translation than *An Enemy of Society*. In *The Lady from the Sea*, Ellida Wangel, the female lead, expresses a desire to divorce her husband in favour of a mysterious Stranger, a murderous sailor who has a powerful sexual hold over her. In the end, she decides of her own volition to stay with her husband, even though she is sexually unfulfilled with him and chafes against the domestic life. That Marx would have recognized in Ellida's irrational fascination with the sailor a parallel with her own attraction to the dishonest and faithlessly womanizing Aveling seems very probable,[36] and is borne out by a letter Marx wrote to a friend, confiding apropos of her irregular relationship with Aveling that 'I was irresistibly drawn to him.' [37] In the play, Ellida describes the mysterious sailor as 'demonic', as 'something that appals – and attracts'.[38] His hold over her is clearly sexual: she laments the 'horrible, unfathomable power he has over my mind'.[39]

If at one level *The Lady from the Sea* dramatizes Marx's fatal attraction to a dangerous man, then she would also have identified with Ellida Wangel's final resignation to a less-than-perfect private life. But the life to which Ellida resigns herself is positively benign in comparison with the miserable situation Marx found herself in with Aveling. Ellida's husband – although she is not attracted to him sexually – loves her and is honest with her; the same cannot be said of Aveling's shabby conduct towards Marx. Dr Wangel is a humane, loving man, resembling Aveling in nothing. The sexual entanglements and disappointments of *The Lady from the Sea*, then, relate inexactly – but none the less poignantly – to Marx's own desires and disappointments.

In a letter to Shaw written in 1885, Marx had declared that she found it 'odd' that people should complain of Ibsen's plays that they

> 'have no end' but just leave you where you are, that he gives no *solution* to the problem he has set you! As if life 'ended off' either comfortably or uncomfortably. We play through our little dramas, and comedies, and

---

[36] This is Ian Britain's suggestion in 'A Transplanted Doll's House'.
[37] Letter to Aaron Rosebury, quoted in Brandon, *The New Women and the Old Men*, p. 22.
[38] *Ibsen; Plays Three*, trans. by Michael Meyer (London: Methuen Drama, 1992), p. 189.
[39] *Plays Three*, p. 158.

tragedies, and farces, and then begin it all over again. If we *could* find solutions to the problems of our lives things would be easy in this weary world.[40]

There is no clear-cut, uplifting end for the main protagonists of *A Doll's House, An Enemy of the People,* or *The Lady from the Sea*: what happens, for good or ill, to Nora Helmer when she slams the door on her husband, the audience never discovers; Dr Stockmann is left homeless, railing against democracy but with only inchoate plans for the future; and Wangel settles for a sexually unfulfilling marital relationship.

One of the few of Ibsen's plays – and it is a play that Marx was passionate about – that does have a definitive close is *Hedda Gabler*. The life and death of Hedda Gabler, arguably Ibsen's most tortured heroine, have powerful resonances with the tragic trajectory of Marx's life. Although it would be facile to read Hedda's life as an allegory for Marx's – there are many more differences than similarities between them – there are all the same sufficient points of contact between the two women's lives to account for her emotional response to the play. Hedda, brought up and heavily influenced by a father who commanded public attention, wishes she were a man. Toting phallic pistols at any man who approaches her sexually, she is torn between a need to conform to bourgeois social conventions and a repressed desire to give expression to her powerful sexuality. There are clear parallels to be made with Marx's troubled adult life: also brought up in the shadow of a father who was a public figure, Marx's political acumen and activities in a man's world confirmed her in her father's view of her as 'more like a boy than a girl'.[41] One of many accolades paid to her by the men of the labour movement in nineteenth-century England was Tom Mann's reflection that she was 'a most capable woman. Possessing a complete mastery of economics, she was able alike in conversation and on a public platform to hold her own with the best.'[42] It was Aveling, Marx reflected, who 'really brought out the feminine in me', and this was in the thirtieth year of her life.[43]

Hedda Gabler, at twenty-nine the same age as Marx when she declared herself as Aveling's common-law wife, rages against the feminine sexuality that she considers will compromise her desire to lead a socially conventional, privileged life. Wild and dangerous as Hedda can be, she has a strong conventional streak in her personality which ultimately confines her field of action. Although infinitely more sympathetic than Ibsen's most troubled female protagonist, Marx too had a conventional, bourgeois dimension to her which she could have enjoyed rather more had she not given rein to the sexual passion that tied her to the impecunious

[40] Eleanor Marx to George Bernard Shaw, 2 June 1885, Shaw Papers, BL Add. MS. 50511, fol. 88v. Quoted by Ian Britain in 'A Transplanted Doll's House', p. 38.

[41] Quoted in Brandon, *The New Women and the Old Men*, p. 22.

[42] Tom Mann, *Memoirs*, quoted in Kapp, II, 331.

[43] Quoted in Brandon, *The New Women and the Old Men*, p. 22.

and dishonest Aveling. In a relationship which offended against bourgeois morality, Marx was at the same time perennially short of money until 1895 when the death of Engels meant that she came into an inheritance which enabled her to buy a house in Sydenham, freed from the ever-present threat of penury that had dogged her adult life. Her enjoyment of her new-found, almost-conventional domesticity is touchingly expressed in a letter to her sister Laura, in which she invites her and her husband, Paul Lafargue, to visit the new house:

> I want Paul badly to help me with the garden! There! The cat's out of the bag. If Paul has any little affection left for me he'll come and teach us to garden. As to our house (I am Jewishly fond of our house in Jew's Walk), voilà. Ground floor: Large room (Edward's study and general room combined); dining room (opens onto back garden), kitchen, scullery, pantry, coal and wine cellars, cupboards, large entrance hall. One flight of stairs (easy), bedroom, spare bedroom (*yours*), servant's room, bathroom (large enough to be another spare room on special occasions). My *study*!!! … Finally, as to furnishing all this I ought to let you know that … Edward … is buying all the furniture that unluckily one can't do without. I want you to know this as it would not be fair to think *I* was paying for it all.[44]

Hedda Gabler's conventional streak reveals itself in a far more ostentatious manner than this: part of her bargain in marrying a man she does not love is the acquisition of a 'liveried footman' and 'the bay mare you promised me'; 'You agreed that we should enter society. And keep open house. That was the bargain.'[45] Her domestic world crumbling about her – her husband is unable to provide her with the trappings of wealth she desires, her lover has shown himself attached to another woman, and she has become the object of sexual blackmail – Hedda takes control of her life in the most violent and destructive way imaginable. Marx's domestic disappointments were less self-inflicted, and even more devastating. The fragile domestic happiness she had attempted to construct for herself in her new home with Aveling in Sydenham was destroyed by her lover's ultimate exercise in infidelity and disloyalty. Accustomed as she was to his sexual philandering, even she could not have guessed that he would marry another woman whilst still living with (and financially dependent on) her. But this is precisely what he did: on 8 June 1897, using his *nom de plume*, Alec Nelson, Aveling married one Eva Frye, a twenty-two year-old actress, at Chelsea Register Office, thereafter returning to his other life as Edward Aveling, 'husband' of Eleanor Marx.

It had not been an easy thing for Marx to live with Aveling as an unmarried woman, and so to discover (as she seems to have done in March 1898) that he had married someone else in preference to her, finally destroyed what little optimism

---

[44] Letter to Laura Lafargue, 10 December 1895, *Daughters*, p. 284.
[45] *Ibsen: Plays Two (A Doll's House, An Enemy of the People, Hedda Gabler)*, trans. by Michael Meyer (London: Methuen Drama, 1991), pp. 271–2.

was left to her after what she described in a suicide note as the 'long, sad years' she had spent with Aveling.[46] Marx evidently felt herself unable any longer, in her own words, to 'begin all over again' with the 'comedies, tragedies and farces' that her personal life had thrown at her. Unable to opt for the sort of honourable compromise which Ellida Wangel chooses in *The Lady from the Sea*, Marx, like Ibsen's most despairing heroine, deliberately brought her life to a close. The poison which Marx used to kill herself powerfully links her to Flaubert's Madame Bovary, the eponymous heroine of the novel which Marx translated into English. But the life and death of this exceptional, gifted daughter of the bourgeoisie can just as fruitfully be apprehended through an understanding of those plays by Ibsen which she both admired and helped to disseminate in nineteenth-century England.

---

[46] Brandon, *The New Women and the Old Men*, pp. 152–3.

Chapter 5

Eleanor Marx and Shakespeare

Gail Marshall

The life of Eleanor Marx is imbued with references to Shakespeare – as is the case for so many women of the nineteenth century. For the Victorians in general the dramatist's female characters, in particular, seem to have taken on an iconic, occasionally even a hagiographic, status and function, and to have acted as archetypes and parameters of the possibilities of contemporary femininity. In the unjustly notorious 'Of Queens' Gardens' section of *Sesame and Lilies* (1864), John Ruskin compares Shakespeare's men and women thus:

> Shakespeare has no heroes;– he has only heroines. There is no one entirely heroic figure in all his plays … Whereas there is hardly a play that has not a perfect woman in it, steadfast in grave hope, and errorless purpose: Cordelia, Desdemona, Isabella, Hermione, Imogen, Queen Catherine, Perdita, Sylvia, Viola, Rosalind, Helena, and last, and perhaps loveliest, Virgilia, are all faultless; conceived in the highest heroic type of humanity.[1]

Ruskin, of course, omits such troubling heroines as Lady Macbeth, and even Beatrice, women clearly not seen by him as an integral part of Shakespeare's testimony to the timeless virtues of womanhood, which in a sleight of hand designed to flatter his listeners, and to collapse the distance between them and Shakespeare's characters, he makes into a universalized 'testimony to the position and character of women in human life'. Ruskin goes on: '[Shakespeare] represents them as infallibly faithful and wise counsellors,– incorruptibly just and pure examples – strong always to sanctify, even when they cannot save'.[2] There is no recognition of a gap between Shakespeare's women and their Victorian counterparts: they both occupy a continuum of idealized femininity.

Such was not the case, however, for Eleanor Marx, whose connections with the playwright are more complex, and straddle, or rather actively unite, both her personal and public political lives. They begin with the admission in her 'Confession' at the age of ten that Shakespeare was her favourite poet.[3] She went on to become a member of the Dogberry Club, a Shakespeare reading group, and

---

1 John Ruskin, 'Of Queens' Gardens', in *Sesame and Lilies* (London: Allen, 1911), pp. 92–3. I am grateful to Bridget Bennett and Andy Todd for their comments on this essay.
2 'Of Queens' Gardens', p. 96.
3 Tsuzuki, p. 17.

the New Shakspere Society, to teach classes on Shakespeare at the Highgate Literary Institution, to review his plays (with Edward Aveling), and to use him as a reference point for both emotional intelligence and integrity in many of her writings. In this essay I look at Marx's various connections with Shakespeare to try to establish precisely what he meant to her, and to examine the ways in which Shakespeare might achieve a radical political potential, rather than simply being used as part of a Ruskinian conservative rhetoric, within the framework of late Victorian socialism. I will argue that Marx's own concern was with the search for an appropriate emotional and political vocabulary rather than for forms of self-definition. So persistent was (and still is) the search for archetypes and answers, that she was herself inevitably simultaneously subjected by others to Shakespeare's defining capacity. However, even these categorizations can be shown to have retained something of the playwright's revolutionary potential.

Eleanor Marx was brought up in a household which rang with Shakespearean cadences and resonances. In his biography of Karl Marx, Isaiah Berlin writes that Marx's 'admiration for Shakespeare was limitless, and the whole household was brought up on him: he was read aloud, acted, discussed constantly. Whatever Marx did, he did methodically. Finding on arrival that his English was inadequate, he set himself to improve it by making a list of Shakespeare's turns of phrase: these he then learnt by heart'.[4] Mrs Marx was herself brought up in a Shakespeare-loving household, and wrote a number of articles on Shakespeare and the London stage for the *Frankfurter Zeitung* in the 1870s. According to Mrs Marx, her eldest daughter Jenny's room was 'a sort of Shakespeare museum'.[5] Eleanor's own participation in the family's worship of Shakespeare was precocious. Chushichi Tsuzuki writes that she knew whole passages from the plays by the time she was three or four years old. Eleanor herself writes vividly to Karl Kautsky forty years later (in January 1898) of this period in her life, and of Shakespeare's part in it. She writes that his works were 'the bible of our house, seldom out of our hands or mouths', and that her 'favourite scenes were the soliloquy of Richard IIIrd ("I can smile and smile and be a villain", which I *know* I loved because I had to have a knife in my hand to say it!) and the scene between Hamlet and his mother!'[6] She recollects that at the line 'Mother, you have my father much offended', she used to look 'very pointedly' at her father.

Their love of Shakespeare clearly involved the Marx family in the fabric as well as the language of their adopted country, for it was through the theatre in addition to their private study that their enthusiasm for the playwright was fed. In particular, the family were supporters of Henry Irving. They were initially attracted to him by his new interpretations of Shakespearean roles, such as his 1874 Hamlet, which involved him in some controversy. According to his grandson

---

[4] Isaiah Berlin, *Karl Marx: His Life and Environment* (Oxford University Press, 1959), p. 262.
[5] Kapp, I, 58.
[6] Tsuzuki, p. 12.

Laurence Irving, the actor steadfastly refused to 'flatter the public taste' with the familiar 'points' of Hamlet's performance, being influenced instead by the more philosophical approach of the American Edwin Booth.[7] Such champions were they of Irving that Mrs Marx wrote an article defending him which Eleanor forwarded to Karl Hirsch for insertion in the *Frankfurter Zeitung*. Her accompanying note defends the actor against the critical attacks on him, adding that Karl Marx himself was a great admirer:

> S'il avait eu le temps Papa aurait lui-même fait une critique sur Mr. Irving qui nous intéresse beaucoup (quoique nous ne le connaissons pas personnellement) d'abord parce que c'est un homme d'un rare talent, et ensuite parce que toute la presse anglaise, par suite des plus misérables intrigues, s'est acharnée contre lui, et a montré contre lui une vraie cabale. En faisant publier la critique de Maman dans la 'Frankfurter' vous nous ferez un grand' plaisir.[8]

The family's enthusiasm for Irving continued when he was no longer a persecuted young actor, but the head of the Lyceum theatre, perhaps one of the most designedly bourgeois institutions in the country, from the late 1870s to the late 1890s, when Irving and Ellen Terry were its stars. In 'My Recollections of Karl Marx', Mrs Comyn recounts how the subscriptions to the Dogberry Club, which met most frequently at the Marxes' house, were spent on tickets to Irving's 'First Nights':

> He used to let the club have the front row of the Dress Circle on these occasions – to my thinking, the best place in the theatre ... Once, before my admission to it, the club presented him with a laurel wreath, and, in receiving it, he kissed the hand of Eleanor, who afterwards preserved the white kid glove his lips had touched as a precious, almost sacred possession.[9]

The Marx family's affiliation is witness to the irrepressibility of theatrical occasions in the Victorian period, and to their ability, matched by the power of Shakespeare's texts, to straddle political and class divides.

It is clear that for Eleanor Marx the playwright's significance was born out of a close-knit family life, and that her subsequent references to him are coloured by that inception. References to Shakespeare often crop up in her letters. She writes to her sister Laura on 19 December 1890 that Engels 'had screwed his courage to the sticking point', and in August of the following year she writes to the same

---

7   Laurence Irving, *Henry Irving: The Actor and His World* (London: Faber & Faber, 1951), pp. 242–3.

8   The letter is dated 25 October 1875, and is quoted in full in Chushichi Tsuzuki, 'Japanese Archives Relating to British Labour History (2)', *Society for the Study of Labour History*, Bulletin 8 (1964), 18–22 (p. 19).

9   Mrs Comyn, 'My Recollections of Karl Marx', *Nineteenth Century and After*, 91 (1922), 161–9 (p. 166).

correspondent, again of Engels and of Pumps, his controversial housekeeper: 'The General is happiest with his drunken enchanter ... 'Tis a Prospero in love with a lower kind of Caliban; for Pumps hasn't Caliban's redeeming qualities.'[10] The references are warm, humorous and intimate, attesting to the depth of her affection for Engels, and also crucially providing a medium in which she can express her love for Laura, through a shared language and through an implicit reference back to their shared childhood. It is arguable that Shakespeare's significance for Eleanor Marx never really exceeded its birth in the heart of her family, even when his significance was later to accrue more overtly political ramifications. Indeed, it is that coincidence of interests that seems to have determined the nature of Shakespeare's appeal and usefulness for her.

Eleanor was the only one of her family to join the New Shakspere Society, which was established in 1874 by the philologist and scholar of early texts, F.J. Furnivall, and which met weekly at University College, London. The Society was inspired in part by patriotic reasons. In Furnivall's opening address, he announced that it was 'the duty of Englishmen to study Shakspere', and that he found it 'humiliating and lamentable' that 'not one in 20 – or shall we say 20,000' has a 'real notion' of the 'the greatest author of the world'. The purpose of the Society was

> by a very close study of the metrical and phraseological peculiarities of Shakspere, to get his plays as nearly as possible into the order in which he wrote them; to check that order by the higher tests of imaginative power, knowledge of life, self-restraint in expression, weight of thought, depth of purpose; and then to use that revised order for the purpose of studying the progress and meaning of Shakspere's mind, the passage of it from the fun and word-play, the lightness, the passion, of the Comedies of Youth, through the patriotism (still with comedy of more meaning) of the Histories of Middle Age, to the great Tragedies dealing with the deepest questions of man in Later Life; and then at last to the poet's peaceful and quiet home-life again in Stratford.[11]

Clearly, Furnivall has already mapped out the shape of the reassuringly coherent developmental chronology of Shakespeare's mind and work. The narrative of the life gives a framework for the chronology of the plays, and we might wonder whether the way in which those two aspects are taken to be synonymous was in itself appealing and even reassuring to Marx. There is a simplicity and optimism about the evolutionary progression to greatness and to understanding which might have appealed to any nineteenth-century reformer.

---

[10] Both letters are quoted Kapp, II, 441, 443.
[11] Opening Speech of the Director, in 'Notices of Meetings. Opening Meeting, Friday 13th March, 1874' in *The New Shakspere Society's Transactions, 1874* (London: Trübner, n.d.), p. vi.

Marx is reported, under the name of Mrs E. Marx, as having become a member of the Society at its meeting on 12 May 1876. A few months later she volunteered to translate a lengthy German paper on 'Shakspere's Use of Narration in His Dramas' from the German of one Professor Delius, and was commended by the Society for her work. The Society's lengthy *Transactions* record little by way of her contributions to discussions following the papers read out at the Society's meetings. On 10 March 1882, she is recorded as having objected to Ruskin's classifying Viola and Juliet together, and as insisting that 'Cordelia must have been beautiful, or else her sisters would not have hated her so.'[12] (She was responding to Ruskin's suggestion, reported in the Society's proceedings, that had she been beautiful Cordelia would never have been so wilfully misunderstood as Shakespeare suggests.) The scarcity and nature of her responses may, however, reflect the Society's view of its women members more accurately than they do Marx's participation in debate.[13]

It was during this period too, of the late 1870s and early 1880s that Marx's love of Shakespeare inspired her desire to be an actress. In June 1881, she made arrangements to take lessons from Mrs Hermann Vezin, and in March of the following year, having studied Juliet with the retired actress, felt sufficiently confident to be able to comment to her sister Jenny that Ellen Terry's Juliet was 'the most disappointing feature' of 'an exquisite production', and that the poison scene was particularly poor.[14] According to Engels, Marx 'modelled herself on Ellen Terry',[15] so she would have watched the performance of Juliet, perhaps the nineteenth century's favourite Shakespearean female part, with particular interest. Prompted perhaps by Terry, Marx was impelled by what Jenny described, in a letter written in April 1882, as the 'prospect of living the only free life a woman can live – the artistic one'.[16] Had the sisters then known more of the actual conditions of the late Victorian stage, and the extent to which actresses' work, far from being a source of freedom, was profoundly bound by economic considerations, and their audiences' desires, their view of the potential of the actress's scope might perhaps have been different. However, apparently ignorant of these considerations, the progressive and excited view Marx took of the stage and specifically of the actress's opportunities was coterminous with her sense of the emotional freedoms and regenerative, liberating aspects represented by Shakespeare.

---

12 'Monthly Abstract of Proceedings', 10 March 1882 in *The New Shakspere Society's Transactions, 1880–6* (London: Trübner, n.d.), pp. 25–31 (p. 30).

13 See Furnivall's remarking 'upon the advantage of having women in the Society', after Miss Latham's paper on waiting-women in the plays, many points of which were new to him (*NSS Transactions, 1887–92*, 9 December 1887, p. 31).

14 25 March 1882, quoted in Kapp, I, 234.

15 5 July 1881, Kapp, I, 222.

16 Quoted in Kapp, I, 234–45.

Marx's lessons with Mrs Vezin, which regrettably did not end in her working as a professional actress, heightened her awareness of a language and set of resources which, as her own writings show, were to remain of crucial importance to her, and indeed helped to determine her assessments of other writers. In the introduction to her 1886 translation of *Madame Bovary*, Marx-Aveling, as she was then known, following her decision to live with Edward Aveling, constructs an introduction to and assessment of Flaubert for her English readers which is largely based on an extended comparison with Shakespeare, most notably on the grounds of the enormous variety of each man's output, and in the quality of their both striving painstakingly for the 'ideal perfection' of the true artist.[17] In part, her assessment of Flaubert seems determined by his own regard for Shakespeare. She approvingly quotes an 1875 letter to George Sand: 'I am reading nothing, with the exception of Shakespeare, whom I have gone through again from end to end. It strengthens one, and puts air into your lungs, as if you were on some high mountain. All else seems mediocre by the side of this tremendous fellow.'[18]

Marx's understanding of the precise nature of this life-affirming quality is elaborated later, when she assesses the nature of Emma Bovary's reality. Emma Bovary is real, not because based on a real woman, but 'real as Hamlet or Lear, Goriot or Eugénie Grandet' are real. Emma's tragedy is that of Shakespeare's characters, who 'act as they do because they *must*. It may be immoral, contrary even to their own personal interests ... but it must be – it is inevitable.'[19] This is a revealing interpretation of reality on the part of the social reformer. For her, it is a condition which inevitably contains the danger of self-destruction, in a world which is not necessarily equipped to assess sympathetically or properly actions which might incidentally act against the perceived good of society or common sense, in their more proper attention to the determining factors of integrity and honesty. Again Marx espouses for Shakespeare's characters an emotional commitment which is its own ineluctable reward, regardless of its seeming results in the social and political world.

We can begin to see in this introduction the seeds of a reading of Shakespeare which explores a fissure between the writer and a society which had come to adopt him as a national emblem.[20] Although, for both Eleanor Marx and her father,

---

17 Introduction to Gustave Flaubert, *Madame Bovary*, trans. by Eleanor Marx-Aveling (London: Vizetelly, 1886), pp. vii–xxii (p. x). Picking up on the popular image of Flaubert's fastidiousness, his weary 'striving after the heaven of the artist – ideal perfection', she writes that Shakespeare too 'had his hours of doubt and despair ... when life seems but too often a striving and a striving, and an ending in nothing'. But she goes on to note: 'It is only we who come after them who know how much that striving has achieved.'

18 Introduction to *Madame Bovary*, p. xi.

19 Introduction to *Madame Bovary*, p. xvi.

20 The 'Bardolatry' which G.B. Shaw so vociferously objected to in the 1890s had already begun by this time. 1879 had seen the opening of the Shakespeare Memorial Theatre in Stratford, and 1878 the commencement of Irving's Shakespeare-dominated lease of the Lyceum.

Shakespeare always signified and was indivisible from a notion of English-ness, that idea was not necessarily coterminous with the England in which they lived. Their Shakespeare was deliberately acquired by learning, and through the mechanism of translation, rather then by their participation in the osmotic process which made Shakespeare the birthright, however neglected Furnivall perceived it to be, of every Englishman. Their Shakespeare could as readily be turned against, as employed to signify, the Victorian period.

The novelist and feminist Olive Schreiner, who was one of Marx's closest friends, responds similarly to Shakespeare. She champions him throughout her letters for the quality of life in his characters, and for his own humanity, writing to her husband in 1911: 'I've just been reading Shakespeare's *Measure for Measure*. How pure and beautiful and sweet he is, but *broadly human*, but with such a high sense of honour always. Never in one instance does he countenance falsehood or disloyalty between human souls.'[21] Later that year, she describes to Havelock Ellis the 'lived' quality of Shakespeare's characters, the extent to which he 'felt his characters'. Schreiner finds both a purity and concentration of emotion in Shakespeare's characters which seems unavailable in contemporary society, and thus articulates the ways in which Shakespeare can be meaningful for women without their having to appeal to the kind of idealizing tendencies associated with earlier Victorian society. We can see in Schreiner's writings the possibility of a Shakespeare who could become politically useful for the late Victorian woman who would read him from a position outside the parameters of conventional power structures.

This is more fully exemplified in Marx's publication (jointly with Edward Aveling), in the same year that her translation of *Madame Bovary* appeared, of *The Woman Question*, a pamphlet in which the Avelings protest against the contemporary situation of women, and most notably the prescription of chastity for those who were unmarried. The pamphlet embraces the kind of emotionally generous Shakespeare invoked in the Flaubert introduction through references to Miranda and Helena in *All's Well that Ends Well*. In their critique of society's treatment of women, Marx and Aveling refer to 'the rigorous social rule that from man only must come the first proffer of affection, the proposal for marriage',[22] and use examples from 'our Shakespeare' to show that 'this is no natural law': 'Miranda, untrammelled by society, tenders herself to Ferdinand. "I am your wife if you will marry me: if not I'll die your maid;" and Helena ... with her love for Bertram, that carried her from Rousillon to Paris and Florence is, as Coleridge has it, "Shakspere's loveliest character."'[23] The examples are very touching, and act in part as a measure of the degeneration of her own century, and its failure to

---

21 *The Letters of Olive Schreiner, 1876–1920*, ed. by S.C. Cronwright-Schreiner (London: T. Fisher Unwin, 1924) pp. 298, 302.

22 *Woman Question*, p. 8.

23 *Woman Question*, p. 9.

advance the claims of women. In more personal terms, in the mismatch between Marx's own situation, and that which the examples conjure up, we see revealed most poignantly the extent of what can only be described as her 'belief' in the emotional structures of Shakespeare, and the gap between that aspirational faith and her own relationship with Aveling.

That relationship was in part based upon a shared enthusiasm for the theatre. Aaron Rosebury reports that she told a friend that 'Our tastes were much the same ... We agreed on Socialism. We both loved the theatre ... We could work together effectively.'[24] In particular they shared a love of Shakespeare. The couple collaborated on a series of 'Dramatic Notes' for *Tinsley's Magazine* in 1890–91, which included a glowing review of the Lyceum's revival of *Much Ado About Nothing*, and a more sceptical account of Lillie Langtry's Cleopatra at the Princess's.[25] But Aveling's writings only serve in fact to show up the distance between them on this shared love. He produced a series of essays on 'Shakespeare the Dramatist' for the first two volumes of Annie Besant's *Our Corner* in 1883,[26] which are an extended version of his 'Hall of Science Thursday Lectures' given on the 'Plays of Shakspere' in the previous year. Nowhere in these writings can we see anything like the sympathetic, even empathic, commitment to Shakespeare espoused by Marx. Rather, Aveling uses Shakespeare as a means of insisting upon his own privileged access to the playwright which he is prepared to share with his listeners. He introduces his remarks with rather bombastic modesty by saying of Shakespeare that 'the innermost thought of him is only comprehended by those rarer minds, to whose fuller comprehension of his words and works haply some of us here may in good time attain'.[27]

Havelock Ellis wrote of Aveling: 'His mental powers were certainly vigorous, though he was devoid of any intellectual originality. All his writings exhibit a receptive power of comprehension and of lucid exposition.'[28] His powers, never very pronounced in these lectures, are those of analysis and tabulation, rather than the more profound and committed form of understanding shown by Marx. Aveling was speaking under a socialist banner, but his reading of Shakespeare is effectively based on exclusivity. Nowhere in his lectures is there the emphasis on a shared access, on the kind of inclusivity espoused by Eleanor and Karl Marx in their writings on Shakespeare. Aveling's Shakespeare has always to be filtered through his own mediating presence. At no point does he suggest ways in which Shakespeare might be directly enabling to his readers.

---

24 Quoted in Kapp, II, 204.
25 See E.B.A. and E.M.A., 'Dramatic Notes', *Tinsley's Magazine*, 46 (1890–91), 276–80.
26 Edward B. Aveling, DSc, 'Shakespeare the Dramatist', 1 (1883), 147–52, 218–22, 272–6, 345–9; 2 (1883), 33–6, 89–93, 207–12, 267–70, 343–6.
27 Edward B. Aveling, DSc, FLS, 'Works of Shakespeare', *Hall of Science Thursday Lectures* (London: Freethought, 1882), Lecture 1, p. 1.
28 Havelock Ellis, 'Eleanor Marx', *Adelphi*, 10 (1935), 342–52 (p. 352). Ellis wrote a second article on Eleanor Marx, 'Eleanor Marx – II', *Adelphi*, 11 (1935), 33–41.

Siegfried Prawer has shown, in his *Karl Marx and World Literature*, how crucial Shakespeare was to Karl Marx's thinking, suggesting indeed that Shakespeare's characters 'aid Marx in conceiving and formulating his own message'.[29] Rather than simply acting as a useful medium or illustration, Shakespeare actually functions as part of the fabric of Marx's writings, just as he was an acquired part of the fabric of his language. In Shakespeare, Prawer suggests, Karl Marx found access to a form of clarification which helped him effectively to assess his own world and, more specifically, that he found an 'image of England that once existed but now has vanished from all but literature; he then uses that image as a means of criticizing the England of his own day'. He goes on to quote Karl Marx himself:

> The emergence of sharp class divisions, extraordinarily complete division of labour, and a so-called 'public opinion' which is manipulated by the Brahmins of the Press have ... brought into being a monotonous sameness of character that would make Shakespeare, for instance, fail to recognise his compatriots.[30]

For Karl Marx, then, Shakespeare and his characters are redolent of a moment that is both potentially persistently desirable, and prelapsarian in specifically English terms.

In Eleanor Marx's critiques of contemporary society too, particularly of the place of women and workers in that society, Shakespeare also seems to represent a prelapsarian, pre-industrial voice signalling possibilities of regeneration through the recuperation of a past characterized by emotional integrity and generosity. However, for Marx, the recuperation of that past is also tinged with a poignant personal longing. She found a brief taste of such a recovery in the cottage which she and Aveling found, just outside Stratford, in 1887:

> One day, walking from Stratford to Bidford, (one of Shakespeare's well-known walks) we saw a farm – near the farm two cottages, one unlet. We inquired, found the rent was two shillings a week and ... decided to rent this lovely little place. It is two miles from Stratford and Dodwell consists of this farm and its two cottages. The farmer at first tried to explain these were only for ... labourers – he could not understand our wanting to come. You would. Downstairs we have a large kitchen – stone-flagged of course, a back kitchen and wash-house in one and a pantry. Upstairs three rooms – two, of course, very small. Besides this we have a quarter of an acre of garden ... Ed. goes out and digs up our potatoes as we need them and we have been sowing all sorts of things. Next spring our garden will be not only ornamental but useful ... There's plenty of room ... I can't tell you how charming this country life is after the hurry and worry and tear of London...Think of it Laura, Shakespeare's Home! We work two or three times a week at his 'birthplace' (by permission of the Librarian of the place) and we have been

---

[29] S.S. Prawer, *Karl Marx and World Literature* (Oxford: Clarendon Press, 1976), p. 85.
[30] *Werke*, XV, 464; quoted in Prawer, *Karl Marx and World Literature*, p. 268.

over his home, and seen the old guild Chapel that stands opposite 'New Place', and the old grammar school – unchanged – whither he went 'unwillingly to school'; and his grave in Trinity Church, and Ann Hathaway's cottage, still just as it was when master Will went a-courting, and Mary Arden's cottage at Wilmecote – the prettiest place of all. Now that I have been in this sleepy little Stratford and met the Stratfordians I know where all the Dogberries and Bottoms and Snugs come from. You'll meet them here today. Just near our 'Kastle' is a bank – many think it Titania's for it is covered with wild thyme and oxlips and violets ... I never knew before how Stratfordian Shakespeare was. All the flowers are Stratford ones and Charlecote I would wager is Rosalind's Arden ... we are settled here till our lessons and other work call us back to London ... Then we get back to Chancery Lane to our teaching and usual dreary round of work.[31]

The potential sentimentality of this letter is redeemed by the anguish which underlies and even impels it. This injects an extraordinary pathos into the personal relief afforded by the cottage, a relief clearly made possible for Marx by its Shakespearean connections.[32]

It was also a relief of a kind which, in its reaching after the harmonizing of nature and of man's efforts, had a distinct place within the English socialist movement. In *Merrie England* (1894), Robert Blatchford describes the industrial counties of England as 'ugly, and dirty, and smoky, and disagreeable'. By comparison, he suggests that the country towns of Southern counties have

> pure air, bright skies, clear rivers, clean streets, and beautiful fields, woods, and gardens; you will get cattle and streams, and birds and flowers, and you will know that all these things are well worth having, and that none of them can exist side by side with the factory system.[33]

In this context then, Marx's Stratfordian idyll, and Shakespeare himself, might be seen to have broader political as well as personal ramifications. As John Lucas notes, it was not unusual for socialist writers of the period, such as Morris and Swinburne, to hanker after a rural vision with, as he puts it, its 'implicit politics of containment and hierarchical structures'.[34] Modern industrialized capitalist societies did, of course, carry their own hierarchies which were clearly even less palatable. For Marx, however, that rural vision confirmed her access to Shakespeare, a poet who gave voice to the 'Dogberries and Bottoms and Snugs' as

---

[31] Quoted in Kapp, II, 209–10.
[32] Tellingly, Aveling's own witness to the Stratford idyll is to be found in his one-act play, 'Judith Shakespeare', which was licensed, and performed, in 1894. The play is an adaptation and abridgement of key scenes from William Black's 1884 novel of the same name.
[33] Robert Blatchford (Nunquam), *Merrie England* (London: Scott, 1894), p. 21.
[34] John Lucas, *England and Englishness: Ideas of Nationhood in English Poetry, 1688–1900* (London: Hogarth, 1990), p. 204.

well as Helena, and enabled an almost visceral satisfaction in shared labour which temporarily overcame her emotional isolation.

Marx's final engagement with Shakespeare is a posthumous one, generated by Yvonne Kapp, who ends the second volume of her biography with Macbeth's words about his wife, 'She should have died hereafter.' The Shakespearean quotation in reference to Marx's suicide, an act which has been seen more often in the context of the *fin de siècle* and the heroines of Ibsen and Flaubert, is striking. Marx's suicide, and indeed life, was far from that of the world-weary lassitude and ineffectualness experienced by such nineteenth-century literary women as Emma Bovary, Hedda Gabler and Rebecca West. Rather her suicide might seem to have been generated by the perception of lost love, wasted sacrifice and thwarted ambition arguably experienced by such heroines as Ophelia, Cleopatra and perhaps most notably Lady Macbeth. We might also look to Wilde's *The Picture of Dorian Gray* (1891) and to Sybil Vane for another example of a woman who, like Marx, believed in the possibility of finding and living out the emotional intensities of Shakespeare, but who is disappointed in the man with whom that dream and that emotional rhetoric had seemed to be a possibility. 'Suicide in Shakespeare' had been discussed at the New Shakspere Society meeting of 13 January 1882, when the Reverend J. Kirkman suggested that in women, 'emotion became uncontrollable, and gave a final momentum' to their action, and further implies that in the case of Lady Macbeth her moral strength was partly responsible for her act. Comparing her with Richard III, he suggests that it was the latter's 'moral cowardice [that] retained him for punishment this side of the act'.[35] Lady Macbeth's suicide thus indirectly becomes a condemnation of a world unfit to appreciate her integrity, rather than an act of despair more appropriate to one of the *fin de siècle*'s 'degenerates'.

It is at this point that the literary critic has to stop short of insisting on a final identification of Eleanor Marx as one of Shakespeare's heroines. However tempting the chance to explain, define, confine the act of suicide, it surely has to be resisted, lest in the cause of one's own anxieties one denies Marx's autonomy, and the very things which attracted her to Shakespeare. The analogy with Lady Macbeth does, however, bear examination in its own right beyond the circumstances of the character's death, for she was a figure with whom Marx had previously been compared. An article in the *Radical* journal of December 1893 describes Marx at a meeting to discuss the possibility of a demonstration in Hyde Park, in the face of the threat of violent suppression, as 'Lady Macbeth Aveling', and goes on to picture the 'lofty scorn' with which she responded to peaceful suggestions. The journalist goes on: 'When the resolution proposing the Hyde Park meeting was read Lady Macbeth turned to Edward, D.Sc., and hissed

---

[35] *The New Shakspere Society's Transactions, 1874, 1880–86, 1887–92* (London: Trübner, n.d.), pp. 14–15.

"C-o-w-a-r-d-s!" between her teeth. It was very fine indeed: something of the "Infirm of purpose! give *me* the daggers!" school of acting'.[36] What was it about Lady Macbeth that tempts both Kapp and the *Radical* journalist to liken Marx to her?

Lady Macbeth was a famously controversial figure during the Victorian period, and was often discussed by the New Shakspere Society, whose recorded opinions were most often split along gender lines. A paper by the Countess of Charlemont in 1876, claiming that Lady Macbeth's devotion to her husband was her sole motivation, was rejected forcibly by Dr Furnivall.[37] A further paper on Lady Macbeth given in 1889 by Beatrice Lamb argued that 'Lady Macbeth was of an unselfish and noble nature, and did what she did only that [Macbeth] might be king'.[38] The *Transactions* record that 'an animated discussion followed, in which almost every one of Miss Lamb's points and conclusions were denied, and declared to be in direct contradiction to Shakespeare's text, though a few speakers defended her'. Ellen Terry, whose performances held a particular interest for Marx, played Lady Macbeth as a devoted wife to mixed responses in 1888. Terry sought to convey the idea that Lady Macbeth was no fiend, but was motivated in her actions by her love for her husband. The part was something of a turning point in the actress's career, her triumph in that role lying not in being found charming, as was her usual critical fate, but in exciting critical dissension and discussion. She herself wrote: 'The critics differ, and discuss it hotly, which in itself is my best success of all'.[39]

An earlier view of Lady Macbeth is given in Anna Jameson's *Characteristics of Women, Moral, Poetical, and Historical* (1832), later published under the title of *Shakespeare's Heroines*. In her comments on Lady Macbeth, she argues that we see in her 'the possible result of the noblest faculties uncontrolled or perverted'. The paradigm informing Jameson's reading is based on what she describes as a fundamental divisibility between person and context, a divisibility which she suggests is camouflaged in the study of history, but which is evident in Shakespeare:

> In history we can but study character in relation to events, to situation and circumstances, which disguise and encumber it; we are left to imagine, to infer, what certain people must have been, from the manner in which they have acted or suffered. Shakespeare and nature bring us back to the true order of things; and showing us what the human being *is*, enable us to judge of the possible as well as the positive result in acting and suffering.[40]

---

[36] Kapp, II, 233–4.

[37] The Countess of Charlemont, 'Gruach (Lady Macbeth)', *NSS Transactions, 1875–76*, pp. 194–9.

[38] 'Monthly Abstract of Proceedings', 3 March 1889, p. 43.

[39] Ellen Terry, *The Story of My Life* (London: Hutchinson, 1909), p. 306.

[40] Mrs Jameson, *Characteristics of Women, Moral, Poetical, and Historical* (London: Bell), pp. 368–9.

Jameson's reading of Shakespeare, which she employs in order to illustrate the breadth of possibilities of which women are capable, and the ways in which contemporary society might be concerned to hamper that potential, has much in common with Eleanor Marx's responses to the playwright, and her turning to him as one who might articulate possibilities apparently unavailable to her elsewhere in contemporary society. Such a response, read alongside the hostile reactions to critical re-evaluations of Lady Macbeth and the conjunction of Eleanor Marx and Lady Macbeth, with all its implications of tragic waste and energy expended with futility, attests to the way in which Shakespeare might be an effective part of the nineteenth century's effort to question modes of femininity, rather than simply seeming effortlessly to confirm the *status quo* in the hands of more conservative writers. Marx's enthusiasm for and commitment to Shakespeare ultimately confirms for herself and for the playwright a revolutionary, critical potential in the late Victorian period.

Chapter 6

Eleanor Marx and Gustave Flaubert

Faith Evans

Eleanor Marx's translation of *Madame Bovary*, a commission she obtained through the novelist and francophile George Moore, was published by the advanced publishing house of Vizetelly in 1886, thirty years after its publication in France and the obscenity trial in which Flaubert was acquitted. It was the first English translation to appear and remained the only English version for many years, and although several more have been undertaken in the past half-century it remains among the most readable. Yet for reasons that I believe were sometimes unconnected with the translation itself, it has often suffered harshly at the hands of the critics. Vladimir Nabokov, for instance, in his reading of *Madame Bovary*, rages against translators in general – 'ignorant, treacherous and philistine'[1] – and Marx in particular. *Lectures on Literature*, published after his death, reproduces a page from his teaching notebook in which he lists what he considers to be some of her mistakes, and includes an appendix containing no fewer than eighteen essay questions on the novel, ranging from 'Discuss Flaubert's use of the word "and"' to 'All translations of *Madame Bovary* are full of blunders ... Describe Emma's eyes, hands, sunshade, hairdo, dress, shoes.'[2] This may seem obsessive but then *Madame Bovary* often inspires devotion. It certainly did in its English translator.

In this essay I first investigate the circumstances surrounding the publication of *Madame Bovary* in France and in England and consider some of the linguistic challenges it poses – issues that Marx herself discusses in the introduction to her translation. I then set Marx's work against a small selection of the translations that have been undertaken since, paying particular attention to *le style indirect libre* that was to have such a marked influence on later writers. Finally, I turn to the vexed question of 'identification'.

Although *Madame Bovary* was the product of many years of work and preparation, the actual writing took Flaubert five years, from the ages of thirty to thirty-five. It was his first novel to be published, and composition was a self-imposed ordeal. He would take a week to write one page. The book went through many drafts, and every weekend he talked through the week's writing with his friend Louis Bouilhet; they would edit and edit until the work was pared down to

---

[1] *Lectures on Literature*, ed. by Fredson Bowers (New York: Harcourt Brace & Co., 1980), p. 143.

[2] *Lectures on Literature*, p. 385.

the barest minimum, with all melodrama removed. A famous example of this economy is the cab scene, when Emma and Léon, her second lover, first make love. None of the sex is described and no characters are identified; we are shown only the exterior of the vehicle as it hurtles around Rouen at increasingly breakneck speed. Finally little scraps of paper are scattered out of the cab window. It is Emma's torn-up letter of farewell to Léon.

Such apparent simplicity is, to say the least, deceptive – it implies so much. Another challenge facing the translator is Flaubert's subtle, often ironic rendering of direct dialogue. By comparison with Balzac or Zola, for example, there is little conversation in *Madame Bovary*, and the writing of it, often in cliché, was an agonizing process. Emma herself does not speak until a full seven chapters into the novel, and when she does it is only seven words, to her little Italian greyhound – 'Pourquoi, mon Dieu! me suis-je mariée?'[3] The early conversations between Emma and Léon, in which they discuss their 'romantic' aspirations, are a triumph of banality.

But it was, of course, less the style of the novel than its supposed obscenity that attracted such widespread attention on its publication, and it was the censorship laws just as much as the 'great reading public' (castigated by Marx in her introduction) that accounted for the long gap between its French and English appearance. In late Victorian England there was a general sense that there was something over-graphic, unwholesome even, about French novels – but this was an attitude that was beginning to be challenged by brave publishers such as Henry Vizetelly. In publishing Flaubert, Maupassant, Baudelaire and Edgar Allan Poe, Vizetelly risked both commercial failure and violation of the Obscene Publications Act of 1857. In fact he was to be summonsed in 1888 for issuing three 'obscene' novels by Zola. According to Stephen Heath, even though *Madame Bovary* was not specifically mentioned at the trial, it was in the air, 'another example of the kind of literature at which the prosecution was aimed':

> The dominant English response, indeed, throughout the century, was very much one of disgust at immorality and recoil from the book's perceived cold-bloodedness, what Matthew Arnold in 1887 called 'the cruelty of petrified feeling'. The same recoil was to continue, enshrined in the influential 'great tradition' of the novel as moral form established by the critic F.R. Leavis in the 1940s, from which perspective Flaubert and Madame Bovary could represent only an immature cynicism, a failing in 'intensity of moral preoccupation.'[4]

---

3   *Madame Bovary* (Paris: Livre de Poche, 1972), p. 52.
4   Stephen Heath, *Gustave Flaubert: Madame Bovary* (Cambridge: Cambridge University Press, 1992), p. 138; see also Karl Beckson, *London in the 1890s* (New York and London: W.W. Norton & Co., 1992), pp. 292–316.

Vizetelly was put on probation for twelve months and the following year received a further summons for the Zola novels, Maupassant's *A Woman's Life* and *Madame Bovary*. He spent three months in Holloway Prison and died soon afterwards. In 1886, however, he was still taking risks – in the same year as Marx's *Madame Bovary* he published a second translation of *Salammbô* by J.S. Chartres which, unlike the first version, was rapturously received.

Marx's translation impressed the critics less. It is clear, though, from the early reviews that they were coloured by the commentators' familiarity with her name and activities, confirming that she and Aveling had acquired a reputation as a famous – or infamous – political couple. (Later in the same year, 1886, they were to be vilified in the London press for their extravagant expenses on a lecture tour of the US.) In a disparaging notice the *Saturday Review*[5] sneers at 'Mrs Aveling's friends in France' – a reference to her revolutionary brother-in-law Paul Lafargue, her ex-fiancé Lissagaray and her work with European socialists.

But this obviously politically-motivated response was accompanied by concern about the translation itself. Most reviewers agreed with the *Athenaeum*[6] which, whilst selecting the book as its 'novel of the week', suggested that 'Mrs Aveling has done her work with more zeal than discretion'. 'Her introduction may be passed over with no further comment than the remark that it is uncritical in itself, and that in its protests against former criticisms of Flaubert it does not show much acquaintance with the subject.' The reviewer complains that her translation is 'laborious':

> Mrs Aveling seems to have thought it incumbent on her to translate as far as possible word for word, and this can never result in anything but an unsatisfactory version when two languages so different in genius as French and English are concerned. Besides, even her word-for-word system has not been successfully carried out.

The anonymous critic proceeds to analyse one long passage, intending to expose the inadequacy of what he considers to be its overfaithfulness to the original, though he diminishes his argument by overlooking a howler which I will examine later. His criticisms refer largely to grammatical and lexical points:

> It is odd that a literal translator should have changed the reference of 'le' from Bovary himself to his remark (the 'grand mot' mentioned just before), though neither 'débonnaire' nor 'vil' suits a thing so well as a person. Moreover, 'débonnaire' itself is not 'offhand', but 'kind', 'complaisant', 'obliging'; and 'vil' is not 'mean' (which has a more restricted sense in English), but 'base'. Yet again, 'conduit' is not so much 'managed' as 'directed', 'guided'.

These rebukes are valid, and it is true that Marx scores low marks on this passage – though it was rather tough to pick on the very last page of the book, making no allowance for the likelihood that she had run out of steam or time.

In addition, Marx's version has become implicated, over the years, in the unprecedented level of close critical attention that Flaubert has received as a writer. Heath describes *Madame Bovary* as 'general cultural fact, an inevitable reference', a seminal influence on later writers from Dostoevsky to D.H. Lawrence. 'What else', asks Heath, 'would Nastasya Filippovna in *The Idiot* (1869) be reading just before her attempted suicide?'[7] If this is true, if *Madame Bovary* is such an immense and all-pervasive book then perhaps, as George Steiner implies in *After Babel*,[8] it is ultimately untranslatable – though I incline to the converse view that its very brilliance makes it virtually indestructible, and that a rhythm or phrase clumsily translated can only shake rather than topple the cumulative stylistic edifice Flaubert so carefully created. Certainly most commentators agree that none of the existing translations is faultless, and some, such as Nabokov, provide their own version, but this is often merely to establish a critical point of their own. What is beyond doubt is that Marx took her translation of a work that had already become such a *cause célèbre* with the utmost seriousness, and that she was fully aware of the hazardous nature of the task.

In her introduction Marx distinguishes between three types of translator: the genius, the hack and the 'conscientious worker', into which final category she places herself. Schlegel and Baudelaire – translators of Shakespeare and Edgar Allan Poe respectively – she describes as 'geniuses', 'but there are few geniuses in the world, and those we have do not, for the most part, devote themselves to the thankless task of translating'. Her work is 'pale and feeble by the side of the original':

> Certainly no critic can be more painfully aware than I am of the weaknesses, the shortcomings, the failures of my work ... That often I have not found the best possible word to express Flaubert's meaning I know; but those who have studied him will understand how impossible it must be for any one of us to give an exact reproduction of the inimitable style of the master. He spent 'days seeking one word'. The consequence is that he invariably gives the one word that fully expresses his meaning ...
>
> My work, then, I know is faulty. It is pale and feeble by the side of its original. Yet, if it induces some readers to go to that original, if it helps to make known to those who cannot study this work of the greatest of French novelists after Balzac, I am content.[9]

***

---

[7] Heath, *Madame Bovary*, p. 139.
[8] Oxford: Oxford University Press, 1975, p. 376.
[9] Introduction to Gustave Flaubert, *Madame Bovary*, trans. by Eleanor Marx-Aveling (London: Vizetelly, 1886), pp. viii–xii (p. xxii). All subsequent references to Marx's introduction are cited parenthetically by page number in the text.

Marx worked on *Madame Bovary* from autumn 1885 to spring 1886 in a house that she and Aveling had rented in Parade Villas, Richmond; his own main project at the time was translating parts of *Das Kapital.* She delivered the translation, complete with introduction, to Vizetelly in May, when they were back in their flat at 55 Great Russell Street, Bloomsbury, and it was published in August. We know that she sought help with some of the medical and legal terminology from her brother-in-law Paul Lafargue in France (and, we can safely surmise, from Aveling), but she was unusually reticent about her work in progress, confessing only to her sister Laura that 'it *has* been work!'[10]

She was thirty. Her father had died in 1883, and in spite of her grief his death had acted as a release, signalling a new phase in her life and giving her the freedom to set up house with Aveling. She had become part of the intellectual Socialist circle that congregated in and around the British Museum, along with George Bernard Shaw, Havelock Ellis and Olive Schreiner, and was beginning to make a name for herself in the literary London of the day. Much of the work she undertook was what she described as 'hack work' but she was also doing projects of her own: editions of plays and translations, to which she usually added strong introductions. She had recently translated Lissagaray's *Histoire de la Commune de 1871* from French, the Factory Acts section of *Das Kapital* from German, and Alexander Kielland's stories from Norwegian. *Madame Bovary* was indeed 'work': a commission, a source of income and, even more importantly, a unique opportunity to align herself with a progressive literary campaign.

That much is clear from Marx's introduction, which is fluently written but entirely uncritical in approach. What interested her most of all as a translator was a book's social interest, its value as a document. It was part of her heritage to champion causes, to be ready for a fight and to have an international outlook: her childhood letters to her sisters Jenny and Laura show that from a very early age she was obsessed by the situation in America, Ireland and Poland. Just as she was partisan in her politics, so was she evangelical in her promotion of the books and authors she admired. She shows herself to be fully aware of Flaubert's slow method of work and the lengths to which he would go in order to remove all traces of Romanticism. She must have recognized the irony implicit in the sharp contrast with her own prodigious, sometimes over-hasty output.

The committed, eloquent tone of Marx's preamble is set by Flaubert's own dedication of *Madame Bovary* to his defence counsel:

> To Marie-Antoine-Jules Sénart, Member of the Paris Bar, ex-President of the National Assembly, and former Minister of the Interior

> DEAR AND ILLUSTRIOUS FRIEND, –

---

[10] *Daughters*, p. 190.

Permit me to inscribe your name at the head of this book, and above its dedication; for it is to you, before all, that I owe its publication. Reading over your magnificent defence, my work has acquired for myself, as it were, an unexpected authority. Accept, then, the homage of my gratitude, which, how great soever it is, will never attain the height of your eloquence and your devotion.

GUSTAVE FLAUBERT (v)

In a similar mood of respect, of reverence even, Marx's fourteen-page introduction begins with a summary of Flaubert's life. She stresses the importance of his medical background in the context of *Madame Bovary* as well as his gift for friendship, the epilepsy which made him a reclusive semi-invalid, his attraction to the East, and his prodigious reading on all subjects: 'philosophy, art, science, poetry, belles-lettres – everything'. Flaubert's trial is introduced with an outburst of republican fervour:

To the eternal honour of Flaubert, this book was presented as immoral by, of all people in the world, the Government of Napoléon the Third. But not even the Bonapartist judges could be induced to condemn Flaubert. As a sop to the Imperial prosecutor, the judgment certainly blamed some portions of the book, but decided that it was on the whole a serious, earnest work, and dismissed the charge against its author. (xi)

Clearly she has studied the transcripts of the trial in detail for she continues with a full account of the charges, chief amongst them Emma's adultery with Rodolphe and Léon. She refers to the 'brilliant defence' of M. Sénart, with its triumphant final question, 'Does the reading of such a book give you a love for vice or inspire you with horror of vice?', before flinging herself into the debate about the 'censorship' of the novel when 'mutilated' sections were first serialized in *La Revue de Paris* in 1856.[11]

She enters the contemporary debate about the comparative strengths of Zola and Flaubert: 'In Flaubert we have the direct antithesis of Zola. He is no photographer, but a great painter, whose men and women live ... He never stops to tell us this or the other is a fact, or to explain why it is a fact; and there is no need. We know it is true and why it must be true.' Still on the offensive, she turns to the complacency and hypocrisy of the bourgeoisie, who accept received ideas about literature and life, and who have branded *Madame Bovary* immoral without reading it for themselves. She contrasts this attitude with that of the 'healthily constituted individual' for whom 'the work contains only the great lessons'.

---

[11] In their efforts to avoid prosecution the editors wanted to shorten the wedding, the agricultural show and the club-foot episode, all of which were eventually reinstated when the book appeared in volume form the following year.

Marx's engagement with issues of the day, both literary and political, make her introduction a true testament to her versatility. But the question remains, to what extent is this commitment matched by her practice, in particular when it comes to *le style indirect libre*, of which Flaubert is the undisputed master? The technique is so called because it is uninhibited by the conventions of either reported speech or quoted dialogue, and is often accompanied by an irony of which the fictional protagonist is unaware. Marx's response to this challenge is to adhere closely (sometimes too closely) to the original. Here is the classic scene involving the carriage that I mentioned at the start – first the original, and then Marx's translation:

Une fois, au milieu du jour, en pleine campagne, au moment où le soleil dardait le plus fort contre les vieilles lanternes argentées, une main nue passa sous les petits rideaux de toile jaune et jeta des déchirures de papier qui se dispersèrent au vent et s'abattirent plus loin, comme des papillons blancs, sur un champ de trèfles rouges tout en fleur.

Puis, vers six heures, la voiture s'arrêta dans une ruelle du quartier Beauvoisine, et une femme en descendit qui marchait le voile baissé, sans détourner la tête.[12]

Once in the middle of the day, in the open country, just as the sun beat most fiercely against the old plated lanterns, a bare hand slipped beneath the small blinds of yellow canvas, and threw out some scraps of paper that scattered in the wind, and farther off lighted like white butterflies on a field of red clover in full bloom.

About six o'clock the carriage stopped in a back street of the Beauvoisine Quarter, and a woman got out; she walked away with her veil down, and without turning her head.[13]

Some later translators have taken a looser approach, but to my mind the exactness of Marx's translation is here justified by the meticulous build-up of information provided by Flaubert: the blinding heat, the open country, the pulled-down yellow blinds, the ungloved hand, which we know to be Emma's just as we know that the rest of her body is otherwise engaged. Without needing to be explicitly told, we take the dispersal of Emma's letter to Léon as the climax, just as we read into her retreating veiled figure a return to propriety and order.

And here is the passage from very late on in the novel which the critic of the *Athenaeum* complained about in 1886. It is a fruitful scene to examine closely as it offers a clear example of the notion that different translations undertaken at different times all produce tolerable, if uneven, results. I start with the original French and go on to look at three of the published translations: Marx's of 1886,

12 Livre de Poche, p. 291.
13 Vizetelly edition, p. 269.

Paul de Man's revised version of this in 1965,[14] and the most recent version, Geoffrey Wall's of 1992.[15]

The scene takes place soon after Emma's death and the day before Charles's own. To their mutual embarrassment Rodolphe and Charles bump into each other in Argueuil market; shortly before, Charles has discovered a cache of billets-doux from Rodolphe to Emma, and his portrait, in a drawer, revealing their affair to him for the first time. The two men go for a beer, and while Rodolphe spouts banalities about everything under the sun without mentioning Emma, Charles works himself into a silent fury. Then he relapses into his usual 'lassitude funèbre':

> – Je ne vous en veux pas, dit-il.
> Rodolphe etait resté muet. Et Charles, la tête dans ses deux mains, reprit d'une voix éteinte et avec l'accent résigné des douleurs infinies:
> – Non, je ne vous en veux plus!
> Il ajouta meme un grand mot, le seul qu'il ait jamais dit:
> – C'est la faute de la fatalité!
> Rodolphe, qui avait conduit cette fatalité, le trouva bien débonnaire pour un homme dans sa situation, comique même et un peu vil.[16]

The scene is bursting with pathetic irony, conveying the placid, slightly bumptious, heartbreaking innocence of Charles, the arrogant, unthinking superficiality of Rodolphe, and the chasm that (as only the omniscient narrator fully realizes) lies between them. The spirit of Emma is there too, overhearing the conversation, agreeing with Rodolphe that Charles is pathetic not to challenge him to a duel: indeed, the scene takes us back to a tryst between her and Rodolphe when, fearing an intruder, she asks him, somewhat to his surprise: 'Have you your pistols?'[17]

None of the selected translations loses sight of this pathos but they approach it in different ways. Here is Marx's:

> Rodolphe was dumb. And Charles, his head in his hands, went on in a broken voice, and with the resigned accent of infinite sorrow.
> 'No, I don't blame you now.'
> He even added a fine phrase, the only one he ever made.
> 'It is the fault of fatality!'
> Rodolphe, who had managed the fatality, thought the remark very off-hand from a man in his position, comic even, and a little mean.[18]

'Dumb' in line 1 is rather strong – the French implies more passivity – and 'accent' in line 2 is a false friend (later corrected by de Man). 'He even added a fine phrase,

---

[14] *Madame Bovary*, trans. by Paul de Man, Norton Critical Editions (New York and London: W.W. Norton & Co., 1965).
[15] *Madame Bovary*, trans. by Geoffrey Wall (Harmondsworth: Penguin Classics, 1992).
[16] Livre de Poche, p. 410.
[17] Vizetelly edition, p. 186.
[18] Vizetelly edition, p. 382.

the only one he ever made' is good, but – something the *Athenaeum* critic overlooked – she is surely wrong to render 'fatalité' as 'fatality' rather than the French word's alternative meaning of 'fate' or 'destiny', which in the context must have been what Flaubert intended. (Marx probably thought it a reference to Emma's recent death.) It follows that in the penultimate line, 'who had managed the fatality' is not right either, though 'offhand', 'comic' and 'mean' are precise. The syntax and structure, which are very clear in this passage, remain as in the original, as they do in the other two translations quoted below.

Here is Paul de Man's version, which he describes as 'A Substantially New Translation Based on the Version by Eleanor Marx Aveling'. It is better than Marx's original, and he corrects some of her blatant errors, including 'fatalité', though he would have done well to keep her 'He even added a fine phrase' rather than substituting 'He even made a phrase'. In the last two paragraphs 'Fate willed it this way' and 'Rodolphe, who had been the agent of this fate' are distinct improvements:

> 'I can't blame you for it,' he said.
> Rodolphe remained silent. And Charles, his head in his hands, went on in a broken voice, with the resigned accent of infinite grief:
> 'No, I can't blame you any longer.'
> He even made a phrase, the only one he'd ever made:
> 'Fate willed it this way.'
> Rodolphe, who had been the agent of this fate, thought him very meek for a man in his situation, comic even and slightly despicable.[19]

De Man provides a useful introductory note to his translation in which he concedes that one of the chief virtues of Marx's version is 'the relatively high degree of fidelity in rendering the cadence of Flaubert's sentence'. He had, he explains, chosen to base his work on hers because whilst other translations may have been more fluent and idiomatic, 'Flaubert himself is neither fluent nor idiomatic (except in conversations), and by adhering more closely to his rhythm, Mrs Aveling sometimes succeeds in conveying Flaubert's carefully controlled syntax.'[20]

Finally, let us look at the most recent version, from Geoffrey Wall:

> – I don't hold it against you, he said.
> Rodolphe sat there in silence. And Charles, his head in his hands, went on in a blank voice with the resigned intonations of infinite sorrow:

---

[19] De Man, pp. 254–5.
[20] De Man, p. xvi. In *The Art of Translating Prose* Burton Raffel takes the opposite view: obsessed with syntactical faithfulness, he fulminates against most of the translations, including Marx's, but admits that 'Aveling makes some amends for her structural insensitivity by being, on the whole, lexically precise' (University Park, PA: Pennsylvania State University Press, 1994), p. 50.

– No, I don't hold it against you any more!
He even added a grand phrase, the only one he had ever uttered:
– Fate is to blame!
Rodolphe, who had controlled this particular fate, thought the man rather soft-hearted for someone in his position, comical even, and slightly despicable.[21]

'Blank voice' in the second paragraph is excellent – more effective than either 'broken' or 'resigned' – and 'intonations' is a better equivalent than the word-for-word 'accent' of Marx and Paul de Man. Wall has got the last paragraph exactly right: 'despicable' is especially good for 'un peu vil'. Many of his equivalents are more suitable for late twentieth-century readers than the earlier versions, but his presentation poses rather more of a challenge. A hundred years after Marx's courageous first effort, this most recent translator has felt sufficiently confident to reinstate much of Flaubert's original punctuation, italicization and paragraphing. Restoring the punctuation has involved not only prefacing dialogue with dashes instead of quote marks, in the French manner, but including Flaubert's unusual and often disconcerting use of commas and semi-colons (a subject discussed at length by Nabokov in *Lectures on Literature*).[22] He has also preserved the very short paragraphs that Flaubert used for emphasis – something he describes in his introduction as 'a form of typographic slow-motion'[23] – and the italicized phrases with which Flaubert drew his reader's attention to cliché. These are bold and effective moves that do not always make for easy reading, but Marx (not to mention Nabokov) would have approved; she too respected Flaubert's grand designs. Which is not say that she necessarily identified with him entirely.

***

Issues of identity involving Flaubert, Marx and Emma Bovary herself have been pursued for more than a century. A recent and particularly ingenious set of speculations occurs in Julian Barnes's novel *Flaubert's Parrot* (1984), in which the narrator deconstructs Flaubert's life as a detective story based on the rival claims of two stuffed parrots to be the inspiration for his story *Un Coeur Simple*. Presumably in silent homage to Nabokov, Barnes includes an exam paper, a sort of teaser, broken down into subjects and warning that 'marks will be deducted for facetious or conceitedly brief answers'. His Psychology question neatly subverts Flaubert's famous phrase 'Madame Bovary, c'est moi' by identifying the novel's heroine with her translator rather than with her creator. He calls Eleanor Marx E1, and Emma Bovary E2:

---

[21] Wall, pp. 285–6.
[22] Nabokov, pp. 171–4.
[23] Wall, p. xxvii.

E1 was born in 1855.
E2 was partly born in 1855.

E1 had an unclouded childhood but emerged into adulthood inclined to
nervous crisis.
E2 had an unclouded childhood but emerged into adulthood inclined to
nervous crisis.

E1 led a life of sexual irregularity in the eyes of right-thinking people.
E2 led a life of sexual irregularity in the eyes of right-thinking people.

E1 imagined herself to be in financial difficulties.
E2 knew herself to be in financial difficulties.

E1 committed suicide by swallowing prussic acid.
E2 committed suicide by swallowing arsenic.

E1 was Eleanor Marx.
E2 was Emma Bovary.

The first English translation of *Madame Bovary* to be published was by
Eleanor Marx. Discuss.[24]

Barnes's question is both witty and deliberately provocative in overlooking the
more subtle possibilities for identification that are permitted by *le style indirect
libre*, where personal intimacy and impersonal knowledge are meshed together to
become indistinguishable. Here, for instance, is the moment with the Italian
greyhound that I referred to at the start, followed by Marx's translation. Emma is
out for a stroll, musing on the state of her marriage:

> Sa pensée, sans but d'abord, vagabondait au hasard, comme sa levrette, qui
> faisait des cercles dans la campagne, jappait apres les papillons jaunes,
> donnait la chasse aux musaraignes ou mordillait les coquelicots sur le bord
> d'une pièce de blé. Puis ses idées peu à peu se fixaient, et assise sur le gazon,
> qu'elle fouillait à petits coups avec le bout de son ombrelle, Emma se
> répétait:
> 'Pourquoi, mon Dieu! me suis-je mariée?'[25]

> Her thoughts, aimless at first, wandered at random, like her greyhound, who
> ran round and round in the fields, yelping after the yellow butterflies,
> chasing the shrewmice, or nibbling the poppies on the edge of a cornfield.
> Then gradually her ideas took definite shape, and, sitting on the grass that
> she dug up with little prods of her sunshade, Emma repeated to herself,
> 'Good heavens! why did I marry?'[26]

---

24 *Flaubert's Parrot* (London: Jonathan Cape, 1984), p. 176.
25 Livre de Poche, pp. 51–2.
26 Vizetelly edition, p. 48.

For all its incidental detail, exactly reproduced by Marx, this is an important passage and a perfect example of *le style indirect libre* at work. Tony Tanner, in *Adultery in the Novel*, cites it as an example of the significance of circling in *Madame Bovary*.[27] The physically circling greyhound leads Emma into a spiritual circling of her own which in turn relates to a larger system of circlings within the novel as a whole. Emma's dilemma, he suggests, is that unlike the greyhound she can never escape from the circle. Mario Vargas Llosa spots this same stylistic circularity in his book *The Perpetual Orgy*, relating it to the novel as a whole: 'The story moves but does not advance, circles round and round in the same place, is repetitive.'[28] He applauds *Madame Bovary* as 'the very exemplar of the closed work, of the book that is a perfect circle'.[29]

It is tempting to speculate further and to continue the idea of circularity, noting that Eleanor Marx was in no better a position than Emma Bovary to break out of the web that she had spun around herself. There was to be no easy exit from the situation created by her attachment to Aveling – the spiralling of debts, the lies, the blackmail. One could even end up with a possible answer to Julian Barnes's exam questions: although twelve years were to pass before she died, during which she gradually distanced herself from Aveling and threw herself into political activity, she did make an unsuccessful suicide attempt early in 1887, the year after the translation was completed.

And Marx's introduction does, it is also true, include along with the defence of Flaubert an equally impassioned account of the character of Emma Bovary herself:

> That there is such a thing as truth Emma is never taught; her ideal of duty is conforming to the prejudices of the world. With such ideas in the place of principles, Emma is turned adrift ... Her life is idle, useless. And this strong woman feels there must be some place for her in the world; there must be something to do – and she dreams. Life is so unreal to her that she marries Bovary thinking she loves him ... She does her best to love 'his poor wretch'. In all literature there is perhaps nothing more pathetic than her hopeless effort to 'make herself in love'. And even after she has been false, how she yearns to go back to him, to something real, to a healthier, better love than she has known. Had he but been anything than what he was![30]

Pleas for a 'healthier, better love' and for strong women to find their place in the world must surely have found powerful echoes in Marx's own life at this time and in her deteriorating relationship with Aveling. She had recently proved her own strength in her decisions to be financially independent while setting up house with him, but she was already well aware of his moral deficiency. 'How natures like Edward's ... are to be envied, who in an hour completely forget anything', she

27 Baltimore: Johns Hopkins University Press, 1979, p. 299.
28 *The Perpetual Orgy*, trans. by Helen Lane (New York: Farrar, Straus & Giroux, 1986), p. 172.
29 *Perpetual Orgy*, p. 10.
30 Vizetelly edition, p. xx.

wrote to Olive Schreiner.[31] She interpreted his womanizing and sponging as a disease, something beyond his control, a compulsion that could be cured by hard work (an attitude to moral lassitude that was not uncommon at the end of the nineteenth century). Other elements with which she might well have identified include Emma's nervous hysteria after her marriage to Charles, her impetuousness and her pursuit of sexual pleasure. The truth is that Marx finds Emma very attractive indeed. 'She is foolish, but there is a certain nobleness about her too. She is never mercenary.'[32]

In the end, though, the temptation to establish absolute links is too great, too personal by far, for not only does it simplify the workings of *le style indirect libre* but it disallows any proper intellectual or professional engagement. After all, that a female translator should wish to identify with Emma's tragedy is less surprising than that there should be clear parallels to be drawn between Emma Bovary and her male creator. Like Emma, Flaubert was often let down by his over-eager anticipation of events (the trip to the East which provided the background for *Salammbô*), and like Emma he was, against his better nature, strongly drawn to Romanticism. His dilemma is chronicled in the many letters he sent to his lover Louise Colet during the book's composition, for example when he was agonizing over the initial love scenes between Emma and her first lover, Rodolphe:

> I have been writing *Bovary* since two o'clock in the afternoon ... I am deep in it, well in the middle; it makes me sweat and catches my throat ... Just now, at six o'clock, just as I was writing the words 'nervous attack', I was so carried away that I groaned aloud, feeling in the depths of my being all that my little woman was then going through. I was afraid I should have a nervous crisis myself ... Today, for instance, I have been man and woman at the same time, lover and mistress together, riding in the forest on an autumn afternoon under the yellowing leaves; and I have been the horses, too, and the leaves, and the wind, and the words they spoke and the red sun that made them blink their eyes that swam with love.[33]

If novelists have to steep themselves so passionately in their characters' identities in order to achieve the goal of impersonality and objectivity, what does that imply for their translators – especially when the original author is no longer available for consultation? The responsibility implied by such commitment was a burden of which Marx was all too aware, and to which she responded to the best of her ability, respecting Flaubert's scrupulous art whilst fully exploring the emotions it evoked.

---

[31] Kapp, II, 27–8.

[32] Marx is surely right in this – the lack of mercenariness is symbolized in the moment when Emma, at the very end of her tether, flings her last sous to the blind beggar.

[33] Gustave Flaubert, *Letters*, ed. by Richard Rumbold (New York: Philosophical Library, 1951) pp. 87–8.

For every act of translation is an encounter, a confrontation with another, be it a character or an author. The skill is not necessarily to reproduce the text precisely but to bring out its uniqueness, to seek in the new language a rhythm and tone that, at best, will convey the voice of the original. The truth of this is supported by the considerable effectiveness of the wide variety of adaptations or dramatized versions of *Madame Bovary* that have been undertaken over the years, many of them carrying an undeniable power that has been achieved without literal access to Flaubert's prose style.[34] The films include Jean Renoir's 1934 version, heavily cut by its original distributor and a Hollywood production directed by Vincente Minnelli which sowed the seed of Mario Vargas Llosa's lifelong devotion to the novel as described in *The Perpetual Orgy*:

> It was 1952, a stifling-hot summer night, a recently opened movie theater in Piura, on the Plaza de Armas with its waving palms; James Mason appeared as Flaubert; Louis Jourdan, tall and svelte, was Rodolphe Boulanger; and Emma Bovary took on visible form by way of the nervous movements and gestures of Jennifer Jones.[35]

Other celluloid versions include a stylish but simplified film with Isabelle Huppert made by Claude Chabrol in the 1980s.

Even more recently, in a 1999 *Woman's Hour* serial adaptation on radio, Juliet Stevenson conveyed Flaubert's irony in a manner that miraculously combined the arrogance of the omniscient narrator with a note of almost perpetual wonder entirely appropriate to Emma. And she managed this even though she was reading not the original, nor even a straight translation of the original, but a much truncated version of Gerard Hopkins's translation.[36]

Most outrageous of all has been Posy Simmonds's illustrated pastiche, serialized in the *Guardian* and later published as a book.[37] 'Gemma Bovery' is the Emma *de nos jours*, a cool but essentially dumb 1990s craftsperson who, whilst living with her inadequate English husband in a cottage in Normandy, has a fling with a local aristocrat in his crumbling château. In true post-feminist style, this is physical desire not romantic love. Gemma meets her untimely end by choking to death on a croissant given to her by an adoring local baker, the main narrator of the story who bears a distant relationship to the young chemist's assistant in Flaubert's original: Justin, the only man (apart from Charles) genuinely to love the heroine. Whereas in the nineteenth-century novel it is Justin who hands Emma the key to the arsenic supply, in Simmonds's cartoon comedy it is the baker who provides the source of her demise by supplying a fatal delicacy.

---

[34] Indeed, Flaubert's plot was borrowed, only seven years after the French publication, by Mary Elizabeth Braddon in *The Doctor's Wife* (London: John Maxwell & Co., 1864; repr. Oxford: Oxford University Press, 1998, ed. by Lyn Pykett).

[35] *Perpetual Orgy*, p. 8.

[36] Oxford: Oxford University Press, 1981.

[37] *Gemma Bovery* (London: Jonathan Cape, 1999).

So bold a popularization might be considered by Flaubert purists as a diabolical liberty but it does attest to the continuing power of *Madame Bovary*, and it might even be argued that in 'updating' the novel for a late twentieth-century British readership and turning it into a comedy of cosmopolitan manners, Simmonds has only taken Flaubertian irony a farcical step further. What is more, she has had the bravura to structure the story as a *bande dessinée*, the cartoon strip so beloved by the French but hitherto a minority taste in Britain.

Hollywood films, radio readings, *Woman's Hour*, *bandes dessinées* – all are innovations beyond the wildest imaginings of the 'hacks', as Marx called them, of the late nineteenth century, but no doubt *Madame Bovary* will continue to be just as attractive to new forms and media throughout the twenty-first century as it was throughout the twentieth. Marx, who was delighted by the way in which the recently-invented typewriter had speeded up her output, relished literary games-playing, as shown in her playful rewriting of *A Doll's House* as 'A Doll's House Repaired', with Nora depicted as the conventional wife. We can be confident that she would have responded to all such *hommages* to Flaubert with her customary humour, open-mindedness and enthusiasm – and that she would be astonished to discover that her translation of *Madame Bovary*, undertaken with such courage and modesty, is still widely in use, a hundred years after her death.

Chapter 7

The Genders of Socialism: Eleanor Marx and Oscar Wilde

Ruth Robbins

In my judgement it is a pretty poor thing to write, to talk without a purpose.

Charlotte Perkins Gilman, *The Living of Charlotte Perkins Gilman*

All art is quite useless.

Oscar Wilde, Preface to *The Picture of Dorian Gray*

In his essay 'The Flight to the Real', Terry Eagleton describes a crisis in contemporary political and cultural theory which arises because of the separation between political activism and intellectual commitment, between practice and theory, and between doing and being. He argues that this separation was not evident in late nineteenth-century culture which adopted positions of 'and/both' rather than 'either/or'. It was 'the period of Aubrey Beardsley *and* the Second International; of aestheticism and anarchism; of decadence and the Dock Strike'.[1] Annie Besant combined spiritualism with industrial agitation. Yeats 'veered between theosophy and Irish Republican Brotherhood', and Oscar Wilde, aesthete and dandy, championed socialism.[2] For Eagleton, these are salutary images of polymathy for an age like ours in which theory has become divorced from political action, despite the mutual necessity of each to the other. He writes that 'the paradox of all social transformation is that it requires as one of its prerequisites a changed human subject, yet ... such reconstructed subjects are as much the product of social transformation as the precondition of it'.[3]

To his list of 'reconstructed subjects' agitating for social transformation, Eagleton might have added Eleanor Marx, socialist theorist *and* socialist activist, translator of Ibsen and Flaubert, would-be actress *and* political orator, author of

---

[1] Terry Eagleton, 'The Flight to the Real', ed. by Sally Ledger and Scott McCracken, *Cultural Politics at the Fin de Siècle* (Cambridge: Cambridge University Press, 1995), pp. 11–21 (p. 12).

[2] Eagleton, 'Flight to the Real', p. 20.

[3] Eagleton, 'Flight to the Real', p. 21.

socialist tracts *and* practical organizer of industrial action and trade unions. Oscar Wilde, on the other hand, whilst clearly a multi-form figure – Eagleton describes him elsewhere as 'socialite and sodomite, Thames and Liffey, Jekyll and Hyde, aristocrat and underdog'[4] – is not quite the champion of socialism that his inclusion in Eagleton's list implies. Although 'The Soul of Man Under Socialism' (1891) can be read as a central statement of Wilde's political and cultural views, and perhaps as a statement that unites politics and culture as Eagleton recommends, it was a strange kind of socialism that Wilde invoked, based not on communalist aspirations for a better future, but on a socialist theory that would provide the ideal conditions for the realization of a new, 'truer' individualism.

Wilde and Marx, from the written evidence, may have shared some of the same ideas, but the similarity of content is belied by the dissimilarity of manner, tone and context in which they each disseminated their ideas. The differences, I want to suggest, arise from the subject position of each, and from their respective sense of audience which in turn has effects on their uses of language. Wilde and Marx probably never met, though Marx was invited to one of Lady Wilde's soirées in 1882. She wrote to her sister Jenny: 'I was asked to a "crush" at Lady Wilde's ... the mother of that very limp and very nasty young man, Oscar Wilde, who has been making such a d—d ass of himself in America. As the son has not yet returned and the mother is nice I may go.'[5] If nothing else, this establishes that their social circles were not widely different. Her judgement of Wilde as 'very limp and very nasty', though, does rather strongly suggest antipathy to Wilde's public persona as an apolitical, purposeless, dandified, useless aesthete. She would certainly have shared Charlotte Perkins Gilman's view that speaking or writing without a purpose is 'a pretty poor thing'.

Wilde, in contrast, took pride in never calling a spade a spade, writing that the man who did so 'should be condemned to use one'.[6] And he regarded the dignity of manual labour as a contradiction in terms. In his socialist writing, the language is poetic and phatic, not persuasive; his politics are aesthetic not practical. Marx, on the other hand, is always deeply in earnest, a most un-Wildean thing to be. She wrote and spoke in a prose that was urgent, rhetorical and which intended to be transitive – her words were supposed to persuade her readers and hearers to the deed. If Wilde's writing said, 'this is how to be', Marx's said, 'this is what to do'.

Writing of Wilde's editorship of the *Woman's World* in the late 1880s, Laurel Brake argues that Wilde constructed his female readership as a group insulted by trivia: 'Instead, women are constructed as serious readers who want (and need) education and acculturation. It is just these qualities rejected as unsuitable for women – a taste for triviality, dress, gossip and pleasures such as music – which are valorized in Wilde's own writing. In this value structure, men are free to be trivial;

---

4   Terry Eagleton, *Saint Oscar* (Derry: Field Day, 1989), p. 64.
5   Kapp, I, 236.
6   Richard Ellmann, *Oscar Wilde* (Harmondsworth: Penguin, 1987), p. 347.

women are not; men may be useless, and women must be useful.'[7] It is men who are constructed as the decorative sex and women who are rendered as practical. This reversal of the separate spheres of ideology is a relatively consistent feature (inasmuch as Wilde was ever consistent) of Wilde's work. It finds its apotheosis in *The Importance of Being Earnest* (1895), in which the male leads, Algy and Jack, are ignorant do-nothings who regard smoking as an occupation, and in which social control and action are wielded by the women. As Gwendolen says of her father: 'Outside the family circle, papa, I am glad to say, is entirely unknown. I think that is quite as it should be. The home seems to me to be the proper sphere for the man. And once a man begins to neglect his domestic duties he becomes painfully effeminate, does he not? And I don't like that. It makes men so very attractive.'[8]

Earnest is a play which renders language almost entirely intransitive and phatic. There is no relationship between what we might loosely term the 'real' and the language that is supposed to describe reality. It is a play which, in Brake's terms, valorizes the trivial and mocks the useful. That same phatic language and camp reversal of usual values also informs 'The Soul of Man Under Socialism', a text that is saturated with the discourses both of proper masculinity, and of social action, but which also invokes those discourses precisely to overturn them. It is only very loosely an essay about socialism as readers both then and now might understand it. It values the 'soul' in an avowedly materialist discourse, and stresses the importance of the individual in a supposedly communal system.

The essay was first published in the 'liberal and erudite'[9] *Fortnightly Review* in 1891, then under the editorship of Frank Harris. It does define socialism in ways that are congruent with other contemporary definitions, for example, that published by Marx and Edward Aveling in their privately printed *Shelley's Socialism* (1888), in which they listed six propositions of what socialism meant 'to some of us':

> (1) That there are inequality and misery in the world; (2) that this social inequality ... [is] the necessary outcome of our social conditions; (3) that the essence of these social conditions is that the mass of the people ... produce and distribute all commodities, while a minority of the people ... possess these commodities; (4) that this initial tyranny of the possessing class over the producing class is based on the present wage system and now maintains all other forms of oppression, such as that of monarchy, or clerical rule, or police despotism; (5) that this tyranny of the few over the many is only possible because the few have obtained ... all the means of production

---

7   Laurel Brake, *Subjugated Knowledges: Journalism, Gender and Literature in the Nineteenth Century* (Basingstoke: Macmillan, 1994), p. 137.

8   Oscar Wilde, *The Complete Works of Oscar Wilde*, ed. by Merlin Holland (Glasgow: Harper Collins, 1994), p. 397. All subsequent references to Wilde's works are to this edition, and are cited parenthetically by page number in the text.

9   Laurel Brake's description in *Subjugated Knowledges*, p. 67.

and distribution of commodities ... (6) ... that the approaching change in
civilized society will be a revolution ... The two classes ... will be replaced
by a single class consisting of the whole of the healthy and sane members of
the community possessing all the means of production and distribution in
common.[10]

In a different style, each one of these propositions is repeated by Wilde. He begins
with the statement that 'Socialism would relieve us the sordid necessity of living
for others', a necessity that arises from the inequalities and miseries of the poor.
The need for revolution, then, comes equally from the miserable conditions of
poverty, and from the effects of those conditions on the rich. Where he differs
from Marx and Aveling is that his emphasis is on the aesthetic effects – the
ugliness – of poverty, on rich and poor alike, rather than on the material effects of
poverty on the poor. There is no economic analysis of the actual processes of
manufacture and distribution of commodities; but there is an analysis of the *effects*
of those systems. One of the effects is the charity of the rich who feel guilty about
their privilege, and end up spoiling their lives 'by an unhealthy and exaggerated
altruism'. This emphasis is wrong, Wilde argues. Rather than trying to keep the
poor alive by individual acts of charity, or in the case of a 'very advanced school',
trying to 'amuse the poor', the proper aim of life is 'to reconstruct society on such
a basis that poverty will be impossible'. 'Charity', he writes, 'creates a multitude of
sins' because it is 'immoral to use private property to alleviate the horrible evils
that result from the institution of private property' (1174). The system itself needs
to be reformed, though the process of reformation or revolution is not really
described.

Wilde's views on charity appear at first sight to be extreme and strange, even as
they are also characteristically witty. In fact, though, arguments about the value of
charity raged in contemporary journals. F.W. Farrars, writing on 'Social Problems
and their Remedies' in the *Fortnightly Review* in 1888, identified the problems
besetting the nation as unregulated population growth, the survival of the unfittest
since the population grew most quickly amongst the poorest classes, urbanization,
and the loss of religious faith, all of which led to prostitution, gambling and the
evils of drunkenness. Farrars argued that the nation could not wait for the laws of
progress to remedy the situation, and he disapproved strongly of charity: 'Still less
is it possible to trust to vague and unorganized instincts of philanthropy ... There
is much existing "charity" which, so far from being beneficial, tends only to
deepen the lazy stream of pauperism and to swell the raging Phlegethon of
drink.'[11] He proposed instead a series of social reforms based on religious belief

---

[10] Edward Aveling and Eleanor Marx-Aveling, *Shelley's Socialism* (privately printed pamphlet,
      1888); quoted in E.P. Thompson, *William Morris: Romantic to Revolutionary* (London:
      Merlin Press, 1977), pp. 331–2.
[11] F.W. Farrars, 'Social Problems and Remedies', *Fortnightly Review*, 49 (1888), 355–63
      (p. 358).

and enlightened legislation – but Farrars saw socialism itself as one of the symptoms of degeneration, and as such it was to be avoided. Indeed, Wilde's strictures on charity perhaps did not seem particularly outrageous to contemporary readers. Only a matter of weeks after 'The Soul of Man' appeared in the *Fortnightly* in February 1891, the *Westminster Review* published an anonymous essay entitled 'The Fetish of Charity' in two parts in March and April. The writer of this piece takes Wilde's views and speaks them more straightforwardly, with a sincerity of tone that is clearly absent from Wilde's own essay. The writer disapproves strongly of the fetish of charity on the grounds of its inefficiency and its tendency to demoralize both donor and recipient. He notes:

> The charitable system (1) invites and creates gross errors of administration. (2) It shifts the duties of the whole community onto the shoulders of a generous minority. (3) It demoralises those who give. (4) It demoralises those who receive. (5) It intensifies the very evils which it was designed to cure.[12]

And in the second essay, imaginatively titled 'The Fetish of Charity, Part II', he went on to argue that charity fosters cant, false pretences, indigence, improvidence and neglect of parental duties in the poor who receive it. He illustrated his argument with the story of the disabled workman who lives from charity, and who makes a better living than his able-bodied neighbour who has to work for his bread. Charity, he wrote, 'makes a trade ... of squalor and disease'.[13] Although this writer does not argue for socialism as the answer to the problem of poverty, he does say that one of the negative effects of charity is that it prevents the worker from demanding his due rate of fair pay for fair work; charity effectively subsidizes capitalism. These arguments from both the *Westminster* and the *Fortnightly* are Wilde's, though the tone and manner is significantly different. And like Wilde, neither writer is able to propose a realistic method of reform – a practical scheme.

The importance of socialism, Wilde argued, is that it will lead necessarily to individualism, an interestingly and paradoxically bourgeois notion of selfhood in this context. At the moment, the poor can have no individualism, since they are so degraded into a mass that they are scarcely even conscious of their own suffering: 'They have to be told of it by other people, and they often entirely disbelieve them ' (1176). But the real problems of private property rebound most of all on those who own it. Private property exacts duties from its owners, and prevents them from realizing their own individuality: 'Private property has really harmed Individualism, and obscured it, by confusing a man with what he possesses ... man thought that the important thing was to have, and did not know that the important thing is to be. The true perfection of man lies, not in what man has,

---

12 Anon., 'The Fetish of Charity', *Westminster Review*, 135 (1891), 301–10 (p. 301).
13 Anon., 'The Fetish Charity, Part II', *Westminster Review*, 135 (1891), 373–84 (p. 374).

but in what man is' (1178). In other words, both the ownership of property, and the lack of it, produce slavish conformity to externally imposed standards that a given subject has not chosen or made. Wilde sees conformity as the most serious threat to the individual because it insists on an 'absolute uniformity of type' (1195). This is a situation that makes art impossible since true art, and the true artist, are never conformist. And the existence of art and artists is the proper measure of the quality of any society, since the artist is the supreme individualist who can only thrive if there is no authoritarian government that enforces any kind of conformity.

Wilde implicitly defines the goal of socialism as being the social organization that allows everyone to live with the freedoms of an artist. All the current systems of government destroy the conditions necessary to the existence of the supreme individualist, the artist:

> All authority is equally bad. There are three kinds of despots. There is the despot who tyrannises over the body. There is the despot who tyrannises over the soul. There is the despot who tyrannises over the soul and body alike. The first is called the Prince. The second is called the Pope. The third is called the People. (1193)

All three systems – monarchy, ecclesiastical rule and democracy – enforce conformity, and mistake conformity for morality. This is a common view in late Victorian socialist writing. Marx and Aveling's 1886 pamphlet *The Woman Question* makes a similar point: 'the customary is the moral', they write, a piece of lazy thinking that makes it easier to dismiss any kind of nonconformity as immorality.[14] Wilde could have said that. Indeed, in 'The Critic as Artist' (1891),[15] Gilbert tells Ernest:

> The security of society lies in custom and unconscious instinct, and the basis of the stability of society ... is the complete absence of any intelligence amongst its members. The great majority of people being fully aware of this, rank themselves naturally on the side of that splendid system that elevates them to the dignity of machines, and rage so wildly against the intrusion of the intellectual faculty ... that one is tempted to define man as a rational animal who always loses his temper when he is called upon to act in accordance with the dictates of reason. (1141)

For Wilde, the power of the people is the most powerful authority in society, and the most likely power to stifle the life of the artist and disrupt the goals of socialism because of its insistence on doing what has always been done, because its morality depends on custom.

---

[14] *Woman Question*, p. 6.
[15] 'The Critic as Artist' was originally published as 'The True Function and Value of Criticism' in *The Nineteenth Century* in July and September 1890. It was collected as 'The Critic as Artist' in *Intentions* in 1891.

The tone of Wilde's arguments in all his writings depends crucially on his sense of audience and on his own subject position in relation to the audience he constructs as his readership. As Regenia Gagnier argues, his prose writings display both cynicism and idealism, with cynicism producing his characteristic wit and distance, and his idealism the seduction of his purple prose: 'This doubleness constituted Wilde's response to the modern bourgeois artist's dilemma between private art and the need for an audience.'[16] In an essay like 'Pen, Pencil and Poison: A Study in Green', published in 1889 in the *Fortnightly Review*, Wilde used the assumptions of the essay genre against themselves. The implied (male) audience of like-minded proper gentlemen was comically coerced – seduced almost, one might say – into assenting to propositions such as 'There is no essential incongruity between crime and culture' (1106). That essay, like 'The Soul of Man', exemplifies Wilde's strategy of using dominant discourses, in particular the vocabulary and assumptions of conformist masculinity against the very assumptions of that discourse, through a tone that resists the certainties that the vocabulary would usually imply. So, in 'The Soul of Man' we read:

> The possession of private property is very often extremely demoralising and that is, of course, why Socialism wants to get rid of the institution … Some years ago people went about the country saying that property has duties … at last, the Church has begun to say it. One hears it now from every pulpit. It is perfectly true. Property not merely has duties, it has so many duties that its possession to any large extent is a bore. It involves endless claims upon one, endless attention to business, endless bother. If property had simply pleasures, we could stand it; but its duties make it unbearable. In the interest of the rich we must get rid of it. (1175–6)

Wilde's point requires the existence of a discourse of *noblesse oblige*; it requires also the Church's discourse of altruism and the Christian denial of earthly pleasures in the expectation of heavenly reward. The joke, as so often with Wilde, depends on the existence of commonly-held beliefs that are then subverted into apparent paradoxes such as getting rid of property to benefit the rich. But whilst the audience may laugh, it will probably not be converted.

With his response to individualism, the technique is slightly different. In this case, Wilde takes standard contemporary ideas about individualism and, instead of reversing the discourse, he pushes the concept to its logical limits, demonstrating in the process that individualism as understood by the nineteenth century is always already a paradox. As Raymond Williams observes in *Keywords*: 'Individual originally meant indivisible. That now sounds like a paradox. "Individual" stresses a distinction from others; "indivisible" a necessary connection.'[17] Williams shows

---

16 Regenia Gagnier, *Idylls of the Marketplace: Oscar Wilde and the Victorian Public* (Aldershot: Scolar Press, 1986), p. 19.

17 Raymond Williams, *Keywords: A Vocabulary of Culture and Society* (revised edition, London: Fontana, 1988), p. 161.

us that 'individualism' is a nineteenth-century coinage which draws on the idea of the individual as a 'unique person' who also has 'his (indivisible) membership of a group'. Individualism makes use of both uniqueness and group membership, and argues for the primacy of the individual's own interests over the interests of the group.[18] On the one hand, then, individualism is bound up with ideas about the uniqueness, self-expressiveness, internal coherence and originality of proper masculinity, ideas expressed by John Stuart Mill in *On Liberty* (1859) who wrote, quoting Wilhelm von Humboldt, that

> the object 'towards which every human being must ceaselessly direct his efforts … is the individuality of power and development'; that for this there are two requisites, 'freedom, and variety of situations'; and that from the union of these arise 'individual vigour and manifold diversity', which combine themselves in 'originality'.[19]

In this model, individualism is not a conformist doctrine, but one that demands originality – nonconformity – as its goal and method. At the same time, however, acceptable individualism also depended on a degree of self-abnegation and conformity, signalled, as James Eli Adams remarks, in the meanings of words like 'restraint' and 'reserve' in Victorian discourses of masculinity (the individual is always male). Restraint and reserve imply that the individual is not to draw attention to himself, and yet he must always behave as if he were being observed. As Adams suggests, 'the masculine, in short, is as much a spectacle as the feminine'.[20]

Masculine individualism is caught up in the paradox of the necessary display of virtue (which is most usually to be understood as conformity to pre-existing moral values) and the necessity not to stand out from the crowd: the Victorian individual is both an aesthete and an ascetic. The Wildean individual on the other hand focuses on his own originality and abandons restraint, taking Mill at his word. The effect is powerful because his implied audience is a homosocial coterie of men – and 'artistic' men at that; men, that is, who are *au fait* with contemporary discourses of masculinity, but who are prepared to divorce themselves from the capitalist and heterosexual modes of production and reproduction sanctioned by dominant versions of individualism. As Lawrence Danson has noted, individualism could mean anything from the very negative view of it as 'individual isolation and social dissolution' to the very positive, which emphasized 'the organic unity of individual and society'.[21] Wilde's individualism,

---

[18] Williams, *Keywords*, p. 165.

[19] John Stuart Mill, *On Liberty* [1859] in Mill, *Utilitarianism; On Liberty; Considerations on Representative Government*, ed. by Geraint Williams (London: Everyman, 1993), p. 125.

[20] James Eli Adams, *Dandies and Desert Saints: Styles of Victorian Masculinity* (Ithaca and London: Cornell University Press, 1995), p. 11. See also his remarks about Newman's 'restraint', pp. 86–103, and about Pater's 'restraint', p. 189.

[21] Lawrence Danson, *Wilde's Intentions: The Artist in His Criticism* (Oxford: Oxford University

as always, refuses the hierarchical valuation of that neat binary of positive and negative: dissolution of the current social order presumably is precisely what socialism aims at, and organic unity is thus itself dissolved as a valued term that can have no positive meaning while it still attaches itself to the *status quo*.

By the by, the soul of woman does not come into it, even in relation to the abolition of marriage and family life under socialism. Men are the implied audience of 'The Soul of Man'. And individualism is the stated aim of socialism, though apart from getting yet-to-be invented machines to do society's dirty work, how this aim is to be achieved is never quite stated.

In other words, 'The Soul of Man' is a text which, from its very title, operates on deliberate misrecognitions (themselves dependent on careful recognitions) of contemporary language codes. The earnestness of contemporary versions of masculinity is invoked only to be debunked. Similarly, the earnestness of contemporary socialist writing, the commonplace attitudes of the activists, are also mocked: in this text, labour is not dignified but disgusting; poverty is unaesthetic; property demoralizes the rich; socialism is not communal. Wilde combines two kinds of knowing joke, against masculinity and against socialism in his essay. But these are jokes told from a position of constructed privilege. It would be difficult to make the joke, and impossible to find it funny, if you lived in real poverty. This does not mean that the joke is unimportant, but it has more to say about 'Man' than 'Socialism', and it explicitly refuses the realm of the practical in its rhetorical strategies, its subject matter, its implied writer and his implied audience.

In the end, Wilde's socialism is a theoretical intervention. As he says himself near the end of the 'The Soul of Man', his ideas about socialism will be attacked as unpractical and as going against human nature:

> This is perfectly true. It is unpractical, and it goes against human nature. This is why it is worth carrying out, and that is why one proposes it. For what is a practical scheme? A practical scheme is either a scheme that is already in existence, or a scheme that could be carried out under existing conditions. But it is exactly the existing conditions that one objects to; and any scheme that could accept these conditions is wrong and foolish. The conditions will be done away with, and human nature will change. (1194)

This is the chicken and egg identified by Eagleton, since changing human nature is the prerequisite as well as the goal of social transformation. And Wilde has nothing to offer in terms of describing *how* socialism will be achieved, concentrating all his attention on why it should be achieved. He proposes ideal ends, but proposes no means – no practice that will make the theory come true. The revolution, finally, is deferred.

Press, 1997), pp. 161–2. Danson here quotes from Steven Lukes, *Individualism* (Oxford: Blackwell, 1973).

The tone of Eleanor Marx's writings could scarcely be more different. Because she seems to write more clearly, her writings on socialist subjects appear simpler, both to read and to write. Her authorial persona is direct, straightforward, sincere, all words of which Wilde, as Jonathan Dollimore has suggested, would have disapproved.[22] Her audience is not implied, but usually very directly and specifically addressed; and her design on that audience is self-evident and overtly stated. This is not to say, however, that Marx's authorial persona is any less constructed than Wilde's. Her use of codes of clarity and sincerity are no less deliberate than Wilde's use and abuse of codes to distort and disguise. Marx's urgency was brave, given that she inhabited none of the structures of privilege, either financially or in terms of gender. Her clarity was calculated because she knew that she was not generally addressing her equals, at least in terms of education and opportunity. There is no coterie language addressed to the discerning few.

Of course, Wilde's own subject position was problematic; indeed, in many ways, more problematic than Marx's, since his same-sex desire was illegal, and required disguise in both life and writing. The disguise he put on, however, that of upper-class masculinity bolstered by a fair degree of economic privilege, was a disguise that lent him power. While living with Aveling had its difficulties, Marx at least was unlikely to be imprisoned on the grounds of her sexual choices. None the less, as Ruth Brandon argues, she was painfully aware of the irregularity of her position as a common-law wife, and of the ammunition that it afforded the enemies of socialism to say that socialism was immoral – immorality for the late Victorians, as Frank Mort has suggested, was always a sexual matter.[23] The letters she wrote in the summer of 1884, explaining her relationship with Aveling, recognize that even amongst those she counted as friends, she could not count on approval for her choice of man and *modus vivendi*. Moreover, she lived in the shadow of the 'solid bourgeois principles of the whole Marx family', and knew how middle-class respectability would respond.[24] A speech delivered on a lecture tour of the United States, in Chicago in November, 1886 shows how she recognized the bases of personal attacks on her and her beliefs, and explicitly answered hostile criticism even when it touched her closely.

Her speech, reported in the American socialist periodical *Knights of Labor*, works on the rhetorical basis of antagonistic assertion, apparent agreement and refutation. It describes what people are saying about socialism, and then it refutes hostile claims point by point. Marx began with the claim that socialists want to

---

[22] Jonathan Dollimore, *Sexual Dissidence: Augustine to Wilde, Freud to Foucault* (Oxford: Clarendon Press, 1991), pp. 14–17.

[23] Frank Mort, *Dangerous Sexualities: Medico-Moral Politics in England since 1830* (London: Routledge & Kegan Paul, 1987), p. 37.

[24] Ruth Brandon, *The New Women and the Old Men: Love, Sex and The Woman Question* (London: Secker & Warburg, 1990), p. 24.

abandon private property, and agreed that socialists did indeed want abolish the private ownership of the means of production and redistribution: 'But this does not mean abolishing private property; it means giving property to the thousands and millions who to-day have none. The capitalists have abolished the "private property" of the working classes, and we intend that this shall be returned to them.' To the claim that socialists are against 'law and order', she assented, given that the current state of law and order made some men millionaires and left others to starve: 'the "order" of today is disorder'.[25] Near the end of the speech, she dealt with the accusation that socialists are sexually immoral, that they favoured free love and disapproved of monogamous marriage – an accusation that she had personal reasons to fear:

> We are told that 'socialists want to have women in common.' Such an idea is possible only in a state of society that looks upon woman as a commodity. To-day, woman, alas, is only that. She has only too often to sell her womanhood for bread. But to the socialist a woman is a human being, and no more to be 'held' in common than a socialistic society could recognize slavery ... We socialists ... want common property in all means of production and distribution, and as woman is not a machine, but a human being, she cannot be held by anyone as a piece of property.[26]

In other words, Marx does assert individuality – including the individuality and humanity of women. Individuality, though, is not quite the same thing as individualism, and Marx is much more concerned with an idea of the individual that stresses the continuity of selfhood with society – the indivisible individual. Unlike Wilde, then, she believed in an individualism that implied individual responsibility, but this could only be acquired 'when all men have collective rights and duties'.[27] This is a slightly different version of the chicken and egg problem. Individuality comes about when collectivism has been established, not before. But Marx does at least propose a plan of action for the achievement of social transformation: 'And now what is to be done? You have to get a strong labor organization ... you must hold together as a party, different from, opposed to all others, one with a distinct platform, and pledged only to the cause of labor ... come and work for the one party that is that of neither thieves nor the robbers, but of honest men and women. Hold together and your victory is assured.'[28]

One of the striking aspects of Marx's writing is her articulation of the doubled oppression of working-class women, and her relative contempt for contemporary middle-class feminist movements. As Yvonne Kapp argues, Marx's feminism was inseparable from her socialism. She was far more interested in the serious material

---

[25] This speech appeared in *Knights of Labor*, 4 December, 1886; quoted in Kapp, II, 161–5 (p. 162).

[26] Kapp, II, 164.

[27] Kapp, II, 163–4.

[28] Kapp, II, 164–5.

oppression of working women than she was in the relative inequalities between middle-class women and their middle-class menfolk. After all, materially speaking, the middle-class woman was still much better off than the woman worker.[29] In *The Woman Question*, she and Aveling argued that most of the manifestations of contemporary feminism were useless to alleviate the sufferings of most women. This was, firstly, because most of the women involved in feminist movements were middle class, and were therefore implicated in the class system of inequality that it was in their interests to shore up; secondly, because their interest in reform was merely partial, and they made no attempt to understand the economic basis of female oppression; and finally, because the middle-class feminist was a liberal not a revolutionary – she sought only to tinker with the existing system, not to reform it thoroughly and completely.[30] Marx championed the voiceless majority of working women whose lot in life was considerably worse even than that of their own husbands: 'The man, worn out as he may be by labour, has the evening in which to do nothing. The woman is occupied until bed-time comes. Often with young children, her toil goes far into, or all through, the night.'[31] Working men are certainly oppressed by the system, but working women are more oppressed since they are used even by working men, as Marx and Aveling argued in *The Woman Question*. Marriage and love are ideologically-motivated shams – but when women are deprived of marriage and love, just as they are generally deprived of education and properly-paid labour, they are oppressed both materially and psychologically. Men and women must therefore work together to overcome the oppressions that undermine them both.

Eleanor Marx does not see a utopian future divorced from the process of achieving it. Her analysis demands action and her emphasis is on *doing* as well as on theorizing. Unlike Wilde, she was practically involved in labour organizations and agitation, helping to found trade union branches amongst low-paid workers, especially in London's East End. She addressed the workers, helping them to organize themselves whilst trying to earn a rather precarious living of her own. With the arrival of socialism, she argued, 'the divorce between art and labour, the antagonism between head and hand work, that grieves the souls of artist without their knowing in most cases the economic cause of their grief, will vanish'.[32] Base and superstructure should exist mutually, each informing the other for mutual benefit. In her address to the Chicago workers, she spoke of there being no qualitative distinction between the work of the architect and the work of the bricklayer: 'one required the other, and so long as each did necessary work each was entitled to the same recognition as an honest laborer; but ... the one is no better than the other. Socialists recognize that all labor is needful – as labor is not

---

29   See Kapp, II, 85–6.
30   *Woman Question*, p. 6.
31   *Woman Question*, p. 9.
32   *Woman Question*, p. 15.

and cannot be recognized to-day.'[33] Thus Marx undertakes 'head work' in the service of those who do 'hand work'. Socialism, in her view, will improve the spiritual as well as the material conditions of the oppressed. In that at least, she is not so far away from Wilde's position in 'The Soul of Man'.

But because her view is practical, and her sense of needing to change the world is so urgent, unlike Wilde, Marx cannot wait for technology to make manual labour unnecessary. In any case, under present conditions, new machines would still belong to the capitalists; they would simply throw the workers out of work, and further depress the price of their labour, thereby cementing their misery.[34] The work of social transformation must begin now, through alternative political organizations. Moreover, Marx does not imagine that unpleasant work will ever be entirely abolished. Rather, in her schema, the unpleasantness will be fairly shared. Her urgency comes from her confrontation of the reality of poverty and her position in relation to both class and gender. As a middle-class woman who had partially lost her caste through both poverty and 'irregular' domestic arrangements, she knew what disprivilege meant. The precariousness of her own existence was a spur to action.

Wilde's position, on the other hand, arises from his ingrained resistance throughout his life and work to the very idea of the 'real'. It is no accident that it is his clever but wicked Lords, Henry Wootton (*Dorian Gray*) and Illingworth (*A Woman of No Importance*) who speak of East End poverty as the problem of slavery: 'and we try to solve it by amusing the slaves', they both say (42, 471). When Lord Henry is asked what change he proposes to solve the problem, he answers: 'I don't desire to change anything in England except the weather.' Intelligence and ethical social actions never meet in Wilde's characters. Only the stupid actually try to *do* anything. And in the short stories such as 'The Happy Prince' or 'The Young King', which both contain detailed analyses of the causes of poverty, there is a flight *from* the real. The plots are resolved by resorting to magic or to God – any solution other than one that requires the reader or writer to contemplate the vigorous action of revolution, or to write in a language that behaves transitively not phatically.

And yet ... the aesthetic is also a political category, as both Marxist and feminist theories attest. The choice Wilde makes has its political dimension, if not precisely a party political one. What brings Marx and Wilde together is the threat that they each offer to the dominant contemporary versions of gender, and especially to the ideas attached to gender within class. Eleanor Marx may have come from a revolutionary family, but they were solidly bourgeois and respectable

---

[33] Quoted in Kapp, II, 163.

[34] *The Woman Question* insists that even if women were equal under capitalist systems, the results would be 'increased competition and more embittered struggle for existence'. The mere creation of new machines and new structures under the existing system without 'larger social change' would still leave proletarian men and all women unfree (p. 6).

too, at least in their own minds. Her life choices left her *déclassée*, with neither the money nor the respectability that designated the middle-class lady. Whilst her own position is exposed, it also works to expose the contradictions inherent in definitions of both respectability and femininity. Writing explicitly of widespread sexual oppression and ignorance in essays like *The Woman Question*, she attacked both the suppression of the sex instinct and the false modesty about sexual matters that produced lies to children about their origins, and left unmarried women with no sexual outlet. The supposed delicacy of femininity is undermined by the ways in which she insistently called a spade a spade.

Wilde too was *déclassé*. But in his highly successful mimicry of the hegemonic class of bourgeois masculinity, he calls its central tenets into question too. In place of a manliness that is supposed to be active, industrious, sincere and practical, he proposed, in his essay on socialism, as elsewhere, a manliness that is passive, idle, artistic, affected and idealistic. Where Marx's language is overt and plan, his subversions are covert and disguised. Straightforwardness is a kind of 'male gift' which Eleanor Marx subversively assumed, and which Oscar Wilde subversively abjured.

Chapter 8

Socialist Feminism and Sexual Instinct: Eleanor Marx and Amy Levy

Emma Francis

At the end of *The Woman Question*, their co-authored essay of 1886 which discusses the English translation of August Bebel's *Woman in the Past, Present and Future*, Eleanor Marx and Edward Aveling bring their argument to a climax by holding out the glittering prize of harmonious heterosexual monogamy that will be made possible by socialist revolution:

> The woman will no longer be the man's slave, but his equal. For divorce there will be no need ... two great curses that help, with others, to ruin the relations between men and women will have passed. Those curses are the treatment of men and women as different beings, and the want of truth. There will no longer be one law for the woman and one for the man ... Husband and wife will be able to do that which but few can do now – look clear through one another's eyes into one another's hearts. For ourselves, we believe that the cleaving of one man to one woman will be the best for all, and that these will find each in the heart of the other, that which is in their eyes, their own image.[1]

This prophecy of mutuality and mutual regard, of a perfect fit of the sexes, mirrors the neatness with which the two main categories of the essay – women and the working class – are compressed into a single analytic model. Under capitalism, Marx and Aveling argue, 'women are the creatures of an organised tyranny of men, as the workers are the creatures of an organised tyranny of idlers' (6). In the socialist utopia envisaged by their essay, intellectual, sexual and economic independence are to be equally the lot of women and men:

> Her education and all other opportunities [will be] as those of man. Like him, she, if sound in mind and body (and how the number of women thus will grow!) will have to give her one, two or three hours of social labour to supply the wants of the community, and therefore of herself. Thereafter she will be free for art or science, or teaching or writing, or amusement in any form. (15)

---

[1] *Woman Question*, p. 16. All subsequent references are cited parenthetically by page number in the text.

The Woman Question seems to waver momentarily over the question of whether single or multiple partners will be the norm: 'Whether monogamy or polygamy will obtain in the Socialistic state is a detail on which one can only speak as an individual. The question is too large to be solved within the mists and miasmata of the capitalistic system' (15). The abolition of the double standard of sexual shame might, the essay argues, necessitate the practice of polygamy for women: 'If the coming society, like European society to-day, regards it as right for man to have mistresses as well as a wife, we may be certain that the like freedom will be extended to women' (16). But Marx and Aveling, in this essay at least, ultimately plump for a happy ending:

> Personally, we believe that monogamy will gain the day. There are approximately equal numbers of men and women, and the highest ideal seems to be the complete, harmonious, lasting blending of two human lives. (15)

Another prophecy of sexual futurism from the second half of the 1880s, 'A Ballad of Religion and Marriage', written by Eleanor's friend Amy Levy offers, by contrast, a quite different prospect for the heterosexuality to come.

> Swept into limbo is the host
>   Of heavenly angels, row on row;
> The Father, Son and Holy Ghost,
>   Pale and defeated, rise and go.
> The Great Jehovah is laid low,
>   Vanished his burning bush and rod –
> Say, are we doomed to deeper woe?
>   Shall marriage go the way of God?
>
> Monogamous, still at our post,
>   Reluctantly we undergo
> Domestic round of boiled and roast,
>   Yet deem the whole proceeding slow.
> Daily the secret murmurs grow;
>   We are no more content to plod
> Along the beaten paths – and so
>   Marriage must go the way of God.
>
> Soon, before all men, each shall toast
>   The seven strings unto his bow,
> Like beacon fires along the coast,
>   The flames of love shall glance and glow.
> Nor let nor hindrance man shall know,
>   From natal bath to funeral sod;
> Perennial shall his pleasures flow
>   When marriage goes the way of God.

> Grant, in a million years at most,
>   Folk shall be neither pairs nor odd –
> Alas! we sha'n't be there to boast
>   "Marriage has gone the way of God!"[2]

Levy is also interested in the changes to sexuality and sexual politics which will result from profound social change, in this case the collapse of theism. But instead of the equity and heterosexual complementarity of Marx and Aveling's vision, Levy hints at a homosocial dystopia, in which men pursue sexual pleasure unchecked by social institutions or romantic loyalties. The political imperative of the poem moves between the genders as it proceeds. What begins as a demand from women for liberation from the confinements of domesticity – the 'round of boiled and roast' – is transformed into a discussion of the greater freedom which will be created for men by the abolition of the distinction between private predilection and public morality. It will be permissible for each man to own to, not to say brag about, having not one or two but 'seven strings unto his bow'.

There are two poems here. The first is produced by an optimistic reading which treats the 'men' of the latter parts of the poem as a generic. In this case, the revolution which dissolves monogamy and its institutions makes the distinction between marriage and a single life meaningless and enhances sexual pleasure and liberation for all. The other poem, which takes Levy's ascriptions of gender – the wholly male pronouns of the second half of the poem – seriously, prophesies the liberation of male desire only and the eclipse of women's political demands; women simply vanish from the poem. The imperative of making a choice between these two poems, and the contrasting sexual politics they delineate, is emphasized by the instability of the metaphor Levy uses to represent the liberation and spread of sexual pleasure – the 'flames of love'. In modern Britain, beacon fires have a ceremonial function in national celebrations. But in ancient and early modern times they were a system of communication used to signal the need to mobilize against the threat of invasion. Unlike Marx and Aveling's *Woman Question*, Levy's poem works to undo the vision of utopia it presents. Given the vicissitudes of her own heterosexual career, the personal consequences of her renunciation of marriage and the mismatch between her own and Aveling's understandings of the significance of their private commitment to each other, Eleanor Marx might have done well to pay some attention to Levy's ironic pessimism.[3]

---

2   Amy Levy, 'A Ballad of Religion and Marriage' (privately printed, n.d.). The copy of this text held by the British Library is inscribed 1915, presumably the date of acquisition. Levy's poetic career began in 1881 with the publication of *Xantippe and Other Verse* (Cambridge: E. Johnson), when she was twenty-one, so the composition of 'A Ballad of Religion and Marriage' can be safely dated to the 1880s. I would argue that its philosophy relates most closely to the work exploring a pessimistic, aggressive account of sexuality that she produced towards the end of her life in the later 1880s.

3   Kapp, II, 678–709 and *passim*.

The Woman Question is part of a crucial moment within the history of British first-wave feminism. Among her contemporaries, Marx was the feminist thinker who made most explicit the need for a link between the question of women's liberation and that of class struggle. But even for those who were not socialists, the climate of discussion changed in the 1880s in ways which caused feminism to chafe at the boundaries of the middle-class assumptions and aspirations which had governed it in the mid-nineteenth century. The pressure at this point in the century of feminism's lengthening intellectual genealogy, its journey from the groundbreaking intervention of Mary Wollstonecraft for women into the agendas of radicalism and Enlightenment, and the articulation of feminism into liberal thought by writers such as J.S. Mill in the mid-nineteenth century, produced the diversification of feminist debate through the lenses of Darwinism and new discourses about sexuality. By the 1880s there was a particularly rich and sometimes contradictory combination of conceptual tools with which feminism could confront the profound social and sexual changes and crises of the time. As Sally Ledger has shown, 'the new socialism, the new imperialism, the new fiction and the new journalism' were accompanied by crucial developments in feminist thinking, which became clustered around the literary and media stereotype of the New Woman, 'as part of that concatenation of cultural novelties which manifested itself in the 1880s and 1890s'.[4]

The comparison of Eleanor Marx's intervention in *The Woman Question* and her other writings about women of the 1880s with her friend Amy Levy's work throws specific light on the British feminist intellectual landscape of the 1880s. During this decade, liberal feminist arguments (often referenced explicitly or implicitly through Wollstonecraft) tend to focus on the legislative and social impediments to women's equality and assume a potentially autonomous and equal female subject. At the same time, they wrestle with the emergent Darwinian arguments which look to a logic of 'instinct' and to deterministic social or biological differences, both in order to explain inequality and conflict between the sexes and to offer solutions to the problem. A comparison of Marx's and Levy's work demonstrates the felicities and blind spots of this combination, which became less possible to sustain in the following decade, when the rhetorical strategies and political stances of feminists became more sharply defined. One of the most important problems at stake in the discussion is still a major impasse within contemporary feminist theory more than a century later. Is it possible to combine a full materialist analysis of women's oppression with a recognition of the imperatives of sexuality, or what we would now call psychic life? And how can we explain the apparent complicity of female sexuality with those aspects of patriarchy which exceed capitalism – the muddying of the waters of political demand by the vagaries of desire?

---

[4]   Sally Ledger, *The New Woman: Fiction and Feminism at the fin de siècle* (Manchester: Manchester University Press, 1997), p. 1.

Amy Levy was born in 1861 into a middle-class Anglo-Jewish family in London, was educated at a girls' high school in Brighton and in 1879 entered Newnham College Cambridge, where she specialized in languages and became the first Jewish woman to pass the Higher Local Examination in 1881. After university she spent some time travelling and teaching in Europe and then settled in Bloomsbury, where she associated with a group of women intellectuals who worked regularly in the British Museum. There she met Eleanor Marx. Both were engaged in translation work, Marx of Ibsen and Levy of 'the German poets Lenau, Heine and others ... She had a peculiar liking for Lenau, the poet of melancholy and human liberation, but her affinity was with Heine, the sublimated essence of Jewish genius', as Marx later reported to Max Beer.[5] When, in September 1889, Levy took her own life, she left behind her a sizeable body of work including short stories, essays of literary and cultural criticism, three collections of poetry and three novels, of which the best known today is *Reuben Sachs* (1888).[6]

Despite the fact that a good deal of this writing was explicitly commercial, written for fashionable periodicals, one of its most consistent themes is the fierce critique of the restrictions of bourgeois femininity, the emotional impoverishment of the lives of middle-class women and the horrors of the marriage market. But if Levy's general theme is the moral bankruptcy and social and sexual limitations of the middle classes in general, it is her own community that draws her most severe criticism. Middle-class Anglo-Jewry is presented as an overdetermined version of Victorian patriarchy, and the constraints it places upon its women are seen as especially frustrating. Eleanor Marx was particularly drawn to *Reuben Sachs* and, in 1889, translated it into German – her only work of translation into, rather than out of German – almost immediately after its first publication.[7]

Reuben is a young and ambitious Tory politician at the start of his career. When the novel opens he has just returned from a convalescent trip to the Antipodes, prescribed for a nervous breakdown brought on by the strain of an unsuccessfully contested parliamentary election. On his arrival in London, he hastens to the house of his cousins, the Leuningers, to see Judith Quixano, an impoverished distant relation of the Leuningers whom they have adopted. Although Judith and Reuben have been in love for some time, his family are determined that they should not marry, as a financially and politically expedient

---

5   Max Beer, *Fifty Years of International Socialism* (London: Allen & Unwin, 1935), p. 72.
6   An excellent modern edition of Levy's work is Melvyn New's *The Complete Novels and Selected Writings of Amy Levy* (Gainesville: University of Florida Press, 1993). All page references to *Reuben Sachs* are taken from this text. Levy's novel was originally published by Macmillan in London in 1888. For further discussion of Levy see Cynthia Scheinberg, 'Canonizing the Jew: Amy Levy's Challenge to Victorian Poetic Identity', *Victorian Studies*, 39 (1996), 173–200; Joseph Bristow, '"All out of tune in this world's instrument": The "Minor" Poetry of Amy Levy', *Journal of Victorian Culture*, 4 (1999), 76–103; and Linda Hunt Beckman's forthcoming *Amy Levy: Her Life and Letters*.
7   Kapp, I, 259–60.

match is vital for Reuben's career. Reuben's mother repeatedly assures herself and the family that 'Reuben can be trusted to do nothing rash'.[8] Indeed, as his career gathers momentum, Reuben makes an active choice to abandon Judith because he recognizes his deepest desires as purely material:

> He had an immense idea of his own market value; an instinctive aversion to making a bad bargain.
> From his cradle he had imbibed the creed that it is noble and desirable to have everything better than your neighbour; from the first had been impressed on him the sacred duty of doing the very best for yourself.[9]

In a symbolic central scene, Reuben is pulled away from a romantic encounter with Judith by the call of political ambition. He arrives late to a party at the Leuningers' house and on seeing Judith talking with another man, becomes aware of how much he is in love with her. He seeks her out, tears up her programme which is filled with the names of other partners and leads her to a private corner of the room. Stating his intention to possess something of her, he unfastens the white flowers pinned to Judith's dress, an act which becomes inflected in the text as a symbolic sexual defloration:

> Judith yielded, passive, rapt, as his fingers fumbled with the gold pin.
> It was like a dream to her, a wonderful dream, with which the whirling maze of dancers, the heavy scents, the delicious music were inextricably mingled. And mingling with it also was a strange, harsh sound in the street outside, which, faint and muffled at first, was growing every moment louder and more distinct.[10]

But at this romantically-charged moment there is a disturbance in the street outside; the long-anticipated death of a Conservative MP is announced, leaving vacant a constituency earmarked for Reuben. Hearing the news, Reuben draws away from Judith: 'on his face was the look of a man who has escaped a great danger'.[11] After leaving her, he drops the flowers and crushes them underfoot.

As critics have noted, during the course of the novel the focus of the narrative shifts from Reuben to Judith and becomes an exploration of the particular effects upon women of the materialism and ambition for status within the Jewish establishment.[12] Judith assents to this ethic as much as anyone else. Realizing that she has no hope of marrying Reuben, she accepts the proposal of Bertie Lee-Harrison, a rich convert whom she does not love, in an attempt to find compensation in wealth and status:

---

8 *Complete Novels*, p. 197.
9 *Complete Novels*, p. 242.
10 *Complete Novels*, p. 258.
11 *Complete Novels*, p. 259.
12 This point is made by Deborah Epstein Nord in her essay '"Neither Pairs Nor Odd": Female Community in Late Nineteenth-Century London', *Signs*, 15 (1990), 752, and by Melvyn New in his Introduction to *Complete Novels*, pp. 29–34.

She had opened up for herself a new field of action; she would be reinstated in the eyes of her world, in Reuben's eyes, in her own ... Material advantage; things that you could touch and see and talk about; these were the only things which really mattered, had been the un-spoken gospel of her life.

Now and then you allowed yourself the luxury of a fine sentiment in speech, but when it came to the point, to take the best that you could get for yourself was the only course open to a person of sense.[13]

Judith's behaviour is determined every bit as much as Reuben's by the desire for worldly advancement. In one sense, her moral failure is worse than his, because the novel makes clear that her family connections embody a commitment to the values of culture rather than self-seeking materialism. Judith comes from stock very different from the worldly-wise families with whom she now lives and associates. Her origins in the Sephardic, Iberian Jewish line mark her out as culturally, socially and physically superior to the Ashkenazic Eastern European Jews from whom the Leuningers have descended. Her father, Joshua, comes from a line of Portuguese merchants, an old Jewish élite. Unable to cope with the cut and thrust of mid-nineteenth-century British commerce, he has withdrawn into scholarship.

Whilst she is considering Lee-Harrison's proposal, Judith visits her parents. Her mother repeats the advice of the Leuninger women, to accept the offer without delay, but her father assures her that she must not consent unless the marriage will make her happy, and that he will always provide a home for her if she decides to refuse. But Judith holds fast to her feeling that there is no alternative for her. Her engagement is announced on the same day as Reuben is returned to Parliament by an overwhelming majority. In the end both Reuben and Judith reap the fruits of their ethical failure. Reuben dies of a heart attack brought on by overwork after being in office for only a few months. The novel concludes with Judith's realization of the mistake they have both made:

It seemed to her, as she sat there in the fading light, that this is the bitter lesson of existence: that the sacred serves only to teach the full meaning of sacrilege; the beautiful of the hideous; modesty of outrage; joy of sorrow; life of death.[14]

The publication of this scathing critique of middle-class mores caused considerable turbulence within the Jewish community and a sensation without. The novel reprinted quickly, going into several editions, and became a byword for the 'intentionally offensive' in Jewish literature, the standard against which all other 'ill-natured fiction of Jewish life was evaluated'.[15]

---

13 *Complete Novels*, pp. 279–80.
14 *Complete Novels*, p. 292.
15 Unsigned review of Mrs Andrew Dean's *Isaac Eller's Money*, in *The Jewish Chronicle*, 2 August 1889, p. 12. An excellent account of the impact of Levy's novel on its contemporary culture is

As well as giving her the opportunity to engage with her own Jewishness (despite the fact the subject was taboo within her own family)[16] it is likely that Eleanor Marx was drawn to the novel because of her taste for closely-observed studies of the moral corruption of bourgeois women, evidenced in some of the other texts she worked upon as a translator and commentator. Judith Quixano can be placed alongside Flaubert's Emma Bovary and Ibsen's Nora Helmer as women whose complicity with bourgeois corruption brutalizes and impoverishes. Judith's fate is a mixture of the two. Like Nora she does come to self-realization about the contradictions of her position, but like Emma Bovary she fails to escape and is ultimately consumed by them.

Reuben Sachs also shares an intellectual structure and combination of arguments to support its feminism with *The Woman Question*. As Gillian Beer has shown in *Darwin's Plots*, during the last third of the nineteenth century different interpretations of Darwin's thought were brought into the service of a variety of social, economic, political and literary narratives.[17] Feminist thinkers of the 1880s engaged enthusiastically with Darwinist argument, and the comparison of Levy with Marx and Aveling reveals something of the range of Darwinisms which feminism was rehearsing.

The Woman Question works with the concept and language of 'instinct', explicitly associated with Darwinism (14), in order to negotiate questions of sexuality and sexual identity. Categories of the 'natural' and the 'unnatural' are put to various uses. On the one hand, there is an attempt to dissolve the significance of sexual division – the argument that women are in some way 'naturally' different from men – in relation to the kinds of work that each might do and the payment that each should receive. Neatly sliding together analyses of gender and class, Marx and Aveling suggest that 'there is no more a "natural calling" of woman than there is a "natural" law of capitalistic production, or a "natural" limit to the amount of the labourer's product that goes to him for a means of subsistence' (7). On the other hand, 'nature' and 'the natural' remain as significant categories in relation to sex.

---

provided by Bryan Cheyette in his essay 'From Apology to Revolt: Benjamin Farjeon, Amy Levy and the Anglo-Jewish Novel, 1880–1900', *Transactions of the Jewish Historical Society of England*, 24 (1982–6), 253–65. In the last decade there has been an upsurge of critical interest in *Reuben Sachs*. Important studies include Bryan Cheyette, 'The Other Self: Anglo-Jewish Fiction and the Representation of Jews in England, 1875–1905', in *The Making of Modern Anglo-Jewry*, ed. by David Cesarani (Oxford: Blackwell, 1990), pp. 97–114; Meri-Jane Rochelson, 'Jews, Gender and Genre in Late-Victorian England: Amy Levy's *Reuben Sachs*', *Women's Studies*, 25 (1996), 311–28. I have learnt a great deal from conversations with Nadia Valman about this novel. Valman's reading of the text is to be published in *Jewish Culture and History*, 3 (2000).

[16] Kapp, II, 174–5, 260.

[17] Gillian Beer, *Darwin's Plots: Evolutionary Narrative in Darwin, George Eliot and Nineteenth-Century Fiction* (London: Routledge & Kegan Paul, 1983).

Much of the essay is concerned with what the authors argue are the deleterious effects upon women of a sexual double standard which condemns so many to celibacy. Statistics for the incidence of lunacy in a variety of European countries as cited by Bebel are scrutinized in order to draw out the point that unmarried women – a category which Marx and Aveling collapse into that of celibate women – are more likely to be insane than their married, that is sexually active, sisters (12–13). It is symptomatic of the pressure exerted by Darwinism on contemporary analysis that these statistics should be related to the issue of sexual behaviour (or the lack of it), rather than to the social and economic consequences for women of the failure to marry.

The Woman Question also considers the marital demography of England, pointing out that in 1870, forty-two per cent of women in the census were unmarried. Again, what is lamented is not the economic vulnerability of these women but the fact that they 'bear upon their brows this stamp of lost instincts, stifled affections, a nature in part murdered' (7). The granting to women of an active and demanding sexuality is a crucial move but it is legitimated by the invocation of a language of naturalness and unnaturalness, health and disease, which is morally loaded and prescriptive.

Marx and Aveling's sexual instinct remains Darwinian rather than proto-Freudian. There is no attempt to tie up sex with or reduce it to reproduction, although the question of reproduction seems to hover uneasily around the discussion. The essay defines chastity as 'the entire suppression of all instincts connected with the begetting of children' (13) but fails to mention children as a consequence of sexual activity at any other point. Sexual instinct is envisaged as having a direction and integrity thwarted and compromised by capitalism: 'It is time for men and women to recognise that the slaying of sex is always followed by disaster. Extreme passion is ill. But the opposite extreme of the sacrifice of healthy natural instinct is as ill' (13). An early commencement of sexual activity is favoured: 'Many of the working class marry young – that is at the natural period.' The essay is also highly critical of sexual anarchists who play fast and loose with gender identity:

> Two extreme forms of the distinction of the sexes that springs from ... their separation are ... the effeminate man and the masculine woman. These are two types from which even the average person recoils with a perfectly natural horror of the unnatural. (12)

I do not think we can reduce this description of the 'diseased forms' of sexuality brought about by capitalism to a simple attack on homosexuality. After all, as Alan Sinfield has shown, in the late 1880s effeminacy was not coterminous with homosexuality and, as a category, the lesbian was even less stable.[18] The more

---

18 Alan Sinfield, *The Wilde Century* (London: Cassell, 1994).

interesting point is that the formulation seeks to take hold of the Darwinian understanding of instinct as a force which, if left unimpeded, will result in development and progress. At present, under capitalism, 'the life of woman does not coincide with that of man. Their lives do not intersect; in many cases do not even touch. Hence the life of the race is stunted' (7).

If Marx and Aveling's Darwinism is an optimistic narrative of perfectibility and advance, Levy's Darwinism represents the other side of the coin, the pessimistic Darwinism of degeneration and extinction. The notion that the Jewish race has overbred and exhausted itself is central to the novel and to Levy's other writings about Anglo-Jewry of the decade.[19] Reuben Sachs's weak heart and nervous breakdown are only two examples of the mental and physical degeneracy which afflicts the community. Kohnthal, a former partner in Sachs and Co., the stockbroking firm which has made the fortunes of the Sachses and Leuningers, has been incarcerated in a lunatic asylum for ten years. Ernest, the eldest Leuninger brother, seems to be in danger of a similar ending: 'He was nervous, delicate; had a rooted aversion to society; and was obliged by the state of his health to spend the greater part of his time in the country.'[20] Ernest cannot cope with parties and devotes himself to morbid games of solitaire. Reuben's doctor tells him that over half of his patients with nervous diseases are Jews, who, in his opinion, 'pay the penalty of too high a civilisation'.[21]

Levy is primarily exploring the vicissitudes of 'racial' rather than 'sexual' instinct, but the discussion does inflect the feminism of the novel and its account of sexuality. Despite his own premature extinction, Reuben's philosophy includes a strong commitment to the survival and regeneration of the Jewish race. The novel makes it clear that an important aspect of Reuben and Judith's mutual attraction is the appeal of race: 'He praised her in the race, and the race in her ... Reuben ... fighting the battle for his people, seemed to her a figure noble and heroic beyond speech.'[22] Part of the tragedy of the failure of their relationship, and of the thwarting of Judith's sexual desires, is the thwarting of this racial instinct. Reuben knows, and the novel knows, that Judith, as a healthy, racially pure and superior Sephardic Jew, represents an opportunity for him to redeem and repair his own degenerate line, to contribute to the regeneration of the race, which he eschews in favour of material greed and social ambition. The text presents this as equally a racial and sexual failure, a racial failure caused by a sexual failure, giving rise to a eugenically-glossed feminism in which the subjection of Judith exacts the price not just of her individual suffering, but also that of the degeneration of her people.

[19] See in particular her story 'Cohen of Trinity', *Gentleman's Magazine*, 226 (1889), 417–24, in *Complete Novels*, pp. 478–85 and her essay 'Jewish Children', *Jewish Chronicle*, 5 November 1886 in *Complete Novels*, pp. 528–31.

[20] *Complete Novels*, p. 204.

[21] *Complete Novels*, p. 198.

[22] *Complete Novels*, p. 240.

This interest in deploying new social and sexual theory inspired by Darwinism exists in Marx and Aveling's essay, as it does in Levy's novel, alongside a continuing dependence upon the categories and arguments of early and mid-nineteenth-century liberal feminisms. Despite their declared disdain for liberal attitudes in *The Woman Question*, and the sharp distinction they draw between their own full economic analysis of women's oppression and the obfuscations of such as J.S. Mill, Marx and Aveling are not above drawing on the rhetorical force of Mill's image of marriage as a form of 'serfdom' (10). In *On the Subjection of Women* (1869), Mill had argued that upon marriage a woman becomes the 'bond-servant' of her husband. Marriage requires a woman to relinquish her property, her children and her person absolutely to the jurisdiction of her husband: 'no amount of ill-usage, without adultery superadded, will free her from her tormentor'.[23] Although Marx and Aveling complain that the feminist thinking and activity which has been inspired by Mill's liberalism is inadequate because it concentrates on 'property, or on sentimental or professional questions' and fails to 'get down through these to the economic basis' (5), their project is not as distant from Mill's as they might wish to think. As Susan Mendus stresses, Mill is concerned not only with making the case for the legal and political equality of women, but also with pointing the way towards the improvement of marriage into the state of intellectual companionship and social complementarity he believes it could and should be.[24] Mill argues that the perfect marriage is between

> two persons of cultivated faculties, identical in opinions and purposes, between whom there exists that best kind of equality, similarity of powers and capacities with reciprocal superiority in them – so that each can enjoy the luxury of looking up to the other, and can have alternately the pleasure of leading and of being led in the path of development ... I maintain with the profoundest conviction, that this, and only this, is the ideal of marriage, and that all opinions, customs and institutions which favour any other notion of it, or turn the conceptions and aspirations connected with it into any other direction, by whatever pretences they may be coloured, are relics of primitive barbarism.[25]

The means proposed by Marx and Aveling might differ from those advocated by Mill but the ultimate aim of heterosexual complementarity and the 'sentimental' rhetoric with which it is described in their essay is taken straight from his work. Similarly, Mary Wollstonecraft's advocacy of co-education in *Vindication of the Rights of Woman* is invoked (12) as part of a plea for integration and for frank

---

23 J.S. Mill, *On the Subjection of Women* (London: Virago, 1983), p. 59.

24 Susan Mendus, 'The Marriage of True Minds: The Ideal of Marriage in the Philosophy of John Stuart Mill', in *Sexuality and Subordination*, ed. by Susan Mendus and Jane Rendall (London and New York: Routledge, 1989).

25 Mill, 1983, p. 177.

discussion of sex by men and women together.[26] As Sally Ledger points out, during the mid-nineteenth century Wollstonecraft became 'liberal feminism's icon'.[27] The importance to *The Woman Question* of these earlier generations of liberal writers should not be underestimated.

Indeed, a comparison of *The Woman Question* with Marx's previous commentary on Bebel, a review of his *Woman in the Past, Present and Future,* which she wrote by herself and which appeared in the supplement to the *Commonweal,* the journal of the Socialist League in July 1885, suggests the extent to which her feminism could sustain itself without the Darwinian preoccupation with sexual instinct which permeates her co-authored work.[28] Whilst it would be quite wrong to suggest that Marx did not take full intellectual responsibility for all the writing to which she ascribed her name, an examination of the terms in which she discusses Bebel's text in her earlier review suggests the specific contribution that Aveling's research into Darwinism made to the perspective of *The Woman Question* and the different emphasis she gave to her feminism when writing alone.[29]

The *Commonweal* review was published in the same month as the *Maiden Tribute of Modern Babylon,* the exposure by the *Pall Mall Gazette* of the widespread sexual trade in little girls in Britain and Europe. As Judith Walkowitz describes, the account, published over four issues of the paper and relating in graphic and dramatic detail the means by which working-class girls, sometimes in their early teens or even younger, were coerced by drugging or physical force or by the penury of their families into prostitution, was 'one of the most successful pieces of scandal journalism of the nineteenth century'.[30] Both in this early review of Bebel and in a separate review of the *Maiden Tribute* which she published in the following issue of the *Commonweal,* in August 1885, Marx is greatly exercised by the issue of prostitution in a way which the later *The Woman Question* is not. In the August 1885 piece she congratulates the *Pall Mall Gazette* on its frank revelations of the problem of prostitution, but insists that parliamentary measures, including the raising of the age of consent from thirteen to sixteen and the enforcing of stiffer penalties for pimping, are inadequate. The purpose of her article is to make a specifically socialist intervention into the problem of prostitution:

---

[26] Mary Wollstonecraft, *Vindication of the Rights of Woman* (Harmondsworth: Penguin, 1983).

[27] Ledger, 1997, p. 37.

[28] Eleanor Marx Aveling, 'Review: *Woman in the Past, Present and Future* by August Bebel (From the German, by H.B. Adams-Walther)', in Supplement to the *Commonweal,* August 1885, pp. 63–4. Subsequent page references are given in the text.

[29] See for example *The Student's Darwin* (London: Freethought Publishing Co., 1881), *Darwinism and Small Families* (London: Besant & Bradlaugh, 1882), and *The Gospel of Evolution* (London: Freethought Publishing Co., 1884). Aveling's scientific Darwinism is discussed in William Greenslade's essay in this volume.

[30] Judith Walkowitz, *City of Dreadful Delight: Narratives of Sexual Danger in Late-Victorian London* (Chicago: University of Chicago Press), 1992, p. 81.

The old Communist manifesto of 1848, our own manifesto of 1885, equally declare that under the present unnatural *régime* we must expect unnatural crimes ...

I maintain that we Socialists alone are truly practical, because we alone dare to go to the root of the ill. Ask a doctor to cure a patient living under absolutely unhealthy conditions in the midst of pestilential air and unsanitary surroundings. He will tell you must change these surroundings if you would save the life of the individual. We but apply to many, to all individuals – i.e. to society – what the doctor applies to the one. We say so long as the human beings are the slaves they are now – whether they be slaves of wealth or of poverty – this disease must continue ... Abolish the *cause* of the disease and the disease will disappear. Why do these poor little children sell themselves? *Because they and their belongings are poor.* They want the money for bread which certain rich individuals, who buy them as they would any other commodity, can give them. And so long as there is a class that must sell its labour power – and the labour power of the poor takes many forms – so long must this iniquity continue.[31]

It is notable that the concepts of nature and the unnatural, of health and disease, are deployed here for a very different purpose than that for which they are used in *The Woman Question*. In the joint work with Aveling the terms are focused on the question of the thwarting of sexual instinct, the 'unnaturalness' of celibacy for women. Here the emphasis is upon the evil and 'unnatural' consequences that follow when women are compelled into (the wrong kind of) sex. Similarly, in her review of Bebel in the previous issue of the *Commonweal*, the issue of sexual instinct is of far less importance than it will have become by 1886. The emphasis of her remarks is upon the need for equal access to education and to labour for women in order to allow them to become fully equal with men in the Socialist state. Her remarks on the question of sexual relations concentrate on Bebel's analysis of marriage and prostitution as two sides of the same coin and the deleterious effects upon women of the stark alternative of markets in which to sell themselves. The concept of sexual instinct is raised, for the only time in this article, in a quotation from Bebel, but his emphasis, which Marx pursues, is on the iniquity of a male sexual instinct gratifying itself by means of the commodification of women. This is more reminiscent of Levy's analysis in her poem 'A Ballad of Religion and Marriage' than the thwarted and deranged female celibates of *The Woman Question*:

The modern *bourgeois* property-marriage 'is regarded by most women as a kind of almshouse ... and the man, for his part, generally counts up the advantages of marriage with the greatest exactitude ... marriage represents one half of the sexual life of the *bourgeois* world and prostitution represents the other. Marriage is the front, and prostitution is the back of the medal.

---

31 Eleanor Marx Aveling, 'The *Pall Mall Gazette*', in Supplement to the *Commonweal*, July 1885, pp. 69–70.

> When a man finds no satisfaction in marriage he generally resorts to prostitution, and when a man for one reason or another remains unmarried, it is again prostitution to which he has recourse. Provision is thus made for men who are celibates by choice or force, as well as for those whom marriage has disappointed, to gratify their sexual instincts in a manner forbidden to women'. (63–4)

Between Marx's first and second commentary upon Bebel, the concept of sexual instinct has changed its emphasis, from something male, dangerous and profoundly implicated with capitalism, to something female and healthy which will be released by socialism.

In addition, the issue of children, repressed in *The Woman Question*, is allowed to surface in the earlier review. Bebel's text engages in aggressive dialogue with Malthus (whom he abominates) and with the question of the implications for population growth of socialism. Marx focuses upon Bebel's assertion that socialism will act as a 'natural' means of regulating population because, when women gain equality and are in a position to choose for themselves the size of their families, they will prefer to keep them small, thus solving the problem of overpopulation. Marx also dwells on Bebel's cheering observations about the joyful experience which motherhood will become in a socialist society. Under socialism, a woman's 'household and her children, if she has any, cannot restrict her freedom, but only increase her pleasure in life. Educators, friends, young girls, are all at hand for cases in which she needs help'.[32] Kapp notes that Eleanor had a great fondness for children and suggests that the fact that her union with Aveling did not produce a family was a matter of sadness to her; she also attributes the failure to produce children to Aveling.[33] One cannot help feeling that the excision of the question of children and mothering from the later essay is a significant repression which bespeaks tension in the partnership of the authors.

In *The Woman Question*, as in the writings of Amy Levy, the deployment of Darwinian categories comes at a price. The essay grants women an active sexuality through the language of instinct, but forces both women and men into prescriptive and restrictive gender identities. The horror which Marx's earlier essay directs at prostitution becomes relocated in *The Woman Question* on to the deviation from gender norms of 'the feminine man and the masculine woman'. Levy, with her more pessimistic view of sexual relations between women and men, is less concerned to shore up a prophecy of the redemption of heterosexuality with a prescriptive account of 'naturalness' of sexual division. If 'A Ballad of Religion

---

[32] 'Review: *Woman in the Past, Present and Future*', p. 64.

[33] Kapp, II, 76. Kapp points out that whilst there can be no conclusive proof that the fertility problems were on Aveling's side, his 'early marriage had been without issue and never in a life of extensive lechery and an era of primitive contraception is a paternity suit ever known to have been brought against him, from which it would not be unfair to draw the conclusion that he was sterile'.

and Marriage' envisages a rampant male sexuality then some of her later lyrics explore an anarchic and ambivalent femininity which slips the noose of organizing repressions, and might be regarded as amongst the most significant 'lesbian' poetry of the late nineteenth century.[34] But Levy's attempt to harness discourses of racial degeneration in order to substantiate her feminism is equally problematic for modern political sensibilities, activating as it does allo-Semitism and even anti-Semitism.[35] We need to think further about Marx's feminist writings and about her relationships with other significant feminist thinkers and activists of the later nineteenth century, such as Olive Schreiner and Clementina Black, both in order to understand the important contribution that she made to feminist intellectual history and to confront afresh the implications of the developments of this crucial period for the dialogue between feminism and socialism and the accounts of gender and sexuality that underpin it.

---

[34] See Emma Francis, 'Amy Levy: Contradictions? – Feminism and Semitic Discourse', in *Women's Poetry, Late Romantic to Late Victorian: Gender and Genre, 1830–1900*, ed. by Isobel Armstrong and Virginia Blain (Basingstoke: Macmillan, 1999), pp. 183–204. Particularly relevant in this context is the 'Love, Dreams and Death' sequence in her final collection of poetry, *A London Plane-Tree and Other Verse* (London: Cameo, 1890).

[35] Allo-Semitism is a term invoked by Bryan Cheyette in *Constructions of the Jew in English Literature and Society* (Cambridge: Cambridge University Press, 1993), p. 8. He argues it is useful in designating discourses which define the Jew simply as other (rather than anti-Semitic discourse which is actively hostile to the Jew).

Chapter 9

'Is this Friendship?':
Eleanor Marx, Margaret Harkness and
the Idea of Socialist Community

Lynne Hapgood

An examination of the friendship between Eleanor Marx and Margaret Harkness gives us a chance to reflect on two closely related aspects of radical life in the London of the 1880s. One is the potential for a new kind of relationship between intelligent, educated women in the socialist arena. The other is the representation of political events in literature – in this case Margaret Harkness's novels, which were partly constructed as a private dialogue with herself, as a means of dealing with the perceived failure of comradeship and, by association, of the socialist community. Both areas present difficulties for the researcher. Historical documentation tends to focus on major events and dominant personalities so that there is an unevenness in the personal record (considerable information about Eleanor Marx; very little about Margaret Harkness, mostly second hand) while novels are notoriously unreliable witnesses to the reality they purport to invoke. In the turbulent atmosphere of the 1880s, when London socialists were few in number, high in profile and zealous in action, it was probably inevitable that the two women should encounter one another. Viewed through the long lens of the history of socialism, or even through the narrower focus of Eleanor Marx's life, their relationship is shadowy and brief, obscured by many others, better known and more fully documented. Even so, reuniting them now promises a distinctive insight into the impact of social and ideological contexts upon individual lives.

In this essay I shall argue that the manner, context and outcomes of the exchange between Marx and Harkness provide an unexpected and illuminating focus on a fundamental conflict for socialist women: the relationship of their public personae to their personal and emotional lives. This was always exacerbated by socialist ambivalence towards women's political role. A Marxist analysis centred on the processes of production and the division of labour had both theoretical problems and practical difficulties when it came to linking class conflict with gender struggle. As the socialist-feminist Ursula Vogel was to express the continuing conflict nearly a hundred years later, in the 1980s: 'love would seem to stand in polar opposition to, and in clear separation from, politics'.[1] If we understand 'love' to cover the network of emotional and sexual feelings, of affection and loyalty, usually associated with the private world, one way of understanding the difficulties Victorian socialist activists faced, and of investigating the friendship between Marx and Harkness, would be to think of it in terms of their attempts to politicize 'love'.

Although both women were socialists, their political experiences were entirely different. Socialism, as we all know, was Marx's life: the intellectual, social and emotional context of her growing up. Harkness's sense of community was also shaped by her early family experiences, but in reaction, a personal quest which began against the background of a country rectory. The daughter of a conventional Church of England parish priest who was completely at odds with his high-spirited and intellectually powerful child, she was born into a family circle within which she never felt comfortable or valued. As her socialist convictions developed, family tensions increased. In 1883, after she decided to give up nursing training at the London Hospital, her father cut all links with her and withdrew her allowance. They were never reconciled. Twenty-nine and unmarried, Harkness had been effectively orphaned by her failure to conform and by her political beliefs.

Long before 1883, she had confided her sense of alienation in letters to Beatrice Potter (later the Fabian social scientist, Beatrice Webb), her slightly younger second cousin and for a time, close friend. She wrote of her isolation again, just before she met Marx, with the illuminating comment: 'I read the papers and have a little political world of my own'.[2] Driven to earn her own living, she settled in London and, after some false starts, survived through journalism and later through novel-writing, a familiar strategy of middle-class female economic necessity not entirely unfamiliar to Marx. As she struggled to work out her role in achieving social justice now and socialism in the future, to understand the conditions of labour for men and women and to resolve the tensions between the religious beliefs she had inherited and the prevailing secularism around her, she moved, drifted or was pushed from friend to friend and from group to group. Sometimes she thought she had found friendship and political sympathy; at other times only a sense of betrayal and misdirection.

Harkness's personal dream of a socialist society, it seems, lay in the transformation of 'a little political world of my own' into a common political vision, and in the transformation of 'wrong and idiotic' words into shared discourse of political concern, and finally in the transformation of the bourgeois family from which she had been rejected into the socialist 'family' or community.

---

[1]   Ursula Vogel, 'Rationalism and Romanticism: Two Strategies for Women's Liberation', in *Feminism and Political Theory*, ed. by J. Evans, et al. (Sage: London, 1986), p. 39.

[2]   Letter to Beatrice, 3 February 1880, item 49, in the Passfield Collection of Beatrice Webb's and Harkness's correspondence in the British Library of Political and Economic Sciences, London School of Economics. See also items 37 and 45.

As far as we know, despite her commitment to socialism, she always remained an outsider, never achieving a unity of personal identity and public community, except for brief and what turned out to be largely delusory moments. Our piecemeal knowledge of her history seems to reflect the fragmentation of her identity rather than to construct it. She is frequently referred to in contemporary sources which present a mixed bag of allegations and accusations, insults and criticisms: occasionally there are counterpointing comments of praise and recognition. Most of these references are in the letters and diaries of political activists (notably Beatrice Webb's), but there are a few of Harkness's own letters, a small portfolio of her articles and reports and, more revealingly, her novels, to which I shall return later.[3]

When Harkness first met Marx, sometime in 1883–4, her belief in the possibility of community still existed. Engels was to initiate their relationship since Harkness could show Marx around and introduce her first-hand to the conditions of work and workers. We do not know exactly when Engels met Harkness. He read a copy of her second published novel, *A City Girl*, which was published by Vizetelly in 1887. Perhaps his enthusiastic and expansive response in a letter to her was the catalyst for their meeting.[4] Even if, at this point, she was little more than a convenient tool, he clearly trusted that her political perspective, her knowledge of the East End and her relationships with workers were valuable and relevant resources to tap. At any rate we do know that during 1888 Harkness was part of Engels's circle,[5] and that when Marx put her theatrical aspirations on hold and began her own social exploration, they spent many hours roaming the East End together as well as with other friends and associates.

The two women met at a crucial period in both their lives. Marx had been living openly with Aveling for some time. She seems to have come to terms with the failed hopes of that relationship and the intense personal unhappiness it had caused her, and was redirecting her political energies under Engels's guidance.[6] Harkness had entered one of the most satisfying periods of her life – her second novel had been published by a celebrated publisher and she too had found political direction working and researching in the East End, as well as a sense of socialist community centred on Engels. As women who met ostensibly because of shared political convictions and a shared political vision, and who, at thirty-three and thirty-four years old respectively, had both reached a point of mature independence, they appear to offer a possible paradigm for friendship between socialist women – that is, the kind of friendship envisioned by Hannah Arendt: a

---

3   See the Margaret Harkness entry by Joyce Bellamy and Beatie Caspar in *Dictionary of Labour Biography, Vol. VIII*, ed. by Joyce Bellamy and John Saville (Basingstoke: Macmillan, 1988), pp. 103–12.
4   Letter of Engels to Harkness, April 1888, in *Marxists on Literature: An Anthology*, ed. by David Craig (Harmondsworth: Penguin, 1975), pp. 269–71.
5   Hyndman names Harkness as a member of the 'Marxist clique' in *Justice*, 28 February 1891.
6   See Kapp, II, 261ff.

relationship not located in a family relationship or a private domestic world but an equal partnership in a community shared by all its members.[7]

And perhaps there were moments of real communion. One characteristic of Margaret's which Beatrice Potter frequently mentions in early diary entries is the genuine compassion she feels for anyone who is suffering and her selfless effort in trying to ameliorate other people's pain.[8] This love of her fellow men and women was at the heart of her socialism and this was the feeling aroused in Marx during her social explorations too. According to Yvonne Kapp, a personal response to the poor and their suffering, and a sense of identification with working peoples' struggles, were opened up to Marx for the first time as she roamed the East End and witnessed the conditions under which so many thousands of men, women and children had to live. In the East End, Yvonne Kapp suggests, something 'extraordinary' happened to her:

> it is the truth that not until now – she was 33 years of age – did Eleanor cross the line between serving a cause and identifying herself with the men and women that cause was intended to serve: the anger and pity she had always felt were crystallised. From now on the seal was set upon her friendship with working men and women.[9]

Marx was the not the first or the last to be profoundly affected by her experiences of poverty in the raw. But another factor was surely the companionship of an equally committed woman deeply moved by the consequences of social injustice and determined to put them right. I have little doubt that the love of humanity which Marx discovered could link the different perspectives of political theory and political practice, was encouraged and shared by Harkness. Her experiences might also have given a political logic to love, extending compassion, commitment and loyalty to the larger community.

What kind of relationship these women developed over the following year is lost to us, eclipsed by the accounts of Marx's political work, her relationship with Aveling and her extended family, and other friendships. The pair re-emerge into the light of history again in their common involvement in the Great Dock Strike of August 1889.

Unexpected and unplanned as it was in Socialist circles, militant Trade Unionists and activists seized the moment to organize thousands of casual labourers. In the back room of 'The Wades Arms' in Poplar, the Strike Committee almost literally bedded in. For five intense weeks, as support came in from the general public and from around the world, and established unions threw their

---

[7]   See Ray Pahl, 'Friendship: the Social Glue of Contemporary Society?', in *The Politics of Risk Society*, ed. by Jane Franklin (London: Polity Press, 1998), pp. 99–119 (p. 109).

[8]   This sense of Harkness's kindness remained unchanged. See *The Diary of Beatrice Webb. Vol. 1 1873–1892. Glitter Around and Darkness Within*, ed. by Norman and Jeanne MacKenzie (London: Virago, 1982), pp. 279, 341, 303.

[9]   Kapp, II, 261.

weight behind the dockers in their confrontation with their employers, the strike held firm until the Dockyard owners, guided by the mediation of Cardinal Manning, agreed to the dockers' terms.[10] Working closely with the committee in 'The Wades Arms' were volunteers, among them Aveling, who came and went, and, in the background, Marx and Harkness, who stayed hour after hour, providing political advice, and administrative and emotional support where it was most useful.

The break-up of the intense comradeship and sense of community which characterized the Strike Committee, and the subsequent parting of the political ways for some of the participants, left Harkness temporarily distraught and stranded. For her, the loss of community outweighed the victory of the political struggle. We know from a letter from Beatrice Potter to Richard Garnett that she was in a desperate emotional state at this time and Beatrice later recorded a visit from Harkness in her diary with irritation and considerable contempt at what she saw as her hysterical and self-important inflation of her own role in the strike. By the end of 1889, about a month after the strike had finished, the personal relationship between Marx and Harkness was formally and publicly closed as well. Sometime in mid-November 1889 Harkness refused to enter Engels's house because Aveling was there. Engels, who had originally introduced the two women to one another, now – acting almost like a stage manager – terminated their relationship.[11]

In making her stand Harkness must have known that she risked her affiliation with the whole 'Marxist clique' as well as any possibility of maintaining her friendship with Eleanor Marx. We do not know what it was she felt so strongly about that she was prepared to take that chance. Whether she had been influenced by Olive Schreiner's tirades about Aveling[12] or whether she was acting on other well-circulated information or whether, as Bernstein suggested, she had suffered some insult at Aveling's hands herself, we have no idea.[13] Whatever the reason, and whatever Marx's reaction might have been (she had never rejected Aveling's critics before), Harkness was from this point outside the 'clique'. Within a month, she had lost two communities – the Strike Committee and the Engels circle – although in neither case, apparently, for ideological reasons.[14]

---

[10] There are many accounts of the Dock Strike 1889 in Labour history. The account produced closest to the events is H. Llewellyn Smith and Vaughan Nash, *The Story of the Dockers' Strike* (London: T. Fisher Unwin, 1889).

[11] Indeed, according to W.O. Henderson, Engels's support of Aveling and his misguided faith in him, long after he realized his inadequacies as a socialist leader, had 'fateful consequences' for the socialist movement as a whole. Harkness was not, of course, Aveling's only critic. See W.O. Henderson, *The Life of Friedrich Engels, Vol. 2* (London: Frank Cass, 1976), p. 685.

[12] As Kapp suggests, II, 261.

[13] Bernstein (1921). Cited in Henderson, p. 202.

[14] Letter from Engels to Laura Lafargue, 16 November 1889 in *F. Engels and Laura Lafargue Correspondence: Volumes I–III, 1959–1963* (London: Moscow Publishing Company and Lawrence & Wishart, 1960), II, 344.

Records of events pass down through history with a seeming clarity and continuity, creating their own hierarchies of contributory factors, social significances and *dramatis personae*. Motivations and responses can be less clear. Trying to trace the role of those individuals designated to be bit players is even harder, while speculating about their individual responses, reactions, antipathies and sympathies moves on to dangerously subjective ground. Yet, even after reminding ourselves of all the limitations which fence interpretation round, the diminishing and eventual termination of the friendship between Marx and Harkness, for all their close proximity and shared political cause, points to a fundamental failure in the fabric of the socialist community. Despite a revolutionary ideology (and even gradualist socialist groups such as the Fabians were in pursuit of revolutionary social change) and despite outward signs of social rebellion, the operations of early socialist groups and campaigns appear to have significantly replicated the existing social structures, tragically failing to transcend bourgeois criteria of class and economic standing, or to reconfigure gender relations. As Ray Pahl argues, 'one of the strongest barriers to pure friendship is structurally conditioned inequality'.[15] It certainly seems likely that Marx's and Harkness's shared identity as middle-class, educated women was mediated, in the mode of bourgeois judgement, by subtleties of different backgrounds and economic standing which would prove more powerful than a shared political objective. Harkness's attachment to any socialist group was always tenuous and contingent on events beyond her control. Sometimes she appeared to have found a foothold in the socialist community only for it to disappear thanks to the turn of political events and changes of allegiances which left her once again on the outside, not just of a political haven but of a class structure dominated by the British upper class and/or an intellectual expatriate élite.

A further obstacle proved to be her own poverty. From 1883, she had been completely self-supporting, usually struggling against lack of funds and having to write to finance her political activities. Many comments about her at this time refer unkindly to her penury. Beatrice Potter, who had an independent income from her successful, entrepreneurial father, reports several small loans and warns another friend to secrecy about her own earnings because 'it makes her [Harkness] so jealous'.[16] Olive Schreiner, who occasionally formed a trio with Marx and Margaret in their explorations of the East End, comments on Harkness's tendency to shadow her every movement.[17] Of the three friends who spent time together in 1888, Marx's and Schreiner's friendship was of longer standing and known to be intensely shared: Harkness would again feel the poor relation. There is a

---

15 Pahl, p. 113.
16 *The Letters of Sidney and Beatrice Webb, Vol. 1*, ed. by Norman Mackenzie (Cambridge: University Press, 1978). See entry for mid-August 1890, p. 177.
17 S.C. Cronwright-Schreiner, *Life of Olive Schreiner* (London: Fisher Unwin, 1924), p. 176. Extract from Schreiner's diary for 4 February 1887.

cumulative sense of a woman constrained by her need to work and by her small means, yet unable to find a foothold in the desired socialist community which would transform class and economic relations. There is an interesting connection here with Aveling's claim that the advent of Socialism would end his poverty and therefore his need to borrow, yet whose financial demands on Marx ultimately threatened her with the poverty he hated.[18] Aveling's argument might be spurious, but it contains sufficient ideological bite to challenge the attitudes of Schreiner and Webb.

There was also a tendency to replicate domestic hierarchies and roles in the political battle. Marx, whose grasp of the ideas behind the formulation of socialism was second to none and who never lost touch with the broader issues, became less and less sure about what she could contribute to socialism as an ideology, and the friendship of individuals became more and more important to her. With the death of Marx (1884) and Engels (1895) and the break-up of her family community, she drew closer to her sister Laura; with her resignation from the Gasworkers Union in 1895, Kapp suggests, she lost touch with the socialist community as a whole in much the same way as Harkness had done at the end of the Dock Strike.[19] The fact that she taught Ben Tillett, one of the leading Trade Union agitators in the 1880s, to read, earning his undying gratitude is a touching if disturbing vignette of the contribution that women felt able to make. Her devotion in supporting and nursing Aveling in the last years of her life, as she had nursed her father until he died, all the while trying to maintain her socialist activities, is a familiar story of Victorian daughters. We have fewer details about Harkness, but many of them suggest that her kindness and compassion to those in trouble were her best and most distinguishing characteristics. It seems that the political energies of these women increasingly needed an emotional and humanist rationale, and in its absence, they had to function as divided selves, pursuing the ideological struggle for social justice with the socialist self while trying to find a role within that framework for the female self.

The perpetuation of traditional female roles is made clear by the part played by Marx and Harkness during the Great Dock Strike. The political focus on male casual labour in the dockyards, and the role of the Unions, effectively displaced them from front-line action. We know from Tom Mann that Marx contributed to the economic debates, but their daily and nightly role was as clerks and counsellors. After the strike, it was the commitment and selflessness of both women to the service of the all-male Strike Committee which was singled out for mention, although (strangely, considering the smallness of the group), neither woman is linked with the other in any account of these dramatic times. In the formal statement issued when the strike was over, Harkness is thanked for her

---

[18] Tsuzuki, p. 328.

[19] Kapp considers this to be a major contributory factor to her decision to commit suicide. See II, 707–8.

contribution, particularly for her 'assistance to the men', and specifically for her role in involving Cardinal Manning in the eventual resolution of the strike.[20] But the most spontaneous expressions of respect, affection and gratitude go to Marx, whose glowing tributes in the personal memoirs of Tom Mann, Ben Tillett and Will Thorne testify to the completeness of her womanly sympathy in her ability to identify herself 'with the men and women that the cause was intended to serve' and to enter their lives.[21] The women's personal interactions during those intense weeks are subsumed by the drama of great events, and their back-room role reveals much about the ambiguity of their position as activists. We can only speculate whether insights into the nature of the relationship between Marx and Harkness were displaced or obscured by the dominance of the male actors at centre stage and by the drama of what was seen as a step forward in the progress of socialism. Perhaps they were divided by the complex tensions caused by emotional ties: at this point, Harkness was very close to H.H. Champion who, in his turn, was suspected of marginalizing Marx.[22] Whatever the reason, by this time their contact appears to have become simply coincidental, structured by the ideological closeness of shared political strategies and objectives but divided by the co-option of their energies into individual campaigns, by their subsequently changing loyalties and by gender roles that had barely changed.

However, these fragments of information, falling on different sides of the private/public divide, point to a model of socialist identity which illustrates the difficulties, often the pain and anguish, facing women activists in the late nineteenth century.[23] Of all these women, the case of Marx is the best known. Celebrated in Tillett's memoirs as having the potential to be 'a greater women's leader than the greatest of contemporary women',[24] Marx's human warmth was recognized by all who worked closely with her. She never lost faith or energy in her political activities, but was slowly undermined and isolated by the loss of her family and the destructive and loveless relationship with Aveling. Despite all her apparent advantages, her 'misfortune was that she had invested love and hope and received nothing in return'.[25] She would appear to have gambled on politicizing a sexual partnership in socialism, and to have lost.

Beatrice Potter, who gives us our clearest and most consistent picture of Harkness, also provides a comparable example of the difficulty of keeping her

---

[20] C. Tsuzuki, *Tom Mann: the Challenge of Labour* (Oxford: Oxford University Press, 1991), p. 67.

[21] Kapp, II, 702.

[22] See *Dictionary of Labour Biography*, p. 107; letter from Engels to Lafargue, 17 October 1889 in *Correspondence*, p. 330.

[23] See my discussion in 'The Novel and Political Agency: Socialism and the Work of Margaret Harkness, Constance Howell and Clementina Black, 1888–96', in *Literature and History*, 3rd Series, 5 (1996), pp. 37–54.

[24] Will Thorne, *My Life's Battles* (London: George Newnes, c. 1925), p. 149.

[25] Tsuzuki, p. 327.

friendship. The intimacy and trust of youth were gradually eroded by Beatrice's success and by her closed-circuit relationship with Sidney Webb, whom she married in 1892. Beatrice attributes this to Harkness's jealousy and unstable temper, and is dismissive of her literary and political achievements. In a striking diary entry in 1889 she records the failure of her friendship with Harkness (and of her friendship with Mary Booth, Charles Booth's wife) in terms which convey with painful clarity the tension between love and politics:

> When you must face life alone, it is better not to deceive yourself with an apparent one-ness of thought of feeling. It can only be temporary; the circumstances of life are too utterly different; there is no real communion of interests and therefore there can be no permanent tie ... Religious feeling, communion with unknown spirits, beings without eyes, creatures of your own imagination who are to you always what you would have them be, are the only safe companions to the lonely mind.[26]

No doubt this knowledge pushed Beatrice toward choosing the kind of relationship that she established with Webb. Her reward was to become the most acclaimed, established and influential woman socialist of her time. Along the way, she sacrificed her passion for Joseph Chamberlain and lost the friendship of not only Harkness but also Mary Booth. She resisted debates on the Woman Question at the Fabian Society and the right of suffrage for women until the turn of the twentieth century. She records the only negative personal account I have come across of Eleanor Marx.[27] In seeking success in a socialist future that in the present stubbornly remained a man's world, she appears to have turned her back, albeit reluctantly, on women. Yet though female friendship failed to save Marx and Harkness in the 1880s, and was to be spurned by Webb later on, for many other early women activists it provided a way of surmounting personal histories, personal tensions and divergences, offering a common cause, a plank across the treacherous quicksand of socialist solidarity.

I have already commented on the unevenness of the historical record in tracing and understanding the friendship of Marx and Harkness. The balance is partially restored by Harkness's novels which shed further light on the private/public dilemma and which, to some extent, tell her side of the story. It is this second perspective – the literary text as surrogate friend and alternative political world – which I now want to discuss. Although from 1883 Harkness used writing as a source of income, her novels are part of her fight for social justice. Like other Victorian women novelists, she used novels rather than public speaking to inform society and to contribute to the debates.

Harkness's novels are quite different from the other slum novels and social problem novels which were so popular at the time in that they have a

---

26   *Diaries, Vol. 1*, entry for 21 February 1889, p. 273.
27   *Diaries, Vol. 1*, pp. 87–8.

distinctiveness which has been categorized by P.J. Keating as 'ideological'.[28] Several of her books contain another, more oblique register as well. I believe that her fictions, however radical their stance on social issues in relation to their readers, provided an uncontentious, safe haven for their author. Within them, she created the 'little political world of my own' which she had nurtured since her isolated young womanhood and which, in the text, runs parallel to and appears to offer a commentary upon her actual socialist activities. She achieves this 'double writing' by handing authorial identity over to 'John Law' (the pseudonym she wrote under), and by entering the narrative as a character who is a 'friend' of the central protagonist.[29] I would further argue that the logic underlying the double identity of 'John Law' and Margaret Harkness was not just the familiar Victorian convention by which women writers felt obliged to adopt strong male pseudonyms, but rather an acknowledgement of the split between the broader socialist analysis of society constructed by the novel's form ('John Law', the structuring male agent) and an individual's personal compassion and concern (Margaret Harkness, the female participant).

This split presupposes a initial conflict between two warring perspectives. Michel Foucault has written about such divisions with considerable insight, showing how it is possible to express impermissible thoughts within a forbidding narrative structure. One of the methods he identifies 'consists of subjecting an utterance [in this case, narrative fiction], which appears to conform to the accepted code [social problem realism] to another code [private voice] whose key is contained within that same utterance so that this utterance becomes divided within itself [author/character]'.[30]

To illustrate how such divisions and strategies operate in Harkness's work, I will look first at a chapter called 'Among the Socialists' in Captain Lobe, written after A City Girl and published in instalments in 1888 before its book publication in 1889.[31] This chapter was being composed while Harkness was at her closest to the Engels household and as she showed Marx around the East End. At precisely the time when she was at her most engaged in the daily reality of socialist politics, she was exploring in her writing what she perceived to be the fundamental weaknesses of the socialist movement: a gaping fissure between theory and practice; between conviction and feeling; between the power of the collective and the uniqueness of the individual.

---

[28] P.J. Keating, *The Working Classes in Victorian Fiction* (London: Routledge, 1972), p. 245.

[29] Robert Caserio in his essay 'G.K. Chesterton and the Terrorist God Outside Modernism', in *Outside Modernism: in Pursuit of the English Novel, 1900–1930*, ed. by Lynne Hapgood and Nancy L. Paxton (Basingstoke: Macmillan, 2000), explores this fictional strategy for registering double meaning.

[30] Michel Foucault, 'Madness, the Absence of Work', *Critical Inquiry*, 21 (1995), 290–98 (p. 294).

[31] John Law, *Captain Lobe: A Story of the Salvation Army* (London: Hodder & Stoughton, 1889).

Captain Lobe is an intriguing novel which has not yet been fully appreciated by critics. Published in the same twelve months as *The Fabian Essays*, Charles Booth's first two volumes of *The Life and Labour of the People in London: East End* and the first instalments of William Morris's *News from Nowhere*, it belongs with a whole range of contemporary approaches to immediate social issues. The central character is a politically naive, spiritually generous and morally accepting Salvation Army officer whose innocent eye provides powerful insights into the nature of poverty and the different ways in which various institutions and individuals were responding to it. The religious affiliation of the central character has probably skewed responses to what seems to me to be an unequivocally socialist novel, although it is certainly not socialist propaganda nor is its vestigial narrative even told from a socialist viewpoint. It is far more profoundly socialist in that its structure decentres contemporary power fields – the church, individualism, philanthropy and charity, gender identities, and political slogans – to reveal the extent of the social exclusion of voice, identity and power from beneath.

In one of the incidental conversations in 'Among the Socialists', anxieties about the socialist project are aired in a long, discursive discussion between an unnamed middle-class woman social worker and Captain Lobe. Their comments are triggered when they hear a socialist agitator talking and catch the cry of 'class oppression'. The conversation takes place as a counterpoint to the inappropriateness of such socialist jargon to the poor and unemployed. The Captain, whose impulse is religious and whose moral purpose is an example of simple goodness and compassion, is entirely unpoliticized. His 'innocent' questions are used to open up the conflicts between the differing rationales of religious and political activity, and conflict between the principles of socialism and the practice of socialists. In a tone of weary helplessness, the unnamed 'lady' admits she is a socialist but that she is frustrated by the socialists' lack of achievement, their internal bickering and in-fighting, and their unrealistic objectives. Even so, she strongly claims that socialism is intellectually correct and that socialism is

> in the air, it is touching everyone and tingeing everything. Many who abhor the name are greater Socialists than those who hold socialistic tenets … With their help Socialism is growing every day, both the sentiment and the economic theory. What it will be in time no one can tell. At present its most helpful sign is an embryonic labour-party. This party is spreading all over the United Kingdom.[32]

It is not impossible that Harkness attempted to share doubts similar to those expressed by this fictional character with Marx, a like-minded activist of her own age witnessing for the first time the poverty and degradation of London's

---

[32] John Law, *Captain Lobe*, p. 158.

underbelly. We know that Marx was becoming increasingly irritated with the factionalism around her at this time.[33] Yet the structure of the chapter and its subsequent history may indicate the difficulties or even dangers of such a conversation. For the unnamed middle-class socialist lady who speaks confidentially to Captain Lobe goes so far as to criticize Hyndman and his Social Democratic Federation (SDF) by name, deploring the incestuous nature of socialist journals such as *Justice* and suggesting that the socialists have lost their way.

If Harkness hoped that 'the little political world of her own' would be protected by its fictional framework, she was wrong. After the novel's publication, the reaction of those members of the SDF circle who knew her was a bitter sense of betrayal. It is possible that Marx also reacted angrily for, despite her own break with the SDF and the constant ideological wranglings of the Engels and Hyndman circles, Hyndman remained in touch with her until her death. Harkness was so distressed that in April of 1889 she wrote to *Justice* herself (and therefore to the audience she had criticized in the novel), claiming that she had tried unsuccessfully to withdraw the chapter before publication. Whether she had in fact tried or now simply wanted to placate her former socialist colleagues, we cannot be sure, but one comment is particularly illuminating. 'We are not a happy family ... To find oneself without a relation or a friend because one is by conviction a Socialist, and then to have vials of wrath poured on one's head, by Socialists, makes one inclined to curse.'[34] Disowned by her blood family as 'idiotic and wrong', able to explore her doubts only through coded 'utterances', and then disowned by her socialist 'family' for daring to question or criticize, she hit a period of misery. The desperation with which she responded to criticisms and personal attacks suggests not just difference of opinion but also the vulnerability she felt when her secret code had been deciphered by the enemy within socialism.

George Eastmont, Wanderer of 1905 is very different from the novels that Harkness wrote in the 1880s and early 1890s. Rather than being a novel which 'co-operates in the social thought and mood of its time' (to use H.G. Wells's phrase),[35] it is an historical novel, and its dedication locates its quasi-fictional status. It tells the story of George Eastmont against the background of the activities of the labour movement from the unemployment demonstrations of the mid-1880s through the great Dock Strike in 1889 to Land Settlement projects and union organization in Australia. The innovatory socialist structure of her earlier novels drops away, leaving a conventional narrative of events with a brooding, romantic aristocratic hero. The major characters – with one exception, the woman strike supporter, Mary Cameron – are thinly disguised versions of

---

[33] Kapp, II, 264.

[34] *Justice*, 20 April 1889, p. 3.

[35] H.G. Wells, 'The Contemporary Novel' (1891) cited in Samuel Hynes, *Edwardian Occasions* (London: Routledge & Kegan Paul, 1972), p. 6.

some of the main players in the Dock Strike: Cardinal Manning, Tom Mann and H.H. Champion. The novel is 'about' socialism but it is not a socialist novel. It demonstrates the collapse of collectivity into individualism, the re-emergence of old class lines, and the equivocal nature of working-class victories subsidized by upper-class money and mediated by employers and church leaders, through a narrative based on labour events in the 1880s. Immediately after the Dock Strike finished Harkness had given Beatrice Webb 'hints of all kinds of mysterious intrigue' and had told of her plan to 'bring it all out in a book'.[36] If *George Eastmont* turned out to be that book then it seems that Harkness's intention was finally to be heard not by the public as with her earlier novels, but by those whose community she had lost – and to be proved right or, at least, to be understood. As Susan Lanser points out in an essay on feminist narratology, sometimes for women 'the act of writing becomes the fulfilment of desire, telling becomes the single predicated act, as if to tell were in itself to resolve, to provide closure'.[37] Even more revealingly there can be seen, throughout the text, a narrative splinter of the grand narrative of the rise and fall of socialism: a coded (auto)biography which shows the failure of love/friendship on the altar of ideology within the socialist community.

Fifteen years after Harkness finally dropped out of active participation in the British socialist movement, she sums up the anguish of political involvement in a novel which looks back on the dramatic events of the Trafalgar Square riots and the Great Dock Strike of 1886–9 through the words of one of the women characters. 'Is this friendship?' Mary Cameron asks herself in a cry of pain, as she finds herself alone after the band of socialists with whom she has worked intensively in support of the striking dockers of 1889 have dispersed to pursue other activities on other socialist battlefields. Then she reflects more soberly:

> She had mistaken mutual sympathy for agreement; now she knew that the desire to do away with poverty was the only thing they had in common … Now she would be unable to help; their friendship would dwindle away, leaving only a memory. Mutability was written on it, as on all other things of life; for friendship has no lasting tie, and what is so frail as human sympathy? Humanity, the great Whole, seemed mere words to her that night … she now craved for some human affection.[38]

This passage from *George Eastmont* is one of those moments in literary fiction when the author's voice breaks through and insists on being heard, loud and clear and unequivocally: to follow Foucault's terminology through, when the 'silent surplus' can finally contain itself no longer. Embedded in this fictional moment is

---

[36] *Diaries, Vol. 1*, entry for 14 November 1889, p. 303.
[37] Susan Lanser, 'Towards a Feminist Narratology', in *Feminisms: An Anthology of Literary Theory and Criticism*, ed. by R. Warhol and Diane Price Lerndl (Basingstoke: Macmillan, 1997), p. 688.
[38] John Law, *George Eastmont, Wanderer* (London: Burns & Oates, 1905), pp. 175–6.

a direct statement of political anguish and loneliness expressed as personal despair, a recognition of how socialism had failed the emotional life of women. In this soliloquy Mary Cameron/Margaret Harkness weeps for the failure of human friendship to survive ideological differences ('she had mistaken mutual sympathy for agreement'); the failure of human friendship to sustain a sense of community ('what is so frail as human sympathy?'); and the poverty of the grand claims of socialist discourse in the face of human need (a capitalized 'Humanity' against the craving for 'human affection'). More disturbingly, she weeps for the reduced significance of friendship and community which the dominance of ideology requires.

The moment of personal desolation and emotional frailty contained in the cry 'Is this friendship?' has an ideological cause which is precipitated by the dividing of the ways after the conclusion of the strike (Harkness's unhappiness was recorded by Beatrice Potter, as I have noted). One group (represented by Charleston/Tom Mann) wishes to continue the fight for unionization and the bettering of workers' conditions. One man (George Eastmont/H.H. Champion) still seeks more radical answers. The woman who has worked alongside them admires and likes Eastmont, maybe even loves him, but his political sympathies are moving him in a new direction. Although their farewell conversation expresses affectionate thanks and comradeship, the unspoken knowledge is that as their political paths diverge their friendship will end. The tragedy of the moment is underlined by the fact that the words just quoted are not spoken by Mary Cameron to Eastmont as he says good-bye but to herself after he has gone. Such an expression of personal feeling falls outside the available historical and ideological discourse, and is inappropriate for the fictional structure she is working within. Her only statements about her personal feelings are addressed to her 'Double'. She continues in words eerily reminiscent of Beatrice Potter's record of the loss of Harkness's friendship:

> Through living by herself she had fallen into some curious habits and one of these was to place her disembodied self in a chair before her, and criticise it. She asked her Double now some plain questions about Eastmont.[39]

If we place the 'fictional grid' (to borrow Carolyn Steedman's phrase)[40] of *George Eastmont* over historical accounts of the Dock Strike, the facts of history and Harkness's fictional account of them cancel each other out. What remains is the narrative of Eastmont and Mary Cameron, a story of failed expectations, of temporary friendship, of socialism as an inadequate substitute or context for sexual 'love'. What is eclipsed is any sense of a female community. Eleanor Marx figures nowhere in either Harkness's realistic or private narrative.

---

[39] John Law, *George Eastmont*, p. 49.
[40] See Carolyn Steedman, p. 29 in this volume.

In seeking to understand what the idea of a socialist community meant for women, I have tried to make explicit the mix of historical documentation and fictional text, deduction and speculation required. I do not want to fictionalize history nor to treat fiction as simply another form of historical document. What I hope to do is to 'thicken' the narrative of history by adding to historical knowledge the understanding offered by a distinctive mode, the impulse of literary production, and, by so doing, to recover some of the personal and private dimensions of a relationship between two women. The ideological perspective on the relationship between Eleanor Marx and Margaret Harkness has as its core agenda the placing of specific events and interaction within the overall progress of socialism. But this obscures and relegates the personal. What Harkness's covert narratives make it possible to understand is that, even as they figured significantly in the development of socialist history, these women were divided in and between themselves by class, gender and economic hierarchies which were only temporarily and intermittently displaced by the struggle for a socialist society in the 1880s and 1890s.

Chapter 10

A Moment of Being:
Miss Marx, Miss Pater, 'Miss Ambient'

Laurel Brake

The lives of Eleanor Marx (1855–98) and Clara Pater (1841–1910) substantially overlap, and both fall into that ambivalent category of their day, 'advanced women', a badge of honour or dishonour depending on the discourse. Both were women who participated in campaigns and other forms of public, civic life without the benefits of much formal education, both used skills in languages to develop their careers, and both lived unconventional sexual lives: Eleanor Marx lived with her (married) lover in a free union and Clara Pater, who also never married, moved in homosocial circles and has been represented as a lesbian.[1] Neither, while indisputably 'advanced', identified unreservedly with what is viewed/constructed as the mainstream of the women's movement of their time, even if from our perspective both are conspicuous among the identifiable pioneers of change for women in the period. But it is their common familial relation with 'men of letters' or, as feminists would have it, their contemporary representation as 'old mistresses',[2] that prompted me initially to compare Clara Pater with Eleanor Marx and, for all the differences in milieus, to explore the parallels their careers invite when set against their respective lovers/fathers/brothers.

This type of representation, characteristically and notoriously a perspective of nineteenth-century masculinist discourse, is limned by Henry James in 'The Author of "Beltraffio"' (1884), when he describes the sister of the artist, a Miss Ambient:

> She had, I believe, the usual allowance of vulgar impulses: she wished to be looked at, she wished to be married, she wished to be thought original ... she had no natural aptitude for an artistic development – she had little real intelligence. But her affectations rubbed off on her brother's renown, and as there were plenty of people who disapproved of him totally, they could easily

---

1 See Virginia Woolf, *The Pargiters*, ed. by M. Leaska (London: Hogarth Press, 1978), and 'Moments of Being. "Slater's Pins Have No Points"', in *A Haunted House and Other Short Stories* (London: Hogarth Press, 1943) pp. 89–95.
2 See Rozika Parker and Griselda Pollock, *Old Mistresses: Women, Art and Ideology* (London: Routledge, 1981). This path-breaking book, deploying feminist tools of analysis, identified and explored gender representation in the field of the visual arts.

point to his sister as a person formed by his influence. It was quite possible to regard her as a warning, and she had done nothing but little good with the world at large. He was the original, and she was the inevitable imitation. I think he was scarcely aware of the impression she produced – beyond having a general idea that she made up very well as a Rossetti; he was used to her, and he was sorry for her – wishing she would marry and observing that she didn't.[3]

Miss Ambient, observed here first by an American outsider and then from the great author-relative's point of view, is a personage mainly defined in terms of her brother, deriving her identity from the ambience of his talent and fame. The great author's wife, Mrs Ambient, is likewise defined, but in opposition to her husband.

Eleanor Marx and Clara Pater were alike prone to such representation, and while they undoubtedly benefited from proximity to their great men, they were in danger of being primarily identified with their respective father's and brother's projects. Rather than a depiction of the displacement or identification of women by their famous relatives, James's commentary on Miss Ambient is a detail of a larger theme, the threat of women to Art and the male Artist. But it should be noted that James's dramatization of the Ambients is written from a point of view common to nineteenth-century male writers. It illustrates the late Victorian male anxiety surrounding the legacy of 'letters' to sisters, daughters and wives which may be also be seen, for example, in *New Grub Street* (1891) where George Gissing fashions Marion Yule as the daughter of an increasingly jaded critic and editor and the girlfriend of a practitioner of the new journalism, torn between two male models of literary work.

However, James's depiction of the Ambients, in its clear location of the household and its inhabitants in the English middle classes and steeped in propriety, also helps identify an important set of differences between Marx and Pater, with respect to class and ethnicity. Marx, a first-generation Briton, stemmed from a Continental, lettered, politically radical, urban, and 'bohemian' family, with extensive connections in Europe. Pater, daughter of an East End surgeon who died when she was an infant, was raised by her mother, aunt and grandmother in impecunious gentility in Middlesex and Kent. It was a household in which the sacrifices seem to have been made for the education of her two brothers rather than for herself and her sister. Marx developed diversely, in the richness of her political and familial culture. Teaching, organizing, translating new and key works by Flaubert and Ibsen, as well as political and philosophical works from German, she also co-authored a pamphlet on *The Woman Question*. Pater's education was somewhat neglected and delayed until in 1869, when she was twenty-eight, she moved to North Oxford with her sister to join their brother, an established Fellow and lecturer only later to become famous. She published nothing that we know of:

---

[3]   *The Complete Tales of Henry James*, ed. by Leon Edel (London: Hart-Davis, 1963), V, 319–20.

as a field classics was overwhelmingly male, and as a late starter, she qualified to teach but lacked the long gestation requisite for scholarship. Although her name appears as a potential contributor to Oscar Wilde's *Woman's World*,[4] in the event it never appears in the contents, and Wilde's connection with the journal was in any case truncated. Evidence of her life is scanty, and largely third-person; traces of her career must be gleaned from official records: she left few letters, and there were no obituaries in the daily press when she died in 1910.

Yet Clara Pater was one of the founders of Somerville College, Oxford in 1879, having participated actively in the Oxford Association for the Education of Women (AEW), out of which the first Oxford women's halls emerged. She tutored at the new institution in both classical and modern languages – Latin, Greek, and German, deputized for the Principal for a year (1885–6), and served as one of the first Resident tutors from 1885 to 1894. In Oxford her colleagues and friends included Mary Arnold and the youthful Mrs Humphry Ward, Charlotte Green, Louise Creighton, Mrs Wood, Vernon Lee, and the Rector of Lincoln College, Mark Pattison; and in London Edmund Gosse and Mary Robinson. Having left Somerville at fifty-three after fifteen years' employment, she removed to London where she worked as a Lecturer in Latin and Greek in the Ladies' Department at King's College, London (1898–1900), and coached the young Virginia Stephen, among others.

Presenting her career like this, as that of a person in her own right, as if she were a nineteenth-century 'independent woman' or our contemporary, is instructive because Pater's life is so demonstrably enacted in the gendered space of her period and class. To begin with, she was very nearly what Mary Taylor calls 'the untaught woman.' Mary Ward, in her *Recollections*, represents Pater at twenty-four or twenty-five as 'intelligent, alive, sympathetic with a delightful humour and a strong judgment but without much positive acquirement. Then after some years [at thirty-three] she began to learn Latin and Greek with a view to teaching.'[5] Mary Taylor's discussion of the phenomenon of the 'untaught woman' in the *Victoria Magazine* of the 1860s presents it as a dysfunction of the heterosexual family, which is blindly dedicated to repeating itself by marrying off its young women:

> No one dare say of the few women who maintain themselves that their industry makes them inferior. It is not found that they deteriorate, or become unfit for the class they belong to. But so long as living in the expectation of being provided for is thought more worthy of respect, the majority, of course, will endeavour to do so. Respect is more to them than money. Competence, friends, the happiness of marriage, all are involved in

4   See Wilde's letter to Wemyss Reid of 1887 in *The Letters of Oscar Wilde*, ed. by Rupert Hart-Davis (London: Hart-Davis, 1962), p. 195.
5   Mrs Humphry Ward, *A Writer's Recollections* (London: W. Collins, 1918), p. 124.

the choice between working and waiting – only waiting; nothing worse than that … So the years that should be passed in active work, or in learning how, are spent in waiting, and the untaught woman is made incapable for life.[6]

It is a fact bound to strike feminist historians that neither Marx nor Pater was more than casually educated. Yvonne Kapp is mincing about Marx's formal education which was for the most part 'irregular' and ended when she was fourteen in 1869, when she travelled to Paris, Manchester and Ireland rather than attend school.[7] But Marx, fourteen years younger than Clara Pater, attended South Hampstead College, whereas it is unknown whether Pater, while her brother Walter went to the King's School in Canterbury and on to Oxford, was ever educated beyond the private tutor at home. There were opportunities in London for both secondary and university education for women. By the 1860s women could attend classes at the university, and after 1866 sit special examinations, and according to Martha Vicinus, Queen's College (open since 1848) and Bedford (from 1849), both at secondary and further education level, 'placed much emphasis in making up deficiencies in their students' education'.[8] Both of these women, who grew up in the period just before the acceleration of the development of higher education for women (in Hitchen, later Girton, College) in 1869, are tantalizingly close to the possibilities it opened up, but neither was enabled or encouraged to take advantage of what was on offer. Both had to find other informal paths to educate themselves. However, both Pater and Marx resumed education later in their lives as adults; they were 'returners'. Pater took advantage of the concentration of women in North Oxford where she moved in 1869, and began to study Greek and Latin in a small tutorial group at the age of thirty-three in 1874–5. Not long afterwards, Marx broke an engagement, and began to train as an actress in the early 1880s at the age of twenty-seven. In the interim, as young adults, both women taught, a well-tried mode of self-education. Pater took private pupils for German, and Marx taught at a boarding school at the age of nineteen, and went on to tutor privately, and to teach Extra-Mural classes.

Our consciousness of the position of their generation helps define our understanding of the life choices they had, and of the shape and meanings of their working lives, however disposed they were to work outside the home (Marx) or forced to earn a living (Pater). Indeed, irrespective of the particulars of the Marx and Pater families, the expectation of marriage and the perpetuation of the domestic woman on behalf of and by young women remained notably widespread among the middle classes. From the 1850s, and particularly in response to the 1861 census that showed a high percentage of unmarried women over twenty,

---

[6] Mary Taylor, 'Our Feminine Responsibility', *The First Duty of Women* (London: Victoria Press, 1870), p. 203.

[7] Kapp, I, 101.

[8] Martha Vicinus, *Independent Women* (London: Virago, 1985), p. 123.

there was considerable debate about redundant women,[9] emigration schemes, 'old maids', and the development of work for middle-class women. But the adherence to marriage as the career of women stunted the development and take-up of further and higher education for women, and their career opportunities, for nearly a century. The strong conceptual link in the mid- and late nineteenth century between higher education for women and paid work (or non-domestic labour) combine to make the refusal of education outside the home part of the posture of waiting *in* the family *for* a family. That was the preferred form middle-class women's apprenticeships (for domestic work) and education took.

The matrix of the domesticated woman, for example, is articulated in the ways in which the discourses of the period normally represent Pater's life – as a mid-century woman entirely contingent on her relations with her family: with Walter on the one hand, the Oxford Fellow, writer of fiction, reviewer and essayist, and with her older sister Hester on the other; and in terms of *lack*, the absence of a husband. Clara Pater's roles – as sister to her (famous) brother, sister to her sister, and as spinster are the reiterated and dominant categories deployed in the odd sentence or paragraph about her which survive. Vernon Lee's description of her first meeting with Miss Pater, when Clara was forty and tutoring at Somerville, is typical: 'To supper there was a Greek scholar, a Mr Arthur Sidgwick, who took up Mary [Robinson]; and Pater with his two sisters, rather gushing old maids.'[10] Even a student, Liz Sheldon, associated with Somerville in 1880, presents Pater, her 'coach', in terms of her brother, her sister and her marital status:

> I'm to go to afternoon tea at Miss Pater's tomorrow. She is a coach whose brother is a fellow, and they live with another old maid sister in a nice house on a nice road. Miss Pater had charge of Somerville for several weeks this term before Miss Lefevre, the real Principal, came.[11]

These discursive accounts of Clara Pater indicate the resistance of language at the time to the notion of the educated, working middle-class woman in general and the female don in particular. D.S. MacColl, one of Walter Pater's male protégés in the early 1880s, draws attention to another factor shaping the discourse which represents Clara: that is North Oxford, the new Oxford housing development in which the Paters lived. Expecting the exotic, MacColl is surprised by a feminized suburb:

> I was invited to Pater's house, a disappointingly suburban villa, and introduced to his sisters, Miss Clara and Miss Hester. The first taught in one

---

[9] See for example W.R. Greg, 'Why are Women Redundant?', *National Review*, 14 (April 1862), 434–60 and Frances Power Cobbe, 'What shall we do with our Old Maids?', *Fraser's Magazine*, 66 (1862), 594–610.

[10] [Violet Paget], *Vernon Lee's Letters*, ed. by Irene Cooper Willis (London: privately printed, 1937), pp. 78–9.

[11] Elizabeth Sheldon, MS Letters, Somerville College, Oxford, 19 November 1880, pp. 51–2.

of the ladies' colleges, the other kept house. She [Hester] had her brother's heaviness of face, a gruffer voice, and the same dry, kind, faintly roguish expression. One of them had worked in crewels, on a panel that hung over the sofa, a scene from Botticelli, but the atmosphere was rather of God than of his enemies.[12]

Besides being suburban, North Oxford was the result of the gradual revolution over a decade before whereby, through the relaxation of the prohibition on married fellows, women began to enter the male world of the university community in Oxford. Until that time, only heads of House were permitted to marry, and the university world was overwhelmingly male. As this changed, many male academics came to live with their wives, daughters and sisters in North Oxford, and Tanis Hinchcliffe suggests that the movement for the education of women in the university was stimulated by the proximity of these activists to each other.[13] A preponderance of the female names on the first committees of the AEW were relatives of male academics who lived in North Oxford. Pater was one of these women who found herself there by virtue of her brother's position in the university. It is through her Somerville career that Mark Pattison invites her to meet Miss Downing, a speaker at a woman's suffrage meeting, and that Pattison records her as a guest. As for the life of Hester Pater there is hardly any trace.

It is perhaps due to the association of the sisters with Walter Pater's reputation for aestheticism in his work and dress, as well as to the interest in fashion which attached to discourse about women, that we owe the pronounced character of their dress and description of it by Sheldon and Lee. Sheldon's first sight of Clara Pater is recorded in terms of her appearance that displaces her name: 'There was a wonderful woman there today, in heavy golden hair and a thoroughly Greek dress. I have no idea who she is, but she seemed to be "some"'.[14] Vernon Lee spies 'the two Miss Paters in fantastic applegreen Kate Greenaway dresses' at a party.[15] Both descriptions of Clara Pater are borne out by the Wirgman portrait done in 1870 when she was twenty-nine.

At all the known points of Clara Pater's life, the gendered parameters of her experience are formative. Her access to education is paralleled with her implication in the family as an unmarried woman, her gendered field of expertise, her experience of the workplace (a female institution), her ambivalent attitude to paid work, and her likely homosocial, sexual orientation. This system of separate (binary) structures bears out the analysis made by Marx and Aveling in their pamphlet of 1886 on *The Woman Question*: 'The life of woman does not coincide with that of man. Their lives do not intersect; in many cases do not even touch.

---

[12] D.S. MacColl, 'A Batch of Memories. XII. Walter Pater', *Weekend Review*, 4 (12 December 1931), 759–60 (p. 759).

[13] See Tanis Hinchcliffe, *North Oxford* (New Haven and London: Yale University Press, 1992).

[14] Sheldon Letters, 12 October 1880, p. 15.

[15] *Vernon Lee's Letters*, p. 153.

Hence the life of the race is stunted.'[16] One aspect of both women's lives which emerges from the comparison is Marx's commitment to heterosexuality and her involvement in the life of the (heterosexual) family, to the point of homophobia. She and Aveling endorse their colleague, Bebel:

> Two extreme forms of the distinction of the sexes that spring from this their separation are, as Bebel points out, the effeminate man and the masculine woman. These are two types from which even the average person recoils with a perfectly natural horror of the unnatural ... the former is less frequent than the latter. But these two types do not exhaust the list of diseased forms due to our unnatural dealing with the sex relations. That morbid virginity, of which mention has already been made, is another. Lunacy is a fourth. Suicide is a fifth.[17]

The Paters also emerge in relief from this comparison, a family unit which, from 1869, involves two sisters living with their homosexual brother, their 'housekeeping' presence providing an appearance of 'order' and coercive limits. There is also the possibility that one or both sisters are homosocial themselves, as Virginia Woolf implies in two fictional portraits of Clara (as Julia Craye in 'Moments of Being. "Slater's Pins Have no Points"' and as Lucy Craddock in *The Pargiters*) and as Vernon Lee suggests in her linking of the sisters with the Souls, a society of forty people in London in the 1880s who sought to 'achieve Platonic friendships'.[18] As a member of staff of a woman's college from 1880, Clara Pater was extremely vulnerable to any whisper of scandal about her brother, as it was believed at the time that the fragile status of the women's colleges was largely dependent on their moral and social respectability. Otherwise, the experiment of sending nubile daughters to pursue residential education outside the protection of home was bound to be vetoed by anxious parents.

Like his sister, Walter Pater was a classicist, a field that afforded him considerable opportunity to explore ancient forms of homosocial culture. His first book in 1873 was denounced for its hedonism, and his second, a novel of 1885, attempted to explain his position in a treatment of ancient Rome. In the 1870s, 1880s, and 1890s Walter Pater steadily published a series of Greek studies that included homosocial elements. He must have been a considerable liability for Clara Pater in her position at Somerville. It is unsurprising that Pater did not open his classes to women students, despite his sister's involvement with Somerville and her advocacy of higher education of women. The field of classics was of course not confined to homosexual men: all male undergraduates were examined in classics. But the contents of the literature brought Platonic love to the attention of all its readers. For this reason classics remained a largely taboo subject for women,

---

16 *Woman Question*, p. 7.
17 *Woman Question*, p. 12.
18 Burdett Gardner, *The Lesbian Imagination* (New York and London: Garland, 1987), p. 548.

although its (selective) inclusion on the syllabus for women students was a big issue in the founding of Newnham in Cambridge and the Oxford halls for women. Clara Pater's choice of Greek and Latin as her subjects is comparable to Eleanor Marx's decision to translate Flaubert and Ibsen. With respect to women, these were all notorious texts to conservatives, and 'advanced' to liberals. An anonymous writer in 1884 in the *Guardian*, an Anglican weekly, comments:

> We think that even the general study of the classics, such is required for Moderations Honours alone, is most undesirable for women. You cannot possibly restrict their reading for the school; and what sort of an introduction to female life the process of breathing the foul atmosphere of the heathen world will be for most of those who are to move in it must be obvious. It is bad enough for men. We all know what controversies have raged over the classics as a means of education on this very account. But these controversies did not include women, who were supposed to be excluded by the nature of the case.[19]

There is no evidence that Clara Pater was a scholar, but even if she had been, it is unlikely that she would have published signed articles in this field at the time, or translations.

Nor was her experience at Somerville without tensions. 'My friends and I were all on fire for women's education, including women's medical education and very emulous of Cambridge, where the movement was already far advanced', wrote Mrs Humphry Ward, who as the young Mary Arnold had worked with Clara, Louise Creighton, Bertha Johnson and Charlotte Green in the AEW in Oxford.[20] Clara Pater's problems at Somerville are various, but from this distance most of them appear systemic rather than personal. First there were chronic problems with the Principal, whose insecurity, ambivalence toward the job, and class consciousness resulted simultaneously in dependence on Clara (who deputized on more than one occasion including a period of two terms), and in jealousy of her as a self-contained woman. Clara's knowledge of classics, modest as it may have been, put the Principal's own claims to status at Somerville, which were based on class and connections, in an unaccustomed shade. Few of these women in the earliest period of higher education at Oxford were 'qualified' or had experience of institutional life, and tensions were bound to arise. Shaw Lefevre, however, went to great pains on her return from an extended leave during which Clara Pater had deputized for her, to prevent Clara's position at Somerville from being formally recognized in the title Deputy or Secretary.

However, there is some evidence to suggest that Clara Pater too found the necessity to do full-time paid work beneath her and uncongenial. She did not apply for the Principal's job when Shaw Lefevre departed in 1889, and in the

---

[19] Anon, *Guardian*, 19 March 1884, p. 427.

[20] Mrs Humphry Ward, *A Writer's Recollections* (London: W. Collins, 1918), p. 152.

summer of 1894 she resigned her resident tutorship, apparently intending to continue her Somerville work on a freelance, part-time basis. When her brother unexpectedly died in July of that year, she quit completely, leaving her job, her networks, her income and Oxford for private life in a terrace in Kensington, at a time when work and a career might have appeared especially welcome. Like Jane Eyre fifty years earlier, the sisters opted in September 1894 to live on their legacy that we know left them immediately 'in great need of money',[21] and Gosse applied for a civil pension on their behalf.

If being Walter Pater's sister was a liability in Oxford, it was more likely to be an asset in London. Clara took private pupils, among them Virginia Woolf, and four years after moving to London she did her two-year stint of teaching for the Ladies' College of King's. In the absence of an explanation from Clara Pater herself for her departure from Oxford in 1894, it may be noted that she, like all unqualified teachers in the first years of the women's colleges, was destined to be overtaken immediately by the first graduates. Her original designation as senior tutor in Greek was dropped once qualified graduates less than half her age joined the staff. As an administrator who was also learned, and a tutor to students whose qualifications outstripped hers as soon as they graduated, Clara's position as a founder, teacher and administrator was anomalous. There may have been much to shun in Oxford and something to go to in London.

Yet another explanation for her apparent dearth of enthusiasm about her job is the gendered issue of 'health'. Just as higher education was alleged to be dangerous to female fertility, so full-time paid work for middle-class women was alleged to be detrimental to health on a number of counts: its lack of diversity, its imposition of exhausting and ignominious routines, its dearth of privacy and, if residential or distant, its loneliness and severance from family protection and love. Henry James's misogynist attribution to Miss Ambient of the 'usual vulgar impulses' of wishing 'to be looked at', 'married' and 'thought original',[22] in combination with her alleged melancholy, proved a fictional hypothesis of the psychology of women situated as Clara and Hester Pater were, unmarried women in the orbit of the male artist. But there is no evidence attaching to either woman that this psychology was theirs. What we have for Clara Pater is sight of three moments that relate to the subject of health in its widest sense, one in 1877, one in about 1885, and one in 1894. Mark Pattison records on 25 June 1877 that he 'call[ed] on Clara Pater, & heard from her confession of her unhappy nihilistic state of mind'.[23] As this sight of Pater's inner life is the only one we have, it is impossible to judge whether it is representative of a deep and abiding melancholia, momentary, or atypical. But an estimate of an early Somervillian, Florence Rich (1884–7), in a letter written fifty

21   Edmund Gosse to William Colles, 8 August 1894, in Walter Pater, *Letters*, ed. by L. Evans (Oxford: Clarendon, 1970), p. 156.

22   *The Complete Tales of Henry James*, ed. by Leon Edel (London: Hart-Davis, 1963), V, 319.

23   Mark Pattison, MS. Diary 1877 Pattison 130, Bodleian Library, Oxford.

years later, uses ambiguous terms which quite specifically obscure this private sphere, and allow for physical and/or psychological explanations of Clara Pater's unfitness or reluctance to assume management when she deputized for the Principal and administered Somerville in 1885–6:

> During her absence Miss Clara Pater took her place. Miss Pater was never very strong, but she understood well how to keep her body in working order, when to rest, when to have a cup of cocoa, and so on, an art that few people understood.[24]

It is notable that while Mark Pattison's view of Clara Pater's psychological state predates Somerville and alludes to her private life, this second glimpse links the unspecified dearth of strength ('never very strong') with the work setting. Is this a way of referring to bouts of nervous exhaustion or depression which are thus prevented? The third glimpse is from the Somerville College Minutes of Council of 11 June 1894 which reveal that Clara Pater's departure was in two stages, the first taking place before her brother's death. Did her health give out? Or did she decide on balance that she was needed at home? Her brother had long been ill with gout, and in early June he was seriously ill with rheumatic fever. Either of these factors – her own or her brother's health – may have led to her resignation in June.

Later reports of the Paters in London, such as those of A.C. Benson (1905) or Virginia Stephen (1900), use tropes to construct the lives of the two women which are similar to those found in the reports of their lives in Oxford of the 1880s; they are viewed as impecunious and waiting for death. But I do not on balance believe them, or think that was the case. When Virginia Stephen writes in 1900: 'Miss Pater ... looks very white and shrivelled poor Love – Don't you think those two old ladies most pathetic, growing old together, and one of them will drop off, and the other will be left. They seem so desolate with no young friends or relations,'[25] she writes from the position of a young woman of eighteen from a large Victorian family. In 1900 Clara Pater was fifty-nine, yet in 1903 Stephen notes 'I should think you might see Totty, and Clara in their red cloaks',[26] and in 1905 she reports: 'Clara, if health permits, is coming in a new Empire gown of scarlet plush, with amber beads, and a little old Lace.'[27] Certainly tropes of deprivation and loss – of health, infirmity and penury – are a characteristic element of the discourse of Virginia Stephen and others around Clara and Totty after their brother's death. They are part of the construction in language not only of the economic dependence of many unmarried Victorian women on fathers and brothers, but of their social dependence and their identity.

---

[24] Florence Rich, MS letter to Helen Darbishire, 31 August 1838, Somerville College, Oxford.
[25] 23 October 1900, *Letters of Virginia Woolf,* ed. by Nigel Nicolson and Joanne Trautmann (London: Hogarth Press, 1975), I, 39–40.
[26] 2 September [1903], *Letters of Virginia Woolf,* I, 93–4.
[27] 23 February [1905], *Letters of Virginia Woolf,* I, 180.

Little positive is known of Clara Pater's life in London. She was not a member of Mrs Ward's Anti-Suffrage League in 1908, nor had she joined Oxford friends such as Charlotte Green and Louise Creighton in signing Ward's 'Appeal Against Suffrage' in the *Nineteenth Century* in 1889. Clara Pater's silence, her history of deeds rather than documents, is a great contrast to the wealth of extant material by and about Eleanor Marx, and the desire of Marx's daughter to perpetuate her father's work and see it disseminated. But as a long-standing witness to her brother's homosexual life and writing, as a participant in the Souls, and as a reader of Greek literature, Clara Pater was fully aware that the prohibitions of her period against writing what she knew to be the case were formidable. Her pamphlet on gender issues could not be written. It is likely that silence was a strategy of choice as well as necessity. Certainly the sisters kept the lid on prospective biographies of their brother for nearly a decade; by restricting access to any remains, refusing interviews and finally arranging an official life to countermand the investigative work of Thomas Wright, they policed their brother's reputation fiercely. There is a distinct possibility that they authorized the destruction of letters and incriminating papers. After the Wilde trials, silence was imperative. In their roles of active guardians of their brother's posthumous reputation, Clara and Hester Pater perpetuated the tendencies of discourse in the period to occlude the individual identities of such women, despite their personal achievements, and to subsume them into the portraits of the artist.

Clara Pater died of cancer on 9 August 1910, and is buried in Holywell Cemetery, Oxford in Walter Pater's tomb, inscribed only as 'sister'. There is no biography. Eleanor Marx died heartbroken in 1898, by her own hand. Tsuzuki's and Kapp's biographies were the first major lives in English. Neither woman was included in the *Dictionary of National Biography* at the time of their deaths. Both will appear in the *New DNB*.

Chapter 11

Radical Voices:
Eleanor Marx and Victoria Woodhull

Bridget Bennett

In Sarah Waters's novel *Tipping the Velvet* (1998), set in the 1880s, there is a scene that has significant implications both for the plot of the novel and for the subjects of this essay. The protagonist, Nan King, sits with her newly-found socialist friends Florence and Ralph Banner discussing their private fantasies of an idealized future, a paradise. As Florence muses she turns away from the others and looks at a picture that has intrigued Nan for some time:

> I turned, to see what it was she was looking at: it was the family portrait, and I guessed she must be looking at her mother. But in the corner of the frame, of course, there was the smaller picture, of the grave-looking woman with the very heavy brows. I had never learned who she was, after all. Now I said to Ralph: 'Who is that girl, in the little photo? She don't half need a hairbrush.'
> He looked at me, but did not answer. It was Florence who spoke. 'That's Eleanor Marx,' she said, with a kind of quiver.
> 'Eleanor Marks? Have I met her? Is she that cousin of yours, who works at the poulterers?' ... Ralph put down his fork. 'Eleanor Marx,' he said, 'is a writer and a speaker and a very great socialist ...'[1]

This is a good, albeit succinct, definition of Marx and it answers Nan's implied question – who on earth is she? The question does not need to be put so starkly, but the preoccupation of the passage (the relation between fame and anonymity, the question of social exclusion – in this instance Nan's) is telling. In this essay I shall ask the same question about two women: one is Marx herself, the other is her contemporary, the American radical Victoria Woodhull.

Both have experienced vacillating reputations despite brilliant achievements. The body of work Marx left on her death is impressive and diverse. It includes translations, editorial work and political tracts. Woodhull's legacy is also remarkable and contains many contradictions and pioneering activities. With her sister Tennessee Claflin she formed the first female brokerage on Wall Street. She was the first woman to run for the American presidency (and she did it more than

---

[1] Sarah Waters, *Tipping the Velvet* (London: Virago Press, 1998), p. 386.

once), and the first person to sue the British Museum for libel – successfully – in her more conservative middle age. Like Marx she was a political activist and pamphleteer, and an editor. She shared Marx's interest in the theatre, supporting herself as an actress for a period. Unlike Marx she was a spiritualist. There are parallels (these and others) between their lives – though there are obvious differences too. Further, there are parallels in the ways in which their lives have been recorded. Marx has been the subject of two significant biographies; one, justly celebrated. Woodhull has been the subject of several, including two that have recently been given serious critical attention.[2] Still, both women often go unrecognized. Woodhull's life intersects with that of Marx to some degree, and there are, at moments, near contacts and entanglements. Marx does not appear to have known Woodhull personally, but she almost certainly knew of her, and despite their differences Woodhull was an important precursor as a public speaker – a celebrated orator – and an activist. The passage this essay opens with suggests the way in which it will be constructed. I will come at Marx tangentially, read her from across the Atlantic, and frame her on the edges of a broader narrative that largely concerns the parallel life of Woodhull.

It was in the 1870s that much of Woodhull's most significant work took place. It was in the 1870s, too, that she finally left the United States for England. As she recanted and repudiated, as she moved up the social scale, it was this decade that she tried to live down. It was also during those turbulent years after the American Civil War, when great social and economic upheavals were irrevocably altering American society, that the paths of Marx and Woodhull met for the first time. So the first part of this essay will look at that textual meeting through an examination of Marx's arrest in France in 1871, and of Woodhull's involvement with publicizing that arrest on the other side of the Atlantic. It will examine the textual elimination of Victoria Woodhull from accounts of American socialism by Eleanor Marx and others and the difficulties this has created in terms of constructing narratives about her.

The second part of the essay will turn to examine the implications of frustrated historical narratives of this kind by looking at the ways in which Woodhull constructed herself through the brilliantly effective publicity machine she created. Finally I will examine how, as a consequence of her own autobiographical imperatives, she was read and inscribed by others, notably Henry James and Harriet Beecher Stowe. James's fictional portrayal of Woodhull mainly

---

[2]   Lois Beachy Underhill, *The Woman Who Ran for President: The Many Lives of Victoria Woodhull* (London: Penguin Books, 1995) and Barbara Goldsmith, *Other Powers: The Age of Suffrage, Spiritualism, and the Scandalous Victoria Woodhull* (New York: Knopf, 1998). Earlier biographies include Johanna Johnston, *Mrs. Satan: The Incredible Saga of Victoria Woodhull* (London, Melbourne: Macmillan, 1967); Emanie Sachs, *The Terrible Siren: Victoria Woodhull* (New York: Harper, 1928); and a pamphlet, *The Lives and Writings of Notorious Victoria Woodhull and Her Sister Tennessee Claflin*, ed. by Arlene Kisner Washington (New Jersey: Times Change Press, 1972).

concentrates upon a social phenomenon – the fortune-hunting American woman with a dubious sexual history. Stowe's, on the other hand, concentrates upon the dangerous, foreign and destabilizing influence of alien political ideologies (represented by a Woodhull-like character) and the threat they pose to American (and domestic) life. These differing fictional representations contain the germ of the ways in which her contemporaries perceived Woodhull, and help to frame a problematical historical narrative. In this essay Marx's erasure of Woodhull will be read against her emergence in fictional and autobiographical forms and will seek to find the two women through a process of negation.

Woodhull's journalistic work started in 1870 with the founding of *Woodhull and Claflin's Weekly* (henceforth the *Weekly*). The journal was named for Woodhull and for Tennessee Claflin, the partner of many of her activities. It was jointly founded by them, Woodhull's second husband James Harvey Blood and the Fourierist Stephen Pearl Andrews, and it ran until 1876.[3] In his seminal work *A History of American Magazines, 1865–1885* (1938) Frank Luther Mott describes its contents in the following terms:

> It discussed the strike in the anthracite coal region of Pennsylvania, defending the strikers. It exposed scandals in insurance companies and bond deals; it was a really valuable muckraker. It printed items about women in industry and business gleaned from here and there. Its articles often represented advanced thought that would have met the approval of liberals of a somewhat later day.

One contemporary described it as having 'voices from the "seventh heaven," and gabblings from a frog-pond' though they added that 'the amazing journal is crowded with thought, and with needed information that can be got nowhere else'.[4]

The first traceable contact between Woodhull and Marx is a textual one and takes place through the *Weekly*.[5] In the late spring of 1871 Eleanor and Jenny Marx travelled from London to Bordeaux to stay with their sister Laura Lafargue, who had recently given birth to her third child. Paul Lafargue had gone to Paris 'to obtain from the Commune *de pleins pouvoirs* to organize the revolutionary army in Bordeaux', as Jenny Marx explained in a letter. Yet though he had written to say he

---

3   *Woodhull and Claflin's Weekly* was suspended from 29 June to 26 October 1872 and from 9 November to 21 December 1872, and appeared with some irregularity in 1873. Frank Luther Mott *A History of American Magazines, 1865–1885*, 3 vols (Cambridge, Mass.: Harvard University Press, 1938), III, 443.

4   Both from Mott, III, 447. For further details of the *Weekly* see Madeleine Stern *We the Women: Career Firsts of Nineteenth-Century America*, Lincoln and London: University of Nebraska Press, 1962 (repr. 1994) p. 260. 'From prostitution and the social evil to free love, abortion and divorce, from suffrage to new employments for women, from spiritualism to puffs for the self-appointed candidate, from currency reform to industrial justice, it ran a wide and ruthless gamut.'

5   Kapp, I, 130.

was on his way home he had not arrived and nothing further had been heard of him. The two sisters decided to go to Bordeaux.[6] By the time they arrived there Lafargue had returned home; however, after the defeat of the Paris Commune it was no longer safe for him to remain. The three sisters, Paul Lafargue and the children fled to Bagnères-de-Luchon in the Pyrenees and from there, warned by a letter from Karl Marx of imminent danger of arrest, Lafargue went over the border to Spain, to what he hoped would be a safe place of refuge. All three sisters went to visit him there, and Laura decided to stay on with him.[7]

When Eleanor and Jenny returned alone they were arrested at the frontier and escorted back to Bagnères-de-Luchon where their house was searched. They were then imprisoned and interrogated. Both sisters recorded the highly traumatic event. Eleanor described it in a long and outraged letter to Wilhelm Liebknecht of 29 December 1871. (Later she would translate Lissagaray's 1876 book *Histoire de la Commune*, which appeared in her 1886 edition as the *History of the Commune of 1871*).[8] Jenny wrote a more detailed public account of it. Her description of her sister's interrogation suggests how much of an ordeal it must have been for Eleanor. Writing of the fact that Eleanor was interrogated until 2 a.m. Jenny calls her 'a young girl of 16, who had been up that day since 5 a.m., and had travelled nine hours on an intensely hot day in August, and had only taken food quite early in Bosot'. Her letter was published in the *Weekly* on 21 October 1871.

At the time of the publication of the letter, the *Weekly* was one of the most important publications of the International Workingman's Association (henceforth IWA) in America. When Eleanor Marx and Edward Aveling visited the United States in 1886, however, it had ceased publication. The following year, the list of influential working-class journals Marx and Aveling mention in their book *The Working-Class Movement in America* (1887) does not include the *Weekly*. This might suggest that they may not have considered it worthwhile adding to their list since it was no longer being published. Yet it has a key place in the history of American socialism which might be thought to make it worth a mention. On 30 December 1871, two months after the publication of Jenny Marx's letter, the *Weekly* became the first American publisher of an English translation of the *Communist Manifesto* and, in the words of one critic, 'had the zest of discovering Marxism for a whole nation'.[9] The *Manifesto* was accompanied by a slightly garbled text that declared:

---

[6]   Letter from Jenny Marx to Ludwig Kugelmann, 18 April 1871 in Kapp, I, 127.

[7]   By this time their youngest child, always sickly, had died, and their remaining son had dysentery. Kapp, I, 128.

[8]   Eleanor Marx Aveling, *History of the Commune of 1871* (London: Reeves & Turner, 1886). Trans. of [Hippolyte-Prosper-Olivier] Lissagaray, *Histoire de la Commune*.

[9]   Paul Buhle, *Marxism in the U.S.A. from 1870 to the Present: Remapping the History of the American Left* (London: Verso, 1987), p. 37.

We reproduce an important document, principally the production of Karl
Marx, the world-famous leader of the 'New Socialism,' which will be read
with great interest at this time, when the progress of the 'International
Workingman's Association' makes the historical evolution so clearly
described in this manifesto one which should be understood by those who
are desirous of comprehending the movement.[10]

This makes it clear that the publication of the *Manifesto* is being conceived of in
relation to developments in the IWA. But it is also Jenny Marx's letter, with its
powerful depiction of her young sister's plight, that provides an important context
for the publication of the *Manifesto*. Further, since the Toulouse press had accused
Eleanor and Jenny of being 'emissaries of the International on the French and
Spanish borders', there was a significant impetus for the journal to publish the
letter, and an explanation for why Jenny should have sent it in the first place.[11]

Eleanor Marx almost certainly knew of the publication of her sister's letter in
October 1871. Likewise, she must have been familiar with the journal's important
part in the furthering of American socialism through its publication of the
Manifesto just two months later. Yet even in her 1896 edition of Karl Marx's
articles for the *New York Tribune*, although she includes a note to describe the
Manifesto (and give the date of its first publication) she does not mention its first
American appearance.[12] Interestingly, by the time she published the articles she
had met, and liked, one of Woodhull's most passionate admirers, Isabella Beecher
Hooker. In *The Working-Class Movement in America* Marx and Aveling wrote that
they passed what they described as 'perhaps the most happy and assuredly the
most peaceful hours of our stay in America' with her.

Beecher Hooker was the half-sister of Harriet Beecher Stowe and Henry Ward
Beecher and was a committed spiritualist and a suffrage activist.[13] Marx and
Aveling had already referred approvingly in *The Woman Question* to Beecher
Hooker's honest discussion of sex with her young son (1886) and she clearly made
an impact on them in person too.[14] The three siblings played crucial roles in

10 Cited in Madeleine B. Stern, *The Pantarch: A Biography of Stephen Pearl Andrews* (Austin and
    London: University of Texas Press, 1968), p. 116. Stern's detailed and witty biography
    contains a great deal of fascinating information about the relationship between Andrews,
    Woodhull and the journal. See especially pp. 103–21.
11 Cited in Kapp, I, 130. It is not clear whether or not she sent the letter anywhere else in
    addition to this.
12 She writes that 'The "Communist Manifesto" has been translated into well-nigh every
    language, and is, again to quote Engels, "the most international production of all Socialist
    literature."' Karl Marx, *Revolution and Counter-Revolution or Germany in 1848*, ed. by
    Eleanor Marx Aveling (London: Swan Sonnenschein; New York: Scribner's, 1896), p. 148.
13 Eleanor Marx and Edward Aveling, *The Working-Class Movement in America*, 2nd edition
    (London: Swan Sonnenschein, 1891), p. 193.
14 As part of a discussion of the advisability of honesty towards children they refer to Isabella
    Beecher Hooker, whom August Bebel had already cited in his 'Die Frau in der Vergangenheit,
    Gegenwart, & Zunkunft': 'In order to satisfy the constant questionings of her little boy of

Woodhull's political life in the United States in the 1870s. Beecher Hooker was as passionate an advocate of Woodhull as Harriet Beecher Stowe was her avowed enemy. Henry Ward Beecher, an antagonist, was, Woodhull claimed, her lover for a period. (This claim is generally accepted – unlike many others Woodhull made.) Stowe went so far as to complain that Hooker's admiration for Woodhull took the form of some sort of possession and critics have argued that Hooker and Woodhull were themselves rumoured to be lovers. On 24 December 1872 Stowe wrote to a friend:

> No one could understand the secret of her influence over my poor sister – incredible infatuation continuing even now. I trust that God will in some way deliver her for she was and is a lovely good woman & before this witch took possession of her we were all so happy together.[15]

One symptom of Beecher Hooker's 'incredible infatuation' with Woodhull was that she spoke about her achievements frequently and passionately. Given her great interest she may well have discussed Woodhull with Marx and Aveling when they visited her, as a leading woman's rights activist, in America. Despite all the evidence that Marx may well (indeed should have) heard of Woodhull, her lack of attention to the *Weekly* may be attributed to many causes, some of them now very difficult or impossible to trace. Some might be inferred. One might be concerned with the sometimes ambivalent, but often hostile, reactions Woodhull could elicit.

Eleanor Marx is certainly not the only figure who ignores or trivializes Woodhull's role in the dissemination of socialist thought in America. Karl Marx's hostility to Woodhull and Claflin is amply documented. In May 1872 he called Woodhull 'Banker's woman, free-lover, and general humbug' and her sister 'in the same line', adding that Section 12 consisted 'almost exclusively ... of middle-class humbugs and worn-out Yankee swindlers in the Reform business'. His notes show detailed knowledge of the *Weekly* between October 1871 and May 1872, and make it clear that he had read at least some part of the edition of 21 October 1871 in which the *Manifesto* appeared, for he quotes from it directly. When he gets to the announcement that Woodhull is to stand for the Presidency he writes of her as the 'laughing-stock of New York and United States'.[16]

---

eight, with regard to his origin, and to avoid telling him fables, which she regarded as immoral, she told him the whole truth. The child listened with the greatest attention, and from the day on which he had heard what pain and anxiety he had caused his mother, clung to her with an entirely new tenderness and reverence. The same reverence he had shown also to other women', *Woman Question*, p. 11.

15 Letter to Mrs. Mary Claflin (no relation), 24 December 1872, cited in Joan D. Hedrick, *Harriet Beecher Stowe: A Life* (New York: Oxford University Press, 1994), p. 377.

16 International Working Men's Association, *Documents of the First International, 1871–1872* (Moscow: Progress Publishers and London: Lawrence & Wishart, 1964–6), pp. 323–9. For more detail see pp. 323–32.

This overt hostility towards Woodhull suggests that, almost without doubt, Eleanor Marx and Edward Aveling took a conscious decision not to include the *Weekly* in their list of significant journals. Again it suggests that Woodhull played a part, albeit an ignoble one, in Marx's imaginative world – as she must have done in Woodhull's, in 1871. Yet acknowledging Woodhull in any way would have led to great difficulty for Marx. Key problems for Woodhull's more hard-line socialist critics were first, her avowal of spiritualism, and second, her outspoken attitude towards sexual freedom for women which, they argued, threatened to alienate conservative immigrants. This anxiety was illustrated in 1872 in Thomas Nast's brilliant and infamous cartoon in which an image of Woodhull, complete with demonic horns and wings, tempts a labouring woman with a sign saying 'Be Saved by Free Love'. The exhausted-looking woman, carrying small children and a drunken husband on her back, tells Woodhull, 'Get thee behind me, Mrs. Satan'. It was Woodhull's central position within Section 12 (one of the American sections) of the IWA that caused her socialist critics real difficulty: had she been a less central figure her 'eccentric' beliefs might have been more acceptable. Given her significance, the issue was how to erase her.

Woodhull's involvement with socialist politics centres on her intellectual friendship with Stephen Pearl Andrews, who had founded the two American sections of the IWA.[17] In 1869 he had first approached the London-based General Council of the International to form an affiliation with the IWA and shortly after that, in 1870, he had met Woodhull for the first time. By the time he formed the American sections he was her valued advisor. The public attention Woodhull was receiving for her women's rights campaigns and successful brokerage firm made her seem to Andrews the ideal honorary president of section 12, a view (as we have seen) not shared by Karl Marx. For some years before she joined the IWA and stood for the presidency she had campaigned for women's suffrage and for 'free love', which she defined as a whole system of economic and social freedoms, and the right to speak out publicly and in print. In early 1871 she petitioned the House Judiciary Committee in Washington, arguing that since the 14th and 15th amendments (which had been adopted to give the vote to black males) already guaranteed women's rights to vote, Congress needed to protect that right. In the November elections later that year she and thirty-two other women tried unsuccessfully to vote.

At the same time as this she was actively involved in spiritualism. In 1871 she was elected president of the American National Association of Spiritualists.[18] Her presidential address assured them that making her president was an act to which they were impelled by the spirit world. This evidence of that world working towards a higher good revealed the fact that dramatic changes were on the way.

---

17 See indexed references in Stern, *The Pantarch*.
18 Johanna Johnston, *Mrs. Satan: The Incredible Saga of Victoria Woodhull* (London, Melbourne: Macmillan, 1967), pp. 295–7.

Such rhetoric allied her both to spiritualism and socialism by attesting to the differing sorts of transformative – revolutionary – possibilities of each.

The first issue of the *Weekly* appeared on 14 May 1870 and the journal served Woodhull and Andrews in a variety of ways. It was an extremely useful platform for Andrews to expound upon his system of science (Universology), his philosophy (Integralism), his practical sociology (Pantarchism or the Pantarchy) and his universal language system, Alwato. For Woodhull, it was to become a way in which she could take her revenge on the enemies she made in her career, as well as in which she could promote the many causes that interested her.

Though Woodhull's association with Section 12 was not one that she considered at all at odds with her public position as a spiritualist and former clairvoyant, or as a Wall Street broker, it was, to say the least, unconventional. As though to demonstrate to sceptics that this latest twist in her public career was not merely wilful eccentricity, she began a fierce attack on the corruption of named capitalists in the pages of the *Weekly*. These included Cornelius Vanderbilt, who had significantly helped her in her earliest days as a broker. For some, though, the personalizing nature of the journal merely demonstrated how frivolous her engagement with socialism was.

Histories of American socialism have sometimes been dismissive of Woodhull's association with it and her historical legacy, particularly in her involvement in the IWA. In his book *Socialism in America* (1970), Albert Fried calls Woodhull and Claflin 'two wild sisters', writing that in the pages of the *Weekly* they 'propagandized not so much for workers' rights as for female suffrage and sexual freedom (which they, at least, had no trouble exercising) and a host of other reforms'.[19] In their edited work *Socialism and American Life* (1952), Donald Drew Egbert and Stow Persons dismiss them as 'two eccentric women'.[20] Though a number of hostile critics have thought of her as a social reformer, Woodhull saw herself as a social revolutionary. This variance in the way in which she was read by others and the way she saw herself is the cause of some of the difficulties her reputation has faced. There are a multitude of ways of reading Woodhull and her problematic – even contradictory – legacy, particularly in relation to women's issues, just as there are with Marx. A second difficulty is the notorious mutual antagonism between the largely German socialists of the IWA in the United States and the Americans of Section 12. Samuel Gompers wrote in his autobiography:

> Section 12 of the American group was dominated by a brilliant group of faddists, reformers, and sensation-loving spirits. They were not working people and treated their relationship to the labor movement as a means to a 'career.' They did not realize that labor issues were tied up with the lives of

---

[19] Albert Fried, *Socialism in America: From the Shakers to the Third International, a Documentary History* (New York: Columbia University Press, 2nd edition, 1992), p. 183.

[20] *Socialism and American Life*, ed. by Donald Drew Egbert and Stow Persons, 2 vols (Princeton: Princeton University Press, 1952), I, 234–5.

men, women, and children – issues not to be risked lightly. Those pseudo-Communists played with the labor movement. This experience burned itself into my memory so that I never forgot the principle in after years.[21]

What made Gompers and others uneasy and later bitter about Woodhull and her associates was not just her avowal of spiritualism and her sexual radicalism, but also her opportunism – and she was undeniably opportunistic. Yet there are others, particularly feminists, who have seen her differently and who have responded to her historical legacy in a more positive light. Feminist critics have often been sympathetic to Woodhull's various projects as she articulated them in the lectures, articles and pronouncements that seemed to pour from her throughout the late 1860s and the 1870s. Recently, Sheila Rowbotham has argued that Woodhull's interest in spiritualism challenged those women activists who preached for transformation through the moral leadership of women by arguing for a social transformation based on agency and self-transformation. She recognizes that Woodhull was above all an individualist, yet she argues that she was one who believed that individuality and communality need not be opposed.[22]

Crucially, too, Woodhull's discussion of social and political reorganization, like that of Marx, was based upon economics. In an article of 1896 called 'Woman Suffrage in the United States' she ends by stating that 'suffrage is only one phase of the larger question of woman's emancipation. More important is the question of her social and economic position. Her financial independence underlies all the rest'.[23]

Her constant reiteration of the economic basis of women's subordination to men was one shared with some other women activists of the period. When Marx and Aveling wrote their account of meeting American women's suffrage activists, however, in *The Working-Class Movement in America*, they criticized them for having too little an account of economics in their considerations of the problems confronting women. Had Woodhull still been involved in the suffrage movement at that point their analysis may well have been quite different. As a woman who had supported herself and a large family financially (and was well known for doing that) Woodhull combined, to a unique degree, a theoretical and rhetorical position with a practical one. This was very compelling to her supporters. Other historians of the labour movement have championed her too.

One key difference between Victoria Woodhull and Eleanor Marx is the relation between Marx's secularism and Woodhull's spiritualism. Paul Buhle has

---

21 Egbert and Persons, I, 234.
22 See Sheila Rowbotham, 'Sensuous Spirits: Victoria Woodhull and Tennessee Claflin' in *Women in Movement: Feminism and Social Action* (New York and London: Routledge, 1992), pp. 77–86.
23 See 'Woman Suffrage in the United States', *The Humanitarian*, 9 (July 1896), No. I, repr. in *The Victoria Woodhull Reader*, ed. by Madeleine B. Stern (Weston, Mass.: M. & S. Press, 1974).

made striking claims about the significance of spiritualism in the history of American socialism and of Woodhull's influence as a woman centrally involved with both. He even goes so far as to argue that spiritualism was 'the American Socialism', writing that spiritualism 'answered the need for a collective, egalitarian vision and nourished indigenous radicalism for decades'.[24]

In recent years the association between spiritualism and radicalism is one that has been explored by a number of social and cultural historians. Woodhull's route into spiritualism is in some ways a classic case. As a girl and young woman she worked as a travelling medium and clairvoyant, cashing in on the massive contemporary interest in spiritualism. Later she worked in California on the stage. The careers of actor/medium were well established for young working-class women: both involved levels of theatricality and mendacity and neither required a formal education. Woodhull went on the stage because she had few other options. Marx's desire to act, however, seems to have emerged from a far more complex set of reasons and to have a set of cultural meanings that are absent from Woodhull's theatrical endeavours. For both Marx and Woodhull stage experience gave them confidence in public speaking, in voice projection and the ability to face an audience.

An avowal of spiritualism could allow young women access to public positions that would have been impossible for them through more conventional routes. Mediums' claims about the unexpected appearance of spirits, their method of giving advice and its efficacy are not at all uncommon in the mid- to late nineteenth century. For women like Woodhull whose class or social position or educational background might not make them obvious candidates for a public social function, such encouragement and authentication from the other world could be extremely useful. She claimed to have been visited on a number of occasions by a figure that turned out to be the Athenian orator Demosthenes. She recounted that in 1868 he visited her in Pittsburgh and told her to go to New York where important work was waiting for her and a house was ready.[25] That Demosthenes should, by implication, pass his mantle on to a woman whose own powers as an orator were to become considerable, suggests the claims she was establishing for herself as a public speaker and those she was making for other women, of all classes and races, too. (Significantly Henry Ward Beecher, the brilliant preacher whose exposure was centrally her responsibility, was often compared with Demosthenes.) In claiming she had experienced this visitation Woodhull was challenging the very basis of men's claims to political, religious and oratorical superiority. When she arrived in New York, and found the house he had

---

[24] Buhle writes: 'The peculiar radical ideology that grew out of the struggle for emancipation of Blacks, women and all Americans, offered a counterpart to Marxism's concentration on the industrial worker', *Marxism in the U.S.A. from 1870 to the Present: Remapping the History of the American Left* (London: Verso, 1987), p. 62.

[25] For fuller details see Underhill, pp. 170–71.

promised her, she visited its library and claimed that the first book she saw was 'The Orations of Demosthenes'. This narrative became a part of the fantasy of Woodhull's development and served an extremely useful function for her in asserting her right to a voice. Women mediums played a significant role in contesting women's right to speak publicly in *ante-bellum* America. Later, the phenomenon of spiritualism, as well as that of women's public speech, found its way into a far greater number of the literary productions of the period than is often recognized – most famously Henry James's *The Bostonians* (1886).[26]

Appearing to speak while in a trance could make women seem passive vehicles for spirit communications which would make their interventions less politically problematic and allow them to make radical interventions while shielding them, in part, from the impact. The invocation of the spirit of Demosthenes is less outlandish than it might sound given the widespread interest in spiritualism in the period. Other women activists such as Elizabeth Cady Stanton 'accepted the theatrical invention of Demosthenes as a bit of poetic license'.[27]

If Woodhull allied her spiritualism with her socialism in ways that can seem bizarre today, it may be useful to remember Cady Stanton's tolerance. For instance, Woodhull claimed that at the time of the fiercest exchange between the Communards and government forces in France – as Marx was travelling to Bordeaux, no doubt – two of her spirit guides (Bonaparte and Josephine as she cosily called them) took her on a journey to Paris, during which she witnessed the events of the moment.[28] For Woodhull, and for many spiritualists, her political radicalism and her spiritualism were not in the slightest bit incompatible. The very history of the emergence of spiritualism in America is tied up with political agitation over abolition and women's rights. Indeed the date invariably (albeit not entirely accurately) associated with its first appearance is 1848. This is also the date of the first publication of the *Communist Manifesto*, and that of the Seneca Falls Declaration of Women's Sentiments, which marked the emergence of a consolidated women's rights movement in America. Yet for sceptical socialist activists such as Eleanor Marx who were engaged with the revolution personally

---

26 For an account of the centrality of women's public speaking to American literary culture and its relation to social change see Caroline Levander, *Voices of the Nation: Women and Public Speech in Nineteenth-Century American Literature and Culture* (Cambridge: Cambridge University Press, 1998).

27 Underhill, p. 172. Underhill writes: 'Later in the year she wrote Woodhull playfully, "Will you ask Demosthenes if there is any new argument not yet made on the 14th and 15th Amendments that he will bring out," assuming rightly, as had Olympia Brown, that Woodhull had enlarged on her spirit guide to pander to the credulous.'

28 'At their behest, Victoria left her body and journeyed to a hill high above the Town Hall of Paris, where she could see that the Palais-Royal, the Ministry of Finance, the Rue de Rivoli, and the Rue Royale were all aflame. As the fire spread, the Porte Saint-Martin, the Hôtel de Ville, the Bastille and Bercy "were belching forth blood-red columns of fire."' Cited in Goldsmith, *Other Powers*, p. 283.

and materially (rather than in trance states), events such as Woodhull's 'visit' to Paris with her exalted spirit guides (had they heard of it) may have been galling.

Woodhull's involvement in both American radical politics and American spiritualism at critical levels reveals a great deal about the opportunities both gave to women who wished to cross over – through class, gender and even race boundaries. As important and ground-breaking work by Logie Barrow, Ann Braude and Alex Owen has demonstrated, nineteenth-century spiritualism, on both sides of the Atlantic, was consistently associated with a radical politics. The work of Braude and Owen has shown that it was a movement that was profoundly available to young women, particularly young working-class women. It offered significant possibilities for women to claim public voices.[29] Spiritualism also provided in some of its practices a form of radicalism in itself, and it encouraged mediums – those who were possessed – to speak publicly while entranced, and then afterwards to speak further about the meanings of the messages they uttered through their persons. The possibilities this offered to a wide range of women were greatly empowering. The insistence on the part of many spiritualists on allying themselves with reforms from animal rights and children's rights to dietary and dress reform, reproductive rights and others turned spiritualism into an arena in which an unusually wide variety of radical activism could take place. The stress, within spiritualism, on individuality was also of key significance for Woodhull and her supporters.

For many of the more conservatively-minded socialists who were members of the IWA, Woodhull's combination of interests suggested a profound lack of understanding of the legitimate aims of socialism. Very soon factionalism within Section 12 was splitting it. In May 1872, after Woodhull announced that she would stand for the American presidency as a candidate for the Equal Rights party, with Frederick Douglass as her vice-president (he was only told of this later) and the *Weekly* supporting her, Section 12 were expelled from the IWA. The journal survived the expulsion and went on to conduct a moral crusade that marked a turn away from international socialism and towards exposing the sexual double standard. This, more than any other of Woodhull's campaigns, damaged her reputation and drew calumny down upon her.

She had been attacked and ridiculed by sections of the press for some years. When the novelists joined in they concentrated on her purported moral degeneracy and, in the case of Harriet Beecher Stowe, allied this to an anxiety about her association with socialist politics. Stowe depicts anxieties about the advances being made by socialism in America as a form of moral panic. This

---

[29] Logie Barrow, *Independent Spirits: Spiritualism and English Plebeians, 1850–1910* (London: Routledge & Kegan Paul, 1986); Ann Braude, *Radical Spirits: Spiritualism and Women's Rights in Nineteenth Century America* (Boston, Mass.: Beacon Press, 1989); Alex Owen, *The Darkened Room: Women, Power and Spiritualism in Late Nineteenth Century England* (London: Virago, 1989).

despite the fact that the socialists associated with Woodhull were equally concerned about her reputation and the impact this would have on future membership of the IWA, and just as desirous of distancing themselves from her. It is interesting to see how similar anxieties would beset Marx some time later when she made her decision to live with Aveling. By this time Woodhull would be safely married to a wealthy British husband.

At the height of Woodhull's fame within women's rights circles, Harriet Beecher Stowe satirized her viciously in her novel *My Wife and I; or, Harry Henderson's History*, serialized in the *Christian Union* (1870–71). The send-up had consequences that Stowe could not have envisaged at the time. She represented Woodhull as Audacia Dangyereyes, 'a somewhat noted character in New York circles' (218). Audacia appears well into the novel in Chapter 23, 'I Receive a Moral Shower-Bath', in which the protagonist Harry Henderson finds himself visited by her in his room. Harry has written a number of articles on the 'Modern Woman', and here he finally meets one. After Audacia scandalizes him by sitting on his desk, holding his hand and stroking his shoulder, he is further shocked when she begins to explain her political and moral beliefs to him:

> 'You've been asserting, in your blind way, the rights of woman to liberty and equality; the rights of women, in short, to do anything that men do. Well, here comes a woman to your room who *takes* her rights, practically, and does just what a man would do. I claim my right to smoke, if I please, and to drink, if I please; and to come up into your room and make you a call, and have a good time with you, if I please, and tell you that I like your looks, as I do ... Come round and take a smoke with me, this evening, won't you? I've got the nicest little chamber that ever you saw.'[30]

Stowe reasserts the moral order when Harry's friend Jim Fellows appears at the door and patronizes and belittles Audacia. Her reply reveals Stowe's anxieties about the way in which the behaviour of woman activists like Woodhull undermined the reactions of 'true women' to social situations and therefore threatened society – especially domestic society – as a whole:

> 'Keep your distance, sir,' said she, giving him a slight box on his ear. 'I prefer to do my own courting. I have been trying to show your friend here how little he knows of the true equality of women, and of the good time coming, when we shall have our rights, and do just as we darn well please, as you do ... The time will come when all women will be just as free to life, liberty, and the pursuit of happiness, as men.'
> 'Good heavens!' said I, under my breath.[31]

---

30 Harriet Beecher Stowe, *My Wife and I, or, Harry Henderson's History* (London: Sampson Low, Marston, Low, & Searle, 1871), p. 218.
31 Stowe, p. 219.

Audacia's appearance in the novel is only fleeting but she manages to force both men to pay out $5 each to subscribe to her paper, *The Emancipated Woman*. Harry has a crisis about it when he realizes that his name will appear on the subscription list and that his aunt and respectable friends might see it. He later describes her paper in terms that suggest the extent to which socialism and activism over sexual rights were tied up together irrevocably in this period of American culture, at least in Stowe's mind. Using highly emotive language he calls the paper 'an exposition of all the wildest principles of modern French communism. It consisted of attacks directed about equally against Christianity, marriage, the family state, and all human laws and standing order, whatsoever. It was much the same kind of writing with which the populace of France was indoctrinated and leavened in the era preceding the first revolution, and which in time bore fruit in blood.'[32]

At this point it seems that for Stowe, to attack 'modern French communism' was equivalent to attacking Woodhull herself, through her association with the IWA. This is how those who recognized Woodhull in Stowe's text would have read the narrative, and this is, ironically, the very moment at which Karl Marx was disassociating himself from Woodhull. Yet when Stowe collected the serialized parts together and published them in book form she took care to deny that the any characters were based on recognizable figures, prefacing the novel with a detailed disclaimer that reads unconvincingly. She explains that any belief that 'certain of the characters are designed as portraits of really existing individuals' comes from 'an imperfect consideration of the principles of dramatic composition'. She then gives a brief account of how the art of characterization comes about before getting to the real point at hand, that of the representation of Audacia (who she does not name in the preface at any point). She continues:

> For instance, it being the author's purpose to show the embarrassment of the young champion of progressive principles, in meeting the excesses of modern reformers, it came in her way to paint the picture of the modern emancipated young woman of advanced ideas and free behaviour. And this character was mistaken for an *individual*, drawn from actual observation. On the contrary, it was not the author's intention to draw an individual, but simply to show the type of a class. Facts as to conduct and behaviour similar to those she has described are unhappily too familiar to residents of New York.[33]

The representation of Audacia centres on the relation between her political aspirations and sexual and moral conduct, juxtaposing this to a relentless debate about maternal and domestic power, which is the dominant theme of the novel. This is quite consistent with Woodhull's representation within the press. Woodhull was furious with Stowe's attack on her and was already planning a

---

[32] Stowe, p. 257.
[33] Stowe, pp. iii–iv.

revenge that would split the Beecher family and create one of the greatest sexual scandals of nineteenth-century America, the Beecher–Tilton affair. Writing in the *Weekly* and following (she claimed) the instruction of the spirit world, Woodhull revealed that Henry Ward Beecher had been having an affair with one of his married parishioners, Elizabeth Tilton. Her revelation, coupled with details of the sexual double standards of other widely-known male figures, would lead to her prosecution, and brief imprisonment, for sending obscene publications through the post. As a consequence of her imprisonment her campaign for the presidency also collapsed and the high point of her political life with it.

Stowe's attack on Woodhull and Beecher Hooker's defence of her might be read as an insignificant spat (albeit with massive consequences) that centres on their relation to their brother Henry Ward Beecher. Yet read differently it goes some way towards helping us consider the ways in which nineteenth-century American women's activism developed in conjunction with spiritualism and the significance of Woodhull as a pivotal figure. Furthermore it reveals that, however distasteful it may have been to Marx, women such as Woodhull were involved with public campaigns in such a way that it allowed other women to follow in their paths. Whether Marx liked it or not, Woodhull was a trailblazer.

Once Woodhull moved to London, however, the way in which she was represented, and the way she represented herself, changed substantially. She created and published a family tree that emphasized her noble origins, occasionally styled herself Woodhall, developed an interest in eugenics and began a lengthy pursuit of a respectable husband. This, purportedly, is the basis for Henry James's novella *The Siege of London* (1882). James describes his protagonist Mrs Headway in brilliant and bitingly subtle terms that suggest Woodhull. 'She had had these episodes – her unions were all unfortunate – and had borne half a dozen names … she had been divorced too often – it was a tax on one's credulity; she must have repudiated more husbands than she had married.'[34] Yet though Woodhull's marriages form compelling narratives and were hugely influential in terms of the direction she took, they are in themselves the least interesting aspects of her life. The narrator attributes her desire to marry the respectable Sir Arthur Desmesne to the fact that she had 'outlived the need of being amused' since she 'had lived a very exciting life, and her vision of happiness at present was to be magnificently bored'.[35] She was tired of a life that had already been too full and saw marriage as a form of escape into some form of peaceful retreat from it.

Victoria Woodhull may well have shared the motivation ascribed to the fictional Mrs Headway, yet this rationale does not fully answer the question of why she largely turned her back on her American past once she moved to England in 1877. It is tantalizing to speculate upon the question of why she tried so

---

34 Henry James, *The Siege of London, The Pension Beaurepas, and The Point of View* (Boston: Osgood, 1883), p. 17.
35 *The Siege of London*, p. 110.

valiantly to erase her past. Was she, like Mrs Headway, tired of life? After years of fighting political battles had she simply had enough if it all? Just as tantalizing is the issue of why Marx erased her own future by her suicide. Both women's collusion in rendering themselves invisible is, ultimately, one fascinating aspect of what they have in common. It is also the least knowable. Perhaps speculations on either woman might find points in common between them. Both Eleanor Marx and Victoria Woodhull had to formulate complex positions for themselves in which the balance between respectability and radicalism was always requiring negotiation. Both had experience of unreliable and duplicitous men. Both had to contend with financial deprivation, attacks upon their families, complicated emotional relationships with siblings. But to say this about these two is to say it about many other women too: ultimately it is reductive and empty. Their legacies and meanings, together and apart, remain problematic and frustrating: yet the stories they told of themselves and have had told about them still keep us coming back for more.

Chapter 12

'Tantalising Glimpses': The Intersecting Lives of Eleanor Marx and Mathilde Blind

Simon Avery

In the postscript to the first volume of her biography, Yvonne Kapp speaks of the 'tantalising glimpses' we get of Eleanor Marx as she flits in and out of other people's reminiscences, letters and lives.[1] In this essay I explore the relationship that existed between Marx and another remarkable nineteenth-century woman, Mathilde Blind, poet, biographer, feminist and freethinking socialist. 'Glimpses' is a particularly apt word in this circumstance, since there exists little evidence of long periods of time spent together. However, there are many parallels between their lives and a number of situations and occasions where we know their lives intersected. Blind and Marx moved in many of the same circles and their opinions and beliefs were remarkably similar on a wide range of social and political issues.

This assumption about their intersecting lives is made, for instance, by William Michael Rossetti in a letter of 1887 to Frederick James Furnivall in which he records his incredulity that Edward Aveling's application for membership of the Shelley Society, of which Rossetti was the chair, might be rejected because of his common-law relationship with Marx:

> While I was absent [at San Remo] a question was raised in the Committee of the Shelley Society whether, if Dr Aveling the socialist were to offer to subscribe to the Society, his subscription should be accepted. The only *serious* objection stated (I gather) is that the so-called Mrs Aveling is in fact not married to him. The Committee decided that they would not accept Aveling's subscription and membership. The decision I regarded as, on various grounds, absolutely monstrous and ludicrous: so I had written that I would resign my seat on the Committee. In consequence of this, the Committee reconsidered the question; and determined to admit Aveling if he applies, and retain me ... I have no personal knowledge of Aveling, nor of Mrs Aveling (said to be Miss Marx): may possibly have met one or other of them some three years ago at Mathilde Blind's.[2]

---

1 Kapp, I, 288.
2 William Michael Rossetti, *Selected Letters*, ed. by Roger W. Peattie (London: Pennsylvania University Press, 1990), p. 504.

Rossetti therefore took it for granted that Marx and Aveling would have been on good social terms with Blind – and, on examination of the evidence, however fragmentary and incomplete it may be, one can see why he did so.

Blind was born in 1841, fourteen years before Marx, yet they were to die within two years of each other (Blind in 1896, Marx in 1898). Like Marx, Blind came from Jewish German stock, her father being a Jewish banker named Cohen. Unlike Marx, however, who increasingly vocalized her Jewishness,[3] Blind seems not to have made any explicit reference to her race in any of the surviving documentation, although her Jewish countenance was often mentioned in the writings of her acquaintances. Indeed, given the fact that she was exposed to Christianity at school, her Jewish ancestry seems to have played little part in her life at all.

A much more important parental influence was offered to Mathilde by her mother Friederike Ettlinger who, following the death of her husband soon after Mathilde's birth, became increasingly involved with campaigns for a unified democratic Germany. Two years later, the revolutionary atmosphere in the family home deepened when Friederike married one of Europe's major revolutionaries and political writers, Karl Blind, who adopted Mathilde and whose name she took. Karl Blind was already well known across Europe as a fervent republican, having been arrested and tried on several occasions for the dissemination of anti-government propaganda, but he is now best remembered for his part in the leadership of the Baden Insurrection of 1848, for which he was arrested and imprisoned for eight months. When a republican government was finally established in 1849, Blind was released from jail and sent to Paris as a state representative. However, the new republicanism did not hold and was soon defeated in Austria and Germany by the forces of reaction, obliging the Blind family to flee first to Belgium and then, following increasing pressure from the French government in the early 1850s, to Britain.

Like the Marxes, who were also expelled from France, Prussia and Belgium following the defeats of the 1848 revolutions, the Blinds were hounded from one European country to another, both families ending up in London. Three years before he had moved to Britain as a political émigré, however, Karl Blind had already made the acquaintance of Karl Marx. As McLellan records,[4] Marx had left his family in Paris in August 1849 and travelled to London in the company of Blind and the Swiss communist Seiler, where he temporarily stayed in Blind's lodgings in Grosvenor Square before his family joined him. Both revolutionaries also briefly sat on the Committee for the Assistance of German Political Refugees, which collected money for the cause through both personal appeals and newspaper campaigns. Links between the Blinds and the Marxes had therefore already started to form before the Blinds took up permanent residence in Britain.

---

[3]   Kapp, II, 510.
[4]   David McLellan, *Karl Marx: His Life and Thought* (London: Macmillan, 1973), p. 226.

After moving to his adopted homeland, Karl Blind, like Marx, continued with his political activities, becoming the London correspondent of almost every radical journal in Germany, as well as writing for major British periodicals including the liberal *Fortnightly Review*. And as with the homes of other political refugees such as the Marxes and the Rossettis, the Blinds' house in Winchester Road became a meeting place and haven for many political visitors, famous revolutionaries and champions of liberty, including Marx himself, Louis Blanc, Ledru-Rollin, Langiewicz, Garibaldi (Eleanor Marx's major hero according to her list of confessions),[5] and Mazzini. As Moncure Daniel Conway, a close friend of Blind, noted in his informative *Autobiography*: 'if any interesting man came, especially from Germany, we were sure to meet him at one of those Sunday evenings in Winchester Road'.[6] Like the young Eleanor Marx, Mathilde Blind was brought up in a household constantly involved in revolutionary and socialist discussion, where she was in continuous contact with many of Europe's leading political thinkers and activists. For both women, the circumstances of their youth remained the major influence on their subsequent lives.

In particular, several contemporary commentators on these Sunday evening meetings at the Blind residence remarked on the close relationship which soon developed between Mathilde and Mazzini. As Conway wrote, 'The delight of Mazzini in her society seemed to some of their political friends to be of importance to the affairs of Germany and France; for Mathilde was well acquainted with such matters and keenly interested in them.'[7] Indeed, like Eleanor Marx, Blind was never hesitant when expressing her views on international affairs, even to the most renowned company, and in 1867 she extended her hero-worship when she dedicated her first volume of poems, published under the pseudonym 'Claude Lake', 'To Joseph Mazzini, the Prophet, Martyr, and Hero … in Undying Gratitude and Reverence'.[8] Mazzini was to remain a particularly important figure for Blind, for twenty-five years later she was to publish her 'Personal Recollections' of him in the *Fortnightly Review*.[9]

Karl Blind's reputation as a republican and revolutionary must have become quickly known both in Britain and the United States, as Conway suggests in his *Autobiography* when he records a visit from 'an agreeable young gentleman'[10] from Ohio who wanted to make his acquaintance. Conway gave him his card as an introduction only to have Karl Blind arrive at his house two days later to report that the man had proposed a scheme for killing the Prince of Wales.

---

5 Kapp, I, 60.
6 Moncure Daniel Conway, *Autobiography, Memoirs and Experiences*, 2 vols (London: Cassell, 1904), II, 61.
7 Conway, *Autobiography*, II, 62.
8 *Poems by Claude Lake* (London: Alfred W. Bennett, 1867).
9 'Personal Recollections of Mazzini', *Fortnightly Review*, 55 (1891), 702–12.
10 Conway, *Autobiography*, II, 61.

However, it was not only Mathilde Blind's stepfather who was involved in revolutionary political politics. In 1866 her seventeen-year-old stepbrother Ferdinand, at that time studying in Tübingen, attempted to assassinate the German Chancellor Bismarck. Several years later Mathilde showed Conway a letter from Ferdinand to a friend in Germany in which he declared that because Bismarck was steadily leading Germany into war and the law considered him too senior to touch, an individual like Ferdinand would have to take him on himself if the country was to be saved:

> As I wandered through the blooming fields of Germany, that were soon to be crushed under the iron heel of war, and saw the number of youths pass by that were to lose their lives for the selfish aims of a few, the thought came quite spontaneously to punish the cause of so much evil, even if it were at the cost of my life.[11]

As Bismarck was returning unaccompanied from the royal palace to the Wilhelmstrasse, Ferdinand Blind attacked him on Unter den Linden. In the struggle that ensued three shots were fired, the first missing Bismarck completely and the other two only grazing his skin. A man who knew how to look after himself, Bismarck had little trouble in disarming his potential assassin who was arrested and subsequently hanged himself in prison. As Lothar Gall argues,[12] Bismarck was able to use the failed assassination both to bolster his position with the German public and reinforce his own strongly-held belief that he was God's chosen instrument. It is a cruel irony that Blind sacrificed himself in the republican cause only to empower further the man he believed to be ruining his homeland.

At this point another intersection between the Blinds and the Marxes occurs, for following Karl Blind's death, Bismarck announced in the Reichstag that his potential assassin had been schooled by Karl Marx. In the 1st May issue of the Social League's journal *Commonweal*, Eleanor Marx took issue with this accusation, arguing that her father had not seen Ferdinand Blind since he was thirteen, and that 'the ridiculous idea that a man like Marx could have spent his time "breeding assassins" only proves how right Marx was to see in Bismarck nothing but a Prussian clodhopper'.[13] So incensed was Eleanor Marx by the accusation that she also sent copies of this notice to the *Sozialdemokrat* and *Le Socialiste*, as well as a copy to Bismarck himself.

Many Germans, however, fully supported Ferdinand Blind. A reporter for the Stuttgart *Beobachter*, for example, the voice of the Württemberg democrats, wrote: 'The attempted murder of this murderer condemned unanimously by an entire

---

[11] Conway, *Autobiography*, II, 61.
[12] Lothar Gall, *Bismarck: The White Revolutionary*, Vol. 1: 1815–1871, trans. by J.A. Underwood (London: Unwin Hyman, 1986), p. 292.
[13] Kapp, II, 89.

people is not in the least surprising. No one will venture to call this young man a bad German who has given his life to free the fathers and from such a monster.'[14] Even Bismarck himself later paid restrained tribute to Ferdinand's patriotism, particularly since

> his dead body became the object of a cult ... ladies of considerable name, whose husbands enjoyed a certain reputation in the scientific world, crowned it with laurels and flowers, and ... this was tolerated by the police – the mass of the ordinary officials, perhaps even some of the higher ones, being rather on his side.[15]

As with the Marx daughters, the political background and radical thinking which surrounded Mathilde Blind was to feed directly into her own life and work, and helped to engender a considerable independence of mind which was evident as early as her school years. Whilst attending the girls' school at St John's Wood, for example, she was introduced to a number of books on geology and, in her own words, she began to worry over 'the strange discrepancies between the account of Creation in Genesis and the history of our globe as revealed to us by the rocks and stones'. She subsequently spent considerable time reading texts such as Butler's *Analogy*, Paley's *Evidences* and Max Muller's *Comparative Mythology*, until 'the veil of Christian sentiments in which I had tried to envelop myself dispersed like a vapour'.[16] Expelled from the school for her atheism – an act which Mathilde Blind would probably have revelled in given its parallels to her beloved Shelley's expulsion from Oxford for the same offence – she mirrored Eleanor Marx and other late nineteenth-century freethinkers in turning to a lifelong commitment to socialist and feminist agendas rather than Christian mythologies.

This rejection of established religion was to form one of the most important bases of Blind's subsequent life and writings. In 1873, for example, she wrote a biography of David Friedrich Strauss, the author of *Das Leben Jesu*, and following in the footsteps of George Eliot, who had translated Strauss's work in 1845, Blind translated Strauss's later text, *The Old Faith and the New*, the work in which he finally abandoned the Hegelian principles to which he had previously adhered and fully embraced materialism. Such freethinking ideas were, of course, typical of the communities to which both Blind and Marx belonged, and a strong sense of positivism, with its emphasis on knowledge being relative to man's social and material conditions, is common to them both.

It is hardly surprising, then, that both grew up to be types of the 'New Woman', that dominant presence in the late Victorian social and psychological landscape who resisted marriage and traditional roles within the family, and

---

[14] Gall, *Bismarck*, p. 292.
[15] Richard Garnett, 'Memoir', in *The Poetical Works of Mathilde Blind*, ed. by Arthur Symons (London: T. Fisher Unwin, 1900), p. 23.
[16] Garnett, 'Memoir', p. 7.

instead committed herself to gaining economic independence, and emancipation and equality in all spheres of existence. For both, this push towards becoming New Women began early with their commitment to self-education. At an early age, Eleanor Marx was already reciting by heart long speeches from Shakespeare, encouraged by her father, as well as reading voraciously and engaging in the intellectual environment provided by the Marx household. Similarly Mathilde was for the most part – and certainly following her expulsion from school – self-educated, reading Kant, Goethe, Schiller and Shakespeare, and teaching herself Latin, Old German and Middle German.

Throughout her life Mathilde Blind was a highly independent woman who chose to remain single, living on her own from 1871, and travelling extensively by herself. Already by 1860, at the age of just eighteen, she had embarked on a lone walking tour through Switzerland. As her autobiographical fragments in the British Library reveal, she used this opportunity to expand her intellectual horizons and escape the limitations of the formal education provided her in England, quickly getting involved with a large group of Swiss radical intellectuals and even attempting to get into lectures in Zurich which were forbidden to women. But perhaps the most powerful experience of the trip was provided by the spectacle of the Alps themselves:

> The Alps, aglow like mountains of roses round a heavenly Jerusalem, receding range beyond range into airier infinitudes of light, a vision like the last part of Beethoven's Ninth Symphony turned into visible form.[17]

Such images of the sublime and their effect were to recur constantly in her later poetic work and from then on she was a frequent visitor to Europe.

On her return to Britain, Blind began to spend considerable time writing and researching, and started to build up a number of contacts with others who shared her passions. One of the most important of these was Richard Garnett, who was in charge of the Reading Room at the British Museum. The correspondence between Blind and Garnett, most of it preserved in the British Library, is voluminous, the friends often writing to each other every day and sometimes twice a day.[18] It was a friendship which was to last throughout Blind's life and there is no doubt about its centrality for both her personal and professional development. The correspondence reflects their constant dialogue about new literary publications and also reveals how much energy Garnett, a poet in his own right, put into finding openings for Blind to get her own work published. He regularly read and commented upon her manuscripts, and contacted publishers, editors and reviewers on her behalf.

---

[17] Garnett, 'Memoir', p. 9.
[18] Blind, Mathilde, Unpublished MSS in the British Library, MSS Add. 61927; 61928; 61929; 61930, fols 1r–55r.

Garnett was also a close friend of Eleanor Marx, frequently meeting her in the Reading Room as it became, in Marx's own words, 'my daily resort'.[19] As Marx spent long hours in the library, attempting to supplement her income by undertaking research and hack work for other writers as well as producing her own political papers, so too her friendship with Garnett developed. By 1882, Garnett was petitioning on her behalf when she wanted to be allowed access to the Reading Room during the so-called 'closed week',[20] and the following year she invited Garnett to her father's funeral (he was unable to attend). It seems highly probable, therefore, that Garnett acted as another lynch-pin in the twisted fates of the Marx and Blind daughters.

One of the strongest links between the two women lies in their mutual love of Shelley, the poet who, in the words of Annie Besant, was 'the hero of the freethinkers' of late Victorian London.[21] Throughout her writing career, Blind was always heavily influenced by the Romantic poets. Her first known work was an 'Ode to Schiller' (1859), and she later edited Byron's letters and poems. Her greatest poetic love was always for Shelley, however, and particularly those poems such as *Prometheus Unbound, Queen Mab, Hellas* and *The Revolt of Islam,* which embody his revolutionary politics. William Michael Rossetti's correspondence reveals the detailed knowledge Blind had of the poet and her immense excitement when she came near to any artefact which might have belonged to him. When Rossetti showed her a fragment of Shelley's skull she slowly brought it to her lips and kissed it 'reverently',[22] whilst Ford Madox Brown records the dogged determination with which Blind tracked down an old woman in Lynmouth who had once met the poet and who possessed a brief note from him in which he acknowledged a debt of £5.[23]

Over the three decades from the 1860s to the 1880s, Blind published many works on her beloved freethinking hero. In 1869, she lectured on Shelley at St George's Hall, a lecture which was later printed in the *Westminster Review* in July 1870, and two years later she published a selection of his poems together with a memoir in which she wrote with enormous enthusiasm of 'this spiritual child of the Revolution' with his 'dauntless championing of the weak against the strong'.[24] Then in 1888, sixteen years after her edited selection, she published another lecture entitled 'Shelley's View of Nature Contrasted with Darwin's'. This work

19 Kapp, I, 192.
20 *Daughters*, p. 157.
21 Kapp, II, 250.
22 William Michael Rossetti, *The Diary of William Michael Rossetti*, ed. by Odette Bornand (Oxford: Clarendon Press, 1977), p. 171.
23 *Ford Madox Brown: A Record of His Life and Works*, ed. by Ford Madox Hueffer (London: Longmans, Green & Co., 1896), p. 268.
24 *A Selection from the Poems of Percy Bysshe Shelley, with a Memoir*, ed. by Mathilde Blind (Leipzig: Tauchnitz, 1872), pp. vi, vii. Also see Mathilde Blind, *Shelley: A Lecture* (London: Taylor, 1870).

was to have tremendous resonances with her later writing on evolutionary theory, but for the moment it is important to stress the socialist politics which she always celebrated in the poet. According to Blind, Shelley had been of the firm conviction that 'if you could only rid society of kings and priests we should immediately enter on the Golden Age, and instead of discord, war, and wretchedness, the earth would become the abode of love and harmony'.[25] This was a line of thinking endorsed by Blind herself since she too believed that if only society could eradicate 'the double yoke of superstition and tyranny', humankind would move to a higher level, which would subsequently allow the liberation of both sexes from ascribed gender roles. Men would become 'kind, sympathetic, and gentle', while women would 'naturally turn into brave, generous and sincere human beings'. Again, Blind's feminist and socialist agendas collapse into one another, as they frequently did for Marx, in a unified vision of hope for the future.

According to William Michael Rossetti, Blind was one of the Shelley Society's most active members,[26] and it seems certain that both she and Marx would have come into contact with each other at the Society's events. Marx and Aveling gave joint papers on Shelley and Socialism to the Society in December 1888 and February 1889, both sessions being chaired by Rossetti, and Blind was due to present a paper on Shelley's women in June 1888, but was prevented from doing so by ill health. Marx was also to publish her own work on the poet entitled *Shelley's Socialism*, which came out in the same year as Blind's paper on Shelley and Darwin.

It was chiefly because of the 1870 *Westminster Review* article on Shelley that Blind made the acquaintance of Ford Madox Brown, with whom a very close relationship developed. Indeed, for several periods of her life she was to live with the Madox Browns, first in Manchester and then at their house in Regent's Park, and from here she first met Swinburne and the Rossettis and established herself as a regular associate of the Pre-Raphaelites. It is clear that many of the male members of the circle were extremely impressed by her character and intelligence. William Michael Rossetti, for example, often mentions her in his correspondence in terms of a close friendship, speaking of her visits to his family and their trips to the theatre, and when he wrote to Walt Whitman in 1875, he referred to her as 'a woman of singular ability and independence of mind'.[27]

Another anecdote reports Madox Brown's badly-executed attempt to convince Dante Gabriel Rossetti of the worth of Blind's writings:

> Brown had called on Rossetti and produced for his perusal and approval a sonnet by Miss Blind; and was put out at finding that it elicited less of

---

[25] Mathilde Blind, *Shelley's View of Nature Contrasted With Darwin's* (London: Shelley Society Paper, first series, 1888), p. 12.
[26] William Michael Rossetti, *Some Reminiscences*, 2 vols (London: Brown, Langham & Co., 1906), II, 388.
[27] William Rossetti, *Selected Letters*, p. 332.

hearty panegyric than he had hoped for. He went off in a huff, after stepping into a dark room, and smashing a screen ... over which he stumbled.[28]

Following this farcical scenario though, Dante Gabriel's response to Madox Brown's written apology reveals his high regard for Blind: 'I always liked her and valued her quite exceptionally, and fully believe that she possesses genius.'[29]

For Madox Brown, however, it was not just Blind's intelligence which attracted him but her beauty as well. He was clearly infatuated with her, installing her at York Place, Cheetham Hill, near his own lodgings, and contriving it so that she 'haunted the households of Madox Brown and his daughter, Lucy',[30] a situation which Emma Brown found extremely taxing. It was even suggested that after Emma's death, Madox Brown wanted to marry Blind, but his daughters vehemently opposed this as they did the suggestion that she should take him to the seaside to convalesce after a bad attack of gout in 1883. Whether she wanted it or not, Blind found herself drawn into the sexual intrigues of the Pre-Raphaelite circle.

She would have been particularly attracted to the Browns' household by the complementary mix of artists and politicians to be found there. From as early as 1863, as Whistler's journal records, 'there was always the most wonderful people, the Blinds, Swinburne, anarchists, poets, and musicians, all kinds and sorts, and in an inner room Rossetti and Mrs Morris sitting side by side in state, being worshipped'.[31] Following the Paris Commune of 1871 (which Karl Marx was accused of having instigated), an international socialist element, including many Communard refugees, frequently gathered there, just as they did at Karl Marx's residence. At the centre of this community, as William Bell Scott records, was Mathilde Blind, whom he described as 'a jolly little red republican, with an immense mop and spread of black hair and in an Indian or Turkish (bright yellow stripes you know) scarf tied across her and hanging behind'.[32]

Another of Blind's political friendships was with the atheist poet James Thomson. Following the publication of *The City of Dreadful Night* in 1870, she invited him to stay at her home in Torrington Square and subsequently he often visited her there. Marx and Aveling also knew Thomson well. Aveling was a prominent member of the National Secular Society and regularly contributed to its newspaper, the *National Reformer*, edited by Charles Bradlaugh and Annie Besant, which was also Thomson's main outlet. The tenets of the Secular Society

28 Helen Rossetti Angeli, *Dante Gabriel Rossetti: His Friends and Enemies* (London: Hamish Hamilton, 1949), p. 51.
29 Angeli, *Rossetti*, p. 52.
30 Angeli, *Rossetti*, p. 50.
31 Philip Henderson, *Swinburne: The Portrait of a Poet* (London: Routledge & Kegan Paul, 1974), p. 57.
32 Teresa Newman and Ray Watkinson, *Ford Madox Ford and the Pre-Raphaelite Circle* (London: Chatto & Windus, 1991), p. 147.

were that one should 'reject all the faiths, or such parts of them as do not seem reasonable ... adopt reason instead of faith, science instead of revelation, nature instead of providence, work instead of worship and prayer, and hold that humanity instead of divinity should occupy the thoughts of men and command their service'.[33] Such tenets squared with both Blind's and Marx's own belief systems and both women attended Thomson's funeral in 1882.

Given her independence and intelligence it is not surprising to find that Blind, like Marx, became increasingly involved in the women's movement. Both wanted to encourage women to move out into the public realm and attempted to achieve this by lecturing on the woman question and female franchise. Although Blind was a competent lecturer – a report in the *Illustrated London News* in May 1870 records that she was able to 'produce a marked effect' upon an audience[34] – she never achieved Marx's status as an orator.

Nevertheless, Blind worked tirelessly in an attempt to better the lot of women, believing, as Marx did, that rather than relying on a few sympathetic men, women must develop strategies for emancipating themselves. In particular, both women looked to education as the way forward. In one of her New York lectures in 1886, Marx argued that education was one of 'the three bombs' which should be thrown among the masses in order to galvanize social change.[35] This was a view with which Blind passionately concurred. She too believed that the lack of educational opportunities for women was the basis of their social inferiority. Many of Blind's lectures on the woman question and on literary themes were therefore directed towards exposing and attempting to remedy educational injustice through a feminist-socialist agenda. Even after her death she sought to continue her campaigns by leaving money to the newly-established Newnham College in order to found a scholarship for Language and Literature.

Blind's extremely strong feminist consciousness was also reflected in her lifelong attraction to strong women. In 1878 she published an article on Mary Wollstonecraft in the *New Quarterly Magazine*,[36] and in the early 1880s, whilst living with the Madox Browns, she worked on two biographies for John Ingram's *Eminent Women* series, one of them the first ever biography of George Eliot. Her interest in the novelist had developed over the years, as her correspondence with Garnett reveals, and her lucidly-written and well-informed life reflects her admiration for her subject matter on every page. 'Will any one deny,' she writes of Eliot, 'that, in the combination of sheer intellectual power with an unparalleled vision for the details of life, she takes precedence of all writers of this or any other

[33] Imogene Walker, *James Thomson (B.V.): A Critical Study* (Ithaca, NY: Cornell University Press, 1950), pp. 43–4.

[34] *Illustrated London News*, 28 May 1870, p. 543.

[35] Kapp, II, 153.

[36] 'Mary Wollstonecraft', *New Quarterly Magazine*, 10 (1878), 390–412.

country?'[37] Praising unreservedly Eliot's 'grasp of abstract philosophical ideas', she proceeds to uphold her as 'the sole outcome of the modern positive spirit in imaginative literature – the sole novelist who has incorporated in an artistic form some of the leading ideas of Comte, of Mazzini, and of Darwin'[38] – ideas, of course, to which Blind herself was constantly drawn. The biography therefore reveals Blind's attempts to align herself with the tradition of strong female writers which Eliot represents.

Three years later in 1886, Blind published her second *Eminent Women* biography, this time on Madame Roland, the wife of Jean-Marie Roland, minister of the French interior in the crucial revolutionary year 1792–3, and a figure whom George Eliot had termed 'still the unrivalled type of the sagacious and sternly heroic yet loveable woman'.[39] Regarded as a tragic heroine by Romantic historians such as Carlyle – a thinker whom Blind held in the highest esteem and whose *The French Revolution* lies behind her own text – Roland had been committed to the revolution in its early stages before becoming its victim as a member of the defeated Girondin faction. Blind's biography celebrates Roland as a politically-engaged heroic figure who should serve as a model of republican thinking for her sex. In her concluding paragraph, she writes:

> In the long, painful process of education through which humanity is slowly advancing towards higher phases of development, the best of systems must remain waste sheets of paper but for the lives of noble men and women capable of transmuting abstractions into realities. Lives that shall illumine the path where others are groping, kindle the moral energies of men; lives such as Mme Roland's stirring her sex to a generous emulation, handing on, as she falls, the sacred tradition of heroes and martyrs.[40]

This teleological model of history, 'advancing towards higher phases of development', was one which underlaid much of Blind's work and philosophy, and was one in which, like her socialist sister Eleanor Marx, she believed women were to have a central role.

In 1890, Blind published her third text celebrating a major female figure, a translation of the journal of the Russian painter Marie Bashkirtseff, who died at the age of twenty-four. Blind saw Bashkirtseff as another model of intellectual woman, immensely learned, highly successful as an artist, intensely passionate, and a socialite who 'remained in regard to moral training as undisciplined as a wild colt'. She was determined that Bashkirtseff's journal – a work which she said was 'breathing and palpitating with life' – should be known in the English-speaking world, but she also had a wider feminist agenda to her translation. As she argues in

---

37 Mathilde Blind, *George Eliot* (London: W.H. Allen & Co., 1883), p. 5.
38 Blind, *Eliot*, pp. 7–8.
39 Blind, *Eliot*, p. 4.
40 Mathilde Blind, *Madame Roland* (London: W.H. Allen & Co., 1886), pp. 254–5.

the preface, Bashkirtseff's journal is particularly interesting 'as a document about feminine nature, of which as yet we know so little. Indeed, most of our knowledge comes to us second-hand, through the medium of men with their cut-and-dried theories as to what women are or ought to be'.[41] On publication, the translation enjoyed great popularity, even being commended by Gladstone, and helped to fuel current debates about female psychology. It is a measure of Blind's erasure from literary history in the twentieth century, however, that whilst she is noted as the first English translator of the journal in the Bashkirtseff entry in *The Oxford Companion to English Literature* (1995), she has no separate entry for herself.

Turning to Blind's poetry, the body of work for which she was most famous in the nineteenth century, we discover a mixture of competing styles.[42] Much of her earlier work is mystical in tone and has much in common with the Pre-Raphaelite work of Christina Rossetti, in both style and subject matter. As Blind was on the periphery of the Pre-Raphaelites, it is not difficult to trace a direct influence here. Indeed, William Michael Rossetti notes that she was in particular 'a very intense admirer of Christina's *Sing Song*'.[43] However, as Blind's poetic career developed, she turned to social and political issues with a commitment which became increasingly predominant in her work, and aligned her poetic ambitions with those of another hero, Elizabeth Barrett Browning. The energy and fervour of *Aurora Leigh* were particularly attractive to Blind as they were to many of the New Woman poets writing in the *fin de siècle*, and they fed into her own major poetic works of the 1880s.

Two of the long poems which she wrote during this highly productive decade were inspired by trips to the Scottish Highlands and reflect the religious and political radicalism to which she was now committed. In *The Prophecy of St Oran*, published in 1881, she relates the story – loosely based on Celtic myth – of a monk who falls in love with a Pictish woman.[44] The monk is punished by being buried alive, but later returns from the dead to deny the truth of the Christian faith and the afterlife. Whilst the volume was praised by *The Times* as 'a remarkable contribution to English Literature',[45] its atheistic argument resulted in its being withdrawn from sale shortly after publication. As William Michael Rossetti speculated to Madox Brown in September of the same year, 'It looks ... very much as if the Publisher had got frightened by somebody about the atheistic character of the book, and had determined to sell it no more'.[46]

---

[41] *The Journal of Marie Bashkirtseff*, 2 vols, trans. by Mathilde Blind (London: Cassell, 1890), I, pp. xiv, vii.

[42] There are selections available in *A Selection from the Poems of Mathilde Blind*, ed. by Arthur Symons (London: T. Fisher Unwin, 1897) and *The Poetical Works of Mathilde Blind*, ed. by Arthur Symons (London: T. Fisher Unwin, 1900).

[43] William Rossetti, *Diary*, p. 170.

[44] Mathilde Blind, *The Prophecy of St Oran and other Poems* (London: Newman, 1881).

[45] Advertisement in Blind, *Eliot*, p. 219.

[46] William Rossetti, *Reminiscences*, II, 400.

Five years later a second trip to the Highlands resulted in *The Heather on Fire*, a social critique on the clearance of the crofters' communities from Highland estates in order to make way for wealthy English and American hunting and shooting parties.[47] This work was more overtly political than anything Blind had published before, and as Richard Garnett wrote: 'It is not too much to affirm that no other English poetess since Mrs Browning could have given utterance with equal energy to the compassion and indignation called forth by such circumstances.'[48] Blind was making her political voice known at the time that Britain was seeing the revival of socialism, and in many ways her poem locks into the new dedication to the working-class struggle which was shared by Eleanor Marx.

It was in 1889, however, that Blind published what is arguably her most accomplished and fascinating poem, *The Ascent of Man*, an epic based upon Darwin's evolutionary theory.[49] Many socialists were committed to the ideas which emerged from *Origin of Species* and *The Descent of Man*, among them, of course, Edward Aveling. As sometime Professor of Comparative Anatomy and Fellow of the Linnean Society, Aveling had published widely on scientific developments, including an undergraduate text on evolution entitled *The Student's Darwin* (1881). Several of the New Women poets, including Constance Naden and Mary F. Robinson, with whom Blind was friendly, were attracted towards the use of Darwin's ideas as a means of reflecting upon various social issues, including gender relations,[50] but there was no other woman poet who dealt with evolutionary theory in such depth as Blind and in a form – the epic – which was itself one which women tended not to employ (the obvious exception being Barrett Browning, to whom *The Ascent of Man* is dedicated).

The first part of the poem, 'Chaunts of Life', records in rich language the development of life from its very first origins within the primeval evolutionary swamp, drawing upon images which merge contemporary developments in Darwinism, electricity and industrialization:

> And vaguely in the pregnant deep,
>   Clasped by the glowing arms of light
> From an eternity of sleep
>   Within unfathomed gulfs of night
> A pulse stirred in the plastic slime
> Responsive to the rhythm of Time.

47 Mathilde Blind, *The Heather on Fire: A Tale of the Highland Clearances* (London: Scott, 1886).

48 Garnett, 'Memoir', p. 28.

49 London: Chatto & Windus, 1889.

50 See Isobel Armstrong and Joseph Bristow with Cath Sharrock, *Nineteenth-Century Women Poets* (Oxford: Clarendon Press, 1996) and Angela Leighton and Margaret Reynolds, *Victorian Women's Poetry: An Anthology* (Oxford: Blackwell, 1995).

> Enkindled in the mystic dark
>   Life built herself a myriad forms,
> And, flashing its electric spark
>   Through films and cells and pulps and worms,
> Flew shuttlewise above, beneath,
> Weaving the web of life and death.[51]

In subsequent pages, Blind maps out the evolutionary process up to the creation of humankind, emphasizing at every stage the dominance of death and destruction engendered by the theory of the survival of the fittest – 'The thickets scream with bird and beast ... Each preys upon the other's life / In inextinguishable strife'[52] – before charting the history of human existence as a similar set of bloody fights to the death. In particular, she highlights the ways in which destruction and brutality have been prescribed by various dominant ideologies, including religion and governmental control.

   The final part of the poem, in many ways the most accomplished, develops this social critique as the female speaker enters an urban matrix reminiscent of Thomson's *City of Dreadful Night*. She encounters an allegorical figure of Love who is 'cast out as weed ... and covered with scars',[53] before following a Pilgrim Soul on a visionary journey where she is witness to the knock-on effects of industrialism and capitalist society – war, famine, disease, prostitution and rape. As she is taken closer, the protagonist is witness to the lives of a working-class family whose poverty leads directly to domestic violence: the murder of the wife by the husband, the husband's slitting his own throat in the back-yard, and their children being left to starve in the streets. The full cost of alienated labour is made horrifically clear.

   Yet within the narrative framework of *The Ascent of Man*, salvation lies with the social outcasts and marginalized groups for whom Blind had spent her whole life fighting. For it is a prostitute, 'a creature / Flung by wanton hands mid lust and crime',[54] who saves the children, feeding them using the money she earns in the economic marketplace through the sale of her body. In combining an astute analysis of the implications of Darwinian theory with a terrifying portrayal of urban dystopia, this poem finally argues that the way forward lies in maternal and humanitarian acts and the kind of 'religion of loving kindness' which Hardy was to propose two years later in *Tess of the D'Urbervilles*. Certainly this was a panacea which would inform the conclusion of many of Blind's socialist poems, including the highly accomplished 'The Street Children's Dance', where the dance of the malnourished and abandoned 'Children mothered by the street' provides a possible hope for a future outside the 'thick defiling crust / Of soul-stifling

---

51 *Ascent of Man*, pp. 9–10.
52 *Ascent of Man*, p. 12.
53 *Ascent of Man*, p. 71.
54 *Ascent of Man*, p. 98.

poverty'.[55] This is a socialist vision which Eleanor Marx would certainly have found attractive.

For many reasons, not least to do with parentage, posterity has been kinder to Eleanor Marx than it has been to Mathilde Blind. Like many Victorian women poets, Blind's existence has until recently been erased by literary history and there remains much recovery work and reassessment to be done. Let us hope, however, that she is eventually given her rightful place on the literary map of late Victorian Britain so that we may be able to flesh out more fully our 'tantalising glimpses' of these two remarkable women.

---

[55] 'Street Children's Dance', in *A Selection from the Poems of Mathilde Blind*, ed. by Arthur Symons (London: T. Fisher Unwin, 1997), pp. 46–7. Later volumes include *Dramas in Miniature* (London: Chatto & Windus, 1891), *Songs and Sonnets* (London: Chatto & Windus, 1893) and *Birds of Passage: Songs of the Orient and Occident* (London: Chatto & Windus, 1895).

Index